Engineering Education for Sustainable Development

T0298931

This book demonstrates how the theoretical concepts of the capabilities approach can be applied in the context of engineering education, and how this could be used to add nuance to our understanding of the contribution higher education can make to human flourishing. In demonstrating the usefulness of the capability approach as a lens through which to evaluate the outputs of engineering education, the author also shows how the capability approach can be informed by, and informs, the concept of 'sustainable development' and discusses what pedagogical and curricula implications this may have for education for sustainable development (ESD), particularly in engineering. As such, the book builds on the work of scholars of engineering education, and scholars of university education at the nexus of development and sustainability.

Engineering employers, educators and students from diverse contexts discuss both the capabilities and functions that are enlarged by engineering education and the impact these can have on pro-poor engineering or public-good professionalism. The book therefore makes an original, conceptual and empirical contribution to our thinking about engineering education research.

The book provides inspiration for both engineering educators and students to orient their technical knowledge and transferable skills towards the public good. It will also be of great interest to students and researchers interested in ESD more generally and to engineers who are interested in doing work that is aligned with the goals of social justice. The book will also appeal to scholars of the capability approach within higher education.

Mikateko Mathebula holds a PhD in Development Studies and is a Senior Researcher at the Centre for Research on Higher Education and Development (CRHED) at the University of the Free State, South Africa. Her research focuses on higher education's contribution to reducing inequalities and advancing social justice.

Routledge Studies in Sustainable Development

This series uniquely brings together original and cutting-edge research on sustainable development. The books in this series tackle difficult and important issues in sustainable development including: values and ethics; sustainability in higher education; climate compatible development; resilience; capitalism and de-growth; sustainable urban development; gender and participation; and well-being.

Drawing on a wide range of disciplines, the series promotes interdisciplinary research for an international readership. The series was recommended in the *Guardian*'s suggested reads on development and the environment.

Engineering Education for Sustainable Development

A Capabilities Approach

Mikateko Mathebula

LONDON AND NEW YORK

from Routledge

First published 2018
by Routledge

2 Park Square, Milton Park, Abingdon, Oxfordshire OX14 4RN
52 Vanderbilt Avenue, New York, NY 10017

Routledge is an imprint of the Taylor & Francis Group, an informa business

First issued in paperback 2019

British Library Cataloguing in Publication Data
A catalogue record for this book is available from the British Library

Library of Congress Cataloging in Publication Data
Names: Mathebula, Mikateko, author.
Title: Engineering education for sustainable development : a capabilities
approach / Mikateko Mathebula.
Description: Abingdon, Oxon ; New York, NY : Routledge, 2018. | Series:
Routledge studies in sustainable development | Includes bibliographical
references and index.
Identifiers: LCCN 2017036421 (print) | LCCN 2017050933 (ebook) |
ISBN 9781315177045 (eBook) | ISBN 9781138038905 (hardback)
Subjects: LCSH: Sustainable engineering. | Engineers–Training of. |
Sustainable development.
Classification: LCC TA170 (ebook) | LCC TA170 .M384 2018 (print) |
DDC 620.0028/6–dc23
LC record available at https://lccn.loc.gov/2017036421

ISBN: 978-1-138-03890-5 (hbk)
ISBN: 978-0-367-88871-8 (pbk)

Typeset in Times New Roman
by Wearset Ltd, Boldon, Tyne and Wear

This book is dedicated to my parents, Godfrey and Virginia Mathebula – the most important teachers in my life

Contents

Illustrations

Acknowledgements

I would like to express my sincere gratitude to all the engineering students, educators and employers who participated in the research from which this book draws. All participants' names are pseudonyms.

I am grateful to the Centre for Research on Higher Education and Development (CRHED), at the University of the Free State. Being a part of CRHED has contributed greatly to my personal and professional development, and has provided a rich space for intellectual stimulation and growth. Excellent research supervision, mentorship and advice was provided by Professor Melanie Walker and Professor Merridy Wilson-Strydom; thank you both for the ongoing inspiration and support you have and do continue to provided me with. Professor Jenni Case, Professor Ann-Marie Bathmaker, and Professor Alejandra Boni provided comments on an early version of this book which helped improve the manuscript; thank you. I am also grateful to the anonymous reviewers whose comments were very useful.

I appreciate greatly, the love and encouragement I have received from my whole family, in particular my parents, Godfrey and Virginia Mathebula and my sisters Makungu Tsotetsi and Vukosi Mathebula. I would like to thank all my colleagues at CRHED, in particular Talita Calitz, Tendayi Marovah and Oliver Mutanga. Onthatile Mlambo, Tumelo Matthias and Jess Kuppan – I am fortunate to have friends like you, who always show unwavering support, whether near or far. Lazlo Passemiers, thank you for the countless conversations, debates and your critical input, which has helped me refine many ideas. I am lucky to have you.

I have always been passionate about learning, and this has a lot to do with the wonderful educators I have had the privilege to be taught by, and so I would also like to thank all the teachers and lecturers who have contributed to my education whether in a personal or professional capacity.

The research reported in this book was supported by the South African Research Chairs Initiative of the Department of Science and Technology and the National Research Foundation of South Africa, grant number 86540.

Abbreviations

CHE	Council on Higher Education
CRHED	Centre for Research on Higher Education and Development
DEAT	Department of Environmental Affairs and Tourism
DESD	Decade of Education for Sustainable Development
DHET	Department of Higher Education and Training
DST	Department of Science and Technology (South Africa)
ECSA	Engineering Council of South Africa
ESD	Education for Sustainable Development
GER	Germany
HDI	Human Development Index
HDRs	Human Development Reports
HRK	*Hochschulrektorenkonferenz* (German Rector's University Council)
HySA	Hydrogen South Africa
IUCN	International Union for Conservation of Nature
MDGs	Millennium Development Goals
NSDS	National Sustainable Development Strategy (Germany)
PLE	Project-led Education
SA	South Africa
SDGs	Sustainable Development Goals
STEM	Science, Technology, Engineering and Mathematics
UB	*Universität Bremen* (University of Bremen)
UCT	University of Cape Town
UN DESA	United Nations Department of Economic and Social Affairs
UNDP	United Nations Development Programme
UNESCO	United Nations Educational, Scientific and Cultural Organisation
VDI	*Verein Deutsche Ingenieure* (Association of German Engineers)
WCED	World Commission on Environment and Development
WSSD	World Summit on Sustainable Development
ZIM	Zimbabwe

Part I

1 Sustainable human development

The overarching goal

Introduction

Historically, universities have played a role in transforming societies by educating decision makers, leaders, entrepreneurs and academics who serve the public good (Lozano, 2013). However, utilitarian and human capital perspectives tend to dominate the way universities are run in current times, resulting in the development of unbalanced, over-specialized and mono-disciplinary graduates (Lozano, 2013) who see education primarily as a means to employment. While education can and should enhance human capital, people and societies also benefit from education in ways that exceed its role in preparing individuals for commodity production in industry (Boni & Walker, 2013). Also, an educational focus on employability and jobs does not say much (if anything at all) about the quality of work, or whether or not people are treated fairly and with dignity at work, or whether they are able to do and to be what they have reason to value as individual professionals or collective citizens (Boni & Walker, 2013). As Boni and Walker (2013) suggest, a human development perspective, with its core values of well-being, participation, empowerment and sustainability could be a good framework to reimagine the purpose of universities, beyond the instrumental goal of creating a workforce out of people.

This opening chapter provides the background of the book through its discussion of debates on the relationships between engineering practice, development and sustainability, as well as the role of these relationships in perpetuating and inhibiting poverty, and engineering education's location within this complex landscape. By introducing the conceptual premise that informs the rationale behind the qualitative research upon which the book is based, namely, the capability approach, the chapter outlines the implications of defining the role of engineering education, and understanding sustainability, from a human development or freedom-centred view. Ultimately, the chapter explores concepts that can enhance our understanding of how to integrate engineering and social justice.

Development

It is necessary to identify, by reference to the freedoms of all people to do and be what they have reason to value, and by what anyone may observe, what allows us to say that certain countries are 'developed' while others are 'developing' (Rist, 2008; Sen, 1999). The point is not to compare two different sets of countries by showing that one has more of this (schools, roads, currency reserves, average calorie consumption, cars, democracy or telephones) but less of that (illiteracy, cultural traditions, children per family, 'absolute poor', time, skilled labour, etc.), while the other set has the reverse (Rist, 2008). Rather, the process of development, whose tempo differs in the two sets of countries and transforms them both quantitatively and qualitatively, does not concern only the countries of the 'South', nor only operations conducted under the auspices of 'development cooperation' (Rist, 2008). It is a global, historically distinctive phenomenon, whose functioning first needs to be critically explored before efforts to sustain it are pursued (Rist, 2008). As Rist argues, it may be objected that the essence of 'development' is not worldwide expansion of the market system:

> Is it not different from mere economic growth? Does it not set itself 'human goals' that conflict with the cynicism of the process presented above? Is it not the generous expression of a real concern for others? Indeed, is it not a moral imperative?
>
> (Rist, 2008: 19)

And perhaps most importantly, despite inevitable mistakes and reprehensible perversions of original intentions, 'does it not aim to put an end to the extreme poverty that is the scourge of most of the world?' (Rist, 2008: 19). These are reasonable questions that represent the hope of improving the conditions of life of the majority of mankind and express a willingness not to be discouraged by past setbacks (Rist, 2008). So how can we explain the inconsistency between such noble goals, and practices that get in the way of their achievement (Rist, 2008)? In keeping with Western tradition, 'development' was initially thought of as an intransitive phenomenon that simply 'happens', but the term 'underdevelopment' evoked not only the idea of change in the direction of particular ends but also the possibility of bringing about such change (Rist, 2008). This suggested that it is possible to 'develop' a region, giving 'development' a transitive meaning (an action performed by one agent upon another) that corresponds to a principle of social organization, while 'underdevelopment' became a 'naturally' occurring (seemingly causeless) state of being (Rist, 2008).

Until this point, global North–global South relations had been organized largely in accordance with the colonizer/colonized opposition, but the 'developed'/'underdeveloped' dichotomy proposed a different relationship (Rist, 2008). Instead of the hierarchical subordination of colony to metropolis, every nation was equal in the eyes of the law, even if it was not (yet) equal in practice (Rist, 2008). Colonized and colonizer had belonged to two different and opposed universes, so that confrontation between them, in the form of national liberation struggles, had appeared unavoidable as a way of reducing the difference (Rist, 2008). Now, however, 'underdeveloped', 'developing' and 'developed' were members of a single family: the one might be lagging a little behind the other, but they could always hope to catch up – so long as they continued to play the same game, and their conception of development was not too different (Rist, 2008).

In this way, 'underdevelopment' and 'developing' are not the opposite of 'development', only its incomplete form; and an acceleration of growth was a logical way of bridging the gap (Rist, 2008). In this comparison, moreover, each nation was considered for itself: its 'development' was mainly an internal, self-made, self-regulating phenomenon, even if it could be 'helped' from outside (Rist, 2008). As Rist argues, the historical conditions that may be used to explain the 'lead' of some countries over others could not enter the argument, since the 'laws of development' are supposedly the same for all, and 'win their way through' with engineering and necessity (Rist, 2008: 41). Not only does this rationale obliterate the effects of conquest, colonization, slave trade, the breaking up of social structures, etc.; it also presents things as if the existence of industrialized countries did not radically alter the context in which candidates for industrialization have to operate (Rist, 2008).

For conventional thinking, the quest for a definition of development therefore lies between two equally irrepressible extremes: (1) the expression of a wish to live a better life, which seems deliberately to ignore the fact that the concrete ways of achieving it would run up against conflicting political choices; and (2) the actions (also often conflicting with one another) that are supposed eventually to bring greater happiness to the greatest possible number (Rist, 2008). The weakness of these two perspectives is that they suggest identifying 'development' quite narrowly: development is presented on the one hand as a subjective feeling of fulfilment that differs from individual to individual, and on the other as a series of actions for which there is no a priori proof that certain actions effectively increase valued freedoms for all people.

Sustainable development

Early discussions on sustainable development began taking place in the 1970s, prompted by concerns raised by the International Union for Conservation of Nature (IUCN) and events such as the 1972 UN Conference on Human Environment (Lélé, 1991; Mebratu, 1998; Robert, Parris & Leiserowitz, 2005). The IUCN sought to bring public attention to ideas of conservation, with an emphasis that species and ecosystems should be used in a manner that allows them to go on renewing themselves indefinitely. The union's 1980 World Conservation Strategy showed how efforts to conserve nature and natural resources needed to be integrated, with a clear understanding of their essential role in human flourishing (see IUCN, 1980).

Debates about the link between finite natural resources and development slowly began to emerge, which brought about views that existing forms of economic expansion would have to be altered (Mebratu, 1998). So the idea of 'sustainable development' essentially arose from apprehensions related to the over-exploitation of natural and environmental resources, the negative impact this would have on production and industrialization processes, and hence on economic activity in the future. Additionally, questionable outcomes caused by fertilizers and monocultures on ecosystems and local economies triggered the UN to be more critical about the long-term effects of large-scale technical projects common to the processes of industrialization (Lucena & Schneider, 2008). This brought widespread attention, arguably for the first time, to questions of how best to manage or sustain 'development'. Since then the social and environmental impact and appropriateness of development activities has garnered increased attention globally, both in the media and in academic literature, and anxieties reported by environmental scientists and ecologists over the years have been recognized by policy makers and economists. These events ultimately sparked the impetus to conceptualize, operationalize and identify indicators of 'sustainable development', in order to generate policies for implementing a national, international and global sustainable development agenda.

The most popular or influential definition of sustainable development is the one formulated by the World Commission on Environment and Development (WCED) in 1987. In the report *Our Common Future*, the WCED described sustainable development as 'development that meets the needs of the present without compromising the ability of future generations to meet their own needs' (WCED, 1987: 43). Although this formulation is often criticized for being too vague, in some ways it is useful in shaping our thinking about what we might want development to look like in the long run. First, it adds a temporal dimension to conceptions of development, prompting us to question how long development can look the way it does, and still be considered as a manifestation of positive change in society. Second, as pointed out by Anand and Sen (1996) and Mebratu (1998) there are two key concepts embedded in this definition:

1   The concept of needs, especially the basic or essential needs of the world's poor, to which priority should be given.
2   The concept of limitations, particularly the restrictions imposed on the natural environment's ability to survive the effects of human activity on it, or to renew its resources (see WCED, 1987).

Thus conceived, we cannot take it for granted that development efforts have a positive effect on or improve the lives of human beings, if they neglect the needs of the poor or limit opportunities for the environment to renew itself so that it might cater for prospective needs of both human and non-human life. Therefore, anyone driven by either long-term self-interest, or concern for poverty, or concern for intergenerational equity would arguably be willing to support the operational objectives stemming from the WCED's definition of sustainable development (Mebratu, 1998). Such a broad definition of sustainable development lends itself to consensus because it is founded upon scientific evidence on environmental degradation, moral and ethical principles about poverty and considerations of long-term self-interest (Repetto, 1986). Therefore, theoretically, this account of sustainable development has the potential for building powerful unanimity (Mebratu, 1998). Indications of the resonance of this definition in shaping mainstream understandings of sustainability is reflected by its widespread use and frequency of citation (Robert et al., 2005).

The three dimensions that have come to be understood as the pillars of sustainable development are: the environment, the economy and society (people). According to Robert et al. (2005), much of the early literature on sustainable development focused on the economic dimension, placing emphasis on the need to maintain productivity levels in industry and wealth in parts of the world where it had been achieved, or providing employment and increasing economic participation for the world's poor. Over time, the social dimension of sustainability has received increased attention, where there is more emphasis on values and goals such as increased life expectancy, education for all and equity (Robert et al., 2005). Within the last five decades, a number of key international milestones[1] signified the increased recognition of sustainability as an important component in development strategies. These include:

- the 1972 UN Conference on the Human Environment;
- the 1992 UN Conference on Environment and Development (UNCED) or 'Earth Summit', where 'Agenda 21' was agreed upon as a blueprint for sustainable development, reflecting global consensus and political commitment to integrate environmental concerns into social and economic decision-making processes;
- the 2000 UN Millennium Summit, where the Millennium Development Goals (MDGs) were adopted, which included eight anti-poverty targets to be accomplished by 2015;
- the 2002 World Summit on Sustainable Development (WSSD), where commitments to sustainable development were reaffirmed alongside a notion of development that aims for equity within and between generations, and poverty eradication placed at the centre of sustainability measures;
- the 2015 UN Sustainable Development Summit, where the 2030 Agenda for Sustainable Development was conceived, which includes a set of 17 Sustainable Development Goals (SDGs) to end poverty, fight inequality and injustice and tackle climate change by 2030 (see DEAT, 2008; UN, 1972, 2012; UNCED, 1992; UNDP, 2015; WSSD, 2002). According to the UN's Global Sustainable Development Report, vast progress has been made on the MDGs, showing the value of a unifying agenda underpinned by specific goals and targets (UN DESA, 2015). While the MDGs aimed at an array of issues that included reducing poverty, hunger, disease and gender inequality by 2015, the new SDGs and the broader sustainability agenda seek to go further than the MDGs to address the root causes of poverty and the universal need for development that works for all people (UN DESA, 2015). Human development features quite strongly in this sustainable development landscape. The human development reports[2] (HDRs) emphasize that human development and sustainability are essential components of the same ethic: the universalism of life claims (UNDP, 2015). As argued in the 2015 report, the strongest argument for protecting the environment, from a human development perspective,

is to guarantee future generations a diversity and richness of choices and substantive opportunities similar to those enjoyed by previous generations (UNDP, 2015).

The last few decades have seen a rise in the promotion of education for sustainable development (ESD) as opposed to a primary focus on education for employment, which has created the impetus for sustainability to become a new paradigm in the complex systems of universities (de la Harpe & Thomas, 2009; Karatzoglou, 2013; Ramos, Caeiro, Hoof, Lozano & Huisingh, 2015). The United Nation's (UN) declaration of the years 2005–2014 as the Decade of Education for Sustainable Development (DESD) is a good example of an initiative to promote education and learning as the basis for a more sustainable world. The major goals of the DESD were to embed sustainable development into all learning spheres, reorient education and develop initiatives that showcase the special role and contribution of education in our pursuit of sustainable development (Tilbury & Mula, 2009). Whereas relevant interest in the DESD has been demonstrated at the regional level and by some nations, the conceptual vagueness of sustainable development (Mebratu, 1998) and the diversity of responses to ESD do not always invite higher education policy makers or practitioners to engage with this agenda (Lozano, 2013). Despite these challenges, the DESD has raised expectations amongst ESD stakeholders, who see this platform as a good opportunity not only to embed ESD at all education levels but also to influence decision-making at government level and to move towards social and economic systemic change (Lozano, 2013). As such, promoting ESD is about engaging and empowering people in and through education, through seeking their commitment to inclusive development and facilitating them in acquiring critical knowledge in order for them to make decisions and bring about changes that are consistent with sustainable development principles.

Locating engineering in sustainable development

Engineering solutions are generally considered as examples of development that work for all people by advancing human productivity and prosperity. This is because engineering activities usually result in the creation of social artefacts that have come to be recognized as manifestations of development, for example, infrastructure in the form of railways, roads and bridges. It is therefore often taken for granted that the education and training received by engineers, subsequently enables them to respond appropriately to the challenges of sustainable development through their contribution to the design and creation of innovative processes and products, like creating biogas[3] from natural waste as a source of renewable energy. However, engineering education has traditionally emphasized mastering technical subject matter at the expense of promoting values that underpin sustainable development; hence, not all engineering contributes to sustainability. To address this problem, higher education institutions, and universities in particular, are increasingly incorporating the humanities and sustainable development content in their engineering programmes (Ahern, O'Connor, McRuaire, McNamara & O'Donnell, 2012; Boni, McDonald & Peris, 2012; Paden, 2007). Measures to incorporate sustainable development concerns in engineering curricula illustrate institutional responses to global action plans for sustainable development such as the DESD. These measures are justifiably often targeted at engineering education because engineers' work cuts across and influences, arguably more directly than any other professional group, the so-called pillars of sustainable development: people, the environment and the economy.

ESD literature (see for example de la Harpe & Thomas, 2009; Fadeeva & Galkute, 2012; Hopkins, 2012; Jones, Trier & Richards, 2008; Karatzoglou, 2013; Lozano, 2013; Mulder & Jansen, 2006) suggests that relevant and appropriate knowledge for sustainable development can be imparted by adding humanities courses to university curricula. In particular, studies that focus on reforming engineering pedagogies to this end recommend approaches such as project-based learning,[4] problem-based learning,[5] back-casting[6] (see Connor, Karmokar, Whittington & Walker, 2014; Fernandes, Flores & Lima, 2012; Fernandes, Mesquita, Flores & Lima, 2014; Schneider, Leydens & Lucena, 2008; Segalás, Ferrer-Balas & Mulder, 2010) and the use of design studios (see Petersen, 2013) as methods to broaden outcomes. These studies suggest that such engineering pedagogies expose students to both technical and qualitative aspects of engineering work, while developing their 'soft skills' and making them knowledgeable about sustainability.

It must be acknowledged that a wider group of professionals (e.g. quantity surveyors, architects, town planners, development aid workers and even contractors and financiers) have knowledge, skills or resources that are applied in the conceptualization and implementation of products and processes that characterize development. For example, town planners deal with the technical and political processes concerned with the use of land, protection and use of the environment, public welfare, and the design of the urban environment, including air, water and the infrastructure passing into and out of urban areas, such as transportation. Engineers often work with professional groups like town planners, and the results of their work frequently positions them at the forefront of development initiatives. It is therefore clear that engineering work cannot be carried out without the input of such professional groups, and engineers have to work within the confines of government regulations or economic and environmental constraints. However, engineering knowledge, which is unbounded in breadth and detail (Trevelyan, 2007), sets engineers apart from their counterparts, giving them technical expertise that can be used to design, construct, and therefore shape (both literally and figuratively) the world in which we live. It can thus be argued that engineers are particularly well placed to help ensure that social artefacts like technology are placed at the service of sustainable development.

As Fernández-Baldor, Boni, Lillo and Hueso (2014) assert, transferring the benefits of technology to society is not a straightforward task. When development aid interventions view technology strictly as a necessary tool for development, attention lies in supplying technological assets or services, and focusing only on technology instead of concentrating on people (Fernández-Baldor et al., 2014). Such approaches to development and development aid projects diminish the potential for social transformation through engineering and technology (Fernández-Baldor et al., 2014). Fernández-Baldor et al. (2014) subsequently ask that we see technological development projects not only as a means to provide an asset or a service, but also as a tool for helping people to shape their own lives and for reducing inequalities. Such a view of technological development projects encourages the idea that professional groups at the forefront of development efforts should embrace values associated with social justice. If such values do not underpin their professional functionings, they might fail to use their knowledge and skills to enhance human development or to solve sustainability problems in a just way. It is therefore important that appropriate conceptions of 'development' are held by professional groups who design, produce and implement technologies in society for the purpose of human progress. This is important, particularly for professional groups like engineers, because their understanding of development determines how they identify or recognize it, as well as how they measure it.

In the section that follows, the capability approach and human development paradigm are put forward as helpful views on development, and arguments are presented on why they serve as a powerful normative lens through which to conceptualize the ends of engineering education. Additionally, 'public-good professionalism' (Walker & McLean 2013) is discussed as a framework within which 'public-good engineering' is conceptualized. This explains how this book uses the capability approach as both a lens for theorizing, and as a site for analysing the contribution engineering education makes to sustainable development.

Conceptual foundation for a normative account of engineering education

The normative account of engineering education provided in this book is grounded in the capability approach (Nussbaum, 2000; Sen, 1999) the human development paradigm (ul Haq, 1995) conceptions of sustainable human development (see Anand & Sen, 1996; Crabtree, 2013; Lessmann & Rauschmayer, 2013; Peeters, Dirix & Sterckx, 2013; Pelenc, Lompo, Ballet & Dubois, 2013), and public-good professionalism (Walker, 2012; Walker & McLean, 2013).

Because a more in-depth discussion of the capability approach and its application to higher education and engineering education research follows in Chapter 2, this section is limited to outlining the approach in order to situate the book theoretically. At the same time, the section discusses ideas and concepts that are related to and inform the capability approach in order to draw attention to the rationale of the book and introduce its theoretical ambitions.

The capability approach

The starting point of the capability approach is Amartya Sen's argument that focusing on the expansion of human freedom as an end of education endeavours, instead of focusing on economic progress, allows economic growth to be integrated into an understanding of development processes as 'the expansion of human capability to lead more worthwhile and more free lives' (Sen, 1992: 295). Based on this view, human freedoms or human capabilities lie at the heart of development (Walker, 2006) where the term 'capabilities'[7] refers to substantive freedoms, or what is effectively possible. When that which is effectively possible has been attained or achieved, it is known as a 'functioning'. Functionings can be described as the realized potential of opportunities, and they are characterized by being and/or doing things that an individual has reason to value, which are (usually) aligned with an individual's aspirations and/or well-being; in capabilities language, 'doings' and 'beings'.

The capability approach draws attention to two distinguishable yet equally important and interdependent aspects of human life, namely well-being and agency (Sen, 1999). Agency is defined as the capacity to initiate an action formulating aims and beliefs, and it requires mental health, cognitive skills and opportunities to engage in social participation (Alkire, 2002). Agency is also distinguished according to agency freedom and agency achievement. According to Sen (1985) agency freedom refers to the liberty an individual has to turn available opportunities into valued outcomes: that is, one's freedom to bring about the achievements one values and tries to produce. Agency achievement refers to the realization of the goals one has reason to pursue (Sen, 1985). However, individual choice can be influenced by the social and relational environment in which one lives, which can result in decisions that are not particularly conducive to individual well-being (Sen, 1985). Such decisions also count as examples of agency.

Thus conceived, 'there is deep complementarity between individual agency and social arrangements' and it is 'important to give simultaneous recognition to the centrality of individual freedom and to the force of social influences on the extent and reach of individual freedom' (Sen, 1985: 206–207). This means that although individuals may be free and able to pursue valued objectives, social arrangements can have an effect on the resultant choice of action individuals may take. For example, budget limitations on engineering projects by senior management in a construction firm may inhibit engineers' freedom and ability to design environmentally friendly products. This could lead to decisions that prioritize economic profit over sustainable engineering practices. This example represents a situation where, despite in theory having the freedom to decide otherwise, an individual may make a decision that is: (1) not necessarily aligned with their intrinsic motivation, (2) may not reflect their aspirations, and (3) has the potential to diminish their professional well-being. Unfortunately, current global economic conditions are not conducive to these freedoms in the engineering industry. Traditional business models that emphasize maximizing profit and minimizing costs dominate industry, with the result that the economic dimension of sustainability is prioritized at the expense of the social and ecological dimensions.

Ideally, one's social environment should offer a space in which the freedom to strive towards intrinsically valued beings and doings is provided. For engineers specifically, their professional environment should offer a space in which they are free to strive towards advancing sustainable development and social justice. Correspondingly, engineering education should offer possibilities to develop graduates' capacities to value the principles of social justice and sustainable development, so that they may have reason to value these ideals and hence work towards them through their professional functionings – that is, so that future engineers might become agents who act and make change happen (Sen, 1999); change that is directed towards social justice. Thus conceived, and drawing on Alkire and Deneulin's (2010) characterization of agency, agentic engineers could be described as individuals who seek to:

1   Pursue goals that they value, in particular, goals that are aligned with the principles of social justice, such as poverty reduction.
2   Apply their effective power, not only according to their individual agency but also according to what engineers can do as members of a group, for example as members of Engineers without Borders, Engineers against Poverty, or as members of communities or political communities.
3   Pursue individual well-being or other reasonable and justifiable objectives that are conducive to societal well-being (displacing local communities for engineering endeavours cannot be understood as agency) and
4   Take ownership of their responsibility as agents who want to achieve those goals.

As mentioned before, the capability approach makes a distinction between well-being and agency freedoms, and well-being and agency achievements; where freedoms are concerned with the real opportunities one has to accomplish what one values, and achievements are concerned with what one actually manages to accomplish (Crocker & Robeyns, 2010). The example that was provided previously (the budget constraints imposed on engineering) illustrates a situation where limits to agency freedom get in the way of agency achievement. As such, the capability approach proposes that the ends of well-being or development be conceptualized, amongst other things, in terms of people's *effective* opportunities to undertake the actions and activities they want to engage in, and to be whom they want to be or achieve desired goals (Crocker & Robeyns, 2010). In the case of engineers, we would therefore ask questions such as, 'What effective opportunities exist for engineers to design, create and implement engineering solutions that serve sustainable development?'

In its account of human diversity in the evaluation of well-being, the capability approach acknowledges the role of contextual factors that influence how free a person is to convert the characteristics of goods or services into a functioning (Crocker & Robeyns, 2010). These elements are defined as 'conversion factors', which can take the form of personal (internal to the individual person), social (the society in which one lives), and environmental (emerging from the physical environment) forces at work (Sen, 2003). Applied to engineering, budget constraints can be seen as social conversion factors that get in the way of engineers' freedom to convert engineering knowledge into sustainable engineering solutions.

As such, the capability approach can be described as a wide-ranging normative framework that can be used narrowly to tell us what information we should look at if we are to judge how well someone's life is going or has gone, and can be used broadly as an evaluative framework within which to conceptualize, measure and evaluate well-being (Crocker & Robeyns, 2010). That is, the capability approach can be used to tell us what information we should look at if we are to judge how well engineering functionings are going or to evaluate and measure professional engineering capabilities. By so doing, it can help to conceptualize 'professional engineering well-being'. This can serve as a basis for identifying educational capabilities and functionings that are necessary to develop engineers who use their agency to secure their own well-being, while at the same time enhancing effective opportunities for all people (but poor people in particular).

However, there are some methodological challenges of the capability approach in this regard. It has been criticized for its failure to identify empirically verifiable categories of capabilities and functionings, which makes it difficult to operationalize empirically (Walby, 2011). Walby addresses the relationship between Sen's theoretical work and its interpretation in the measurement of justice, where the central question asked is whether it is possible to develop a meaningful operationalization of Sen's philosophical distinctions between capabilities and functionings. Walby (2011) identifies a few problems with Sen's preference for capabilities (opportunities) rather than functionings (achievements) as the basis of, or indicators for, social justice.

These challenges are:

* identifying the most important capabilities;
* mapping the philosophical difference between capabilities and functionings onto a distinction between empirical categories; and
* evaluating potentially incommensurable categories.

Another possible limitation of the approach is that it does not provide an actual formula for interpersonal comparisons of well-being, nor does it offer sufficient guidelines for its operationalization or clear methods of identifying valuable capabilities (Crocker & Robeyns, 2010). However, it is important to note that attempts have been made to do so, as exemplified by the Human Development Index (HDI)[8] (UNDP, 2015) and the Multidimensional Poverty Index (MPI)[9] (Alkire, Jindra, Aguilar, Seth & Vaz, 2015). Furthermore, Sen's ideas constitute the core normative principles of a development approach that has evolved in the HDRs, because they offer a favourable alternative view on human development. This view is not limited to seeing only resources and income as indicators of development (Walby, 2011). Therefore, the capability approach (despite these limitations) provides a good starting point for a more holistic examination and understanding of the purposes of engineering education, because it encourages us to consider individual opportunities to achieve well-being in higher education. It therefore, also prompts us to consider how the effective individual capabilities of professional agents contribute to the well-being of others and to societal well-being. This is because it defines development as pertaining to the positive processes of social, economic and political change that broaden valued capabilities (Alkire, 2002; Sen, 2003). Looking at higher education through a capabilities lens, its purpose is not merely to enable employment by imparting skills and knowledge that are needed in the economy. Instead, the capability approach inspires us to ask how valued opportunities (and functionings) are being widened for individuals because of higher education. This makes the capability approach well suited for use as a framework under which the value of higher education (and engineering education more specifically) can be examined beyond its economic utility.

If one defines well-being primarily according to its economic dimension, it is easy (and appropriate) to evaluate the work engineers do as a contribution to (economic) development. This is because transforming natural resources into means of production for industrialization and expanding infrastructure or advancing technology are all examples of engineering outcomes that are indispensable to economic development. For these reasons, it is often taken for granted that engineering outcomes contribute to development and ultimately improve human well-being. However, if one looks at well-being from a capabilities perspective, engineers' contribution to development would be evaluated differently; according to the freedoms of *all* people to live lives that they consider valuable.

According to Fukuda-Parr (2003), this evaluative account of development and well-being provided the robust conceptual foundation for Mahbub ul Haq's human development paradigm (ul Haq, 1995). The next subsection shows how the capability approach and human development paradigm interrelate and inform each other to contribute to the basis of the normative account of engineering education posited in this book.

Human development

The human development paradigm is founded on the idea that the purpose of development is to improve human lives by expanding the range of people's capabilities and functionings. Therefore, the capability approach conceptualizes development as freedom to be and do what one has reason to value, while the human development paradigm conceptualizes the purpose of development according to the expansion of the range of those freedoms, with particular attention being paid to the lives of the vulnerable and poor. Examples of general human capabilities and functionings include being healthy and well nourished, knowledgeable or able to participate in community life (Nussbaum, 2000). According to Anand and Sen (1996), human development, in the form of people being better educated, more healthy or less debilitated, etc., is not only constitutive of a better quality of life, but also contributes to one's productivity and ability to make a larger contribution to human progress and material prosperity. However, we need to avoid seeing human beings as merely the means of production and material prosperity, because that is the danger of an approach that sees people as 'human capital' (Anand & Sen, 1996).

Rejecting an exclusive concentration on people as human capital is central to the human development paradigm. However, it does not deny the commanding role of human capital, human resources or a human workforce in enhancing production and substantial wealth. There is no denial that the quality of human life can be further increased by material prosperity that is advanced by human development (Anand & Sen, 1996). Nevertheless, from a human development perspective, development is ultimately about removing the obstacles or challenges that limit the range of things a person can do or be in life. Examples of obstacles include illiteracy, ill health, lack of access to resources, or lack of civil, political, or economic freedom (Fukuda-Parr, 2003). In engineering education, an example of an obstacle to a wide set of professional capabilities is educating engineers for the sole purpose of employment. If engineering education focuses too heavily on technical skills for employment's sake, and neglects cultivating engineers' humanity, it becomes an obstacle to widening engineering graduates' capabilities and functionings both within the workplace and outside of it.

Too heavy an emphasis on technical expertise, to the exclusion of developing transversal skills like critical thinking, diminishes engineers' professional capabilities. Narrowing engineering education outcomes to technical knowledge limits students' opportunities to establish, show and improve their knowledge of and commitment to sustainability challenges. This gets in the way of achieving social justice, because it limits engineering students' effective freedom to channel their skills and knowledge explicitly towards solving problems such as extreme poverty.

As ul Haq (1995) states, treating human beings as only a resource for the production process clouds the centrality of people as the ultimate end of development. As such, human development is concerned both with building human capabilities through investment in education and health and with using those capabilities fully through an enabling framework for growth and employment (ul Haq, 1995). This means that the human development model regards economic growth as being of vital importance, but it pays equal attention to its quality and distribution, its link to human lives and its sustainability (ul Haq, 1995). The difference between economic growth or utilitarian models of development and the human development model is that the former prioritize the expansion of income and its uses, while the latter embraces the enlargement of *all* human choices, ranging from economic and political, to social and cultural (ul Haq, 1995). As Boni and Walker (2013) posit, a human development perspective, with its core values of well-being, participation, empowerment and sustainability could be a good framework within which to rethink and reimagine a different vision of the university. This is because a human development framework advances the notion that, while education can enhance human capital, people also benefit from education in ways that exceed its role in commodity production (Boni & Walker, 2013). That is, human development highlights both the instrumental *and* the intrinsic values of education and higher education.

To summarize, the human development paradigm questions the presumed (automatic) positive relation between expanding income or economies and expanding human freedoms. It reminds us that there is more to the well-being experienced by human beings than their personal economic positions, or their economic contributions to society. For these reasons, it serves well to aid the exploration of broader values associated with university learning, as it encourages an investigation of what graduates gain from higher education, beyond skills for employability. If engineering education is to contribute to engineers' human development it should produce engineering graduates who can in turn contribute to the human development of others through their personal and professional capacities. That is, engineering education should enhance graduates' personal and professional capabilities, so that they might in turn enhance the capabilities of others through their citizenship and employment.

Questions about education and its contribution to human development cannot be addressed without making considerations about ways to sustain desirable levels of human development. The discussion in the next section considers the conceptual contribution sustainable development makes to the capability approach and human development paradigm.

Public-good professionalism

Walker and McLean (2013) propose a view of professionalism grounded in the view that university-based professional education (of nurses, doctors, lawyers, engineers, teachers, social workers, economists and so on) ought to contribute to our opportunities to choose and to live in ways we find meaningful, productive and rewarding both individually and collectively to the good of society. The position advanced by Walker (2012) is that capabilities and functionings should not be left entirely unspecified for comparative assessments of justice. Rather, they should point to what it is that people (professional engineers in this case) ought to try to become for their own good lives and for the lives of others to flourish (Walker, 2012). As Walker (2012) argues, in order for us to adjudicate or evaluate what forms of professional practice are right and good, some professional and social ideal towards which we aspire ought to be identified. To develop our power through education is then also to have a view on which powers are worth developing, and which ones not (Walker, 2012). Similarly, to develop graduates' skills, knowledge and effective power through engineering education is then also to have a view on which professional capabilities and functionings are worth cultivating, and which ones not. More importantly, this judgement should be made with a particular focus on sustainable human development. That is, the capacities worth developing through engineering education have to be assessed according to their relevance for public-good professionalism or engineering that supports sustainable human development.

Sen (2009) emphasizes that as a key feature of justice, we need to recognize that capability is effective power. Thus conceived, if someone has the effective power to make a change that will reduce injustice in the world, there is a strong social argument for doing just that (Sen, 2009; also see Walker & McLean, 2013). Furthermore, research on social change suggests that if (professional) elites are sufficiently socially aware, they can play a significant role in transformative development, not only through quality in public services, but also by broadening civic participation and consolidating democratic reforms (Walker, 2012: 823). Thus, central to Walker and McLean's (2013) account of professional capabilities, is the assumption that professional education has the potential to form agents who understand and respond to the plights of others and who have acquired through their university education the competencies, knowledge and values to contribute to human development. In this context, if university graduates have effective power to contribute positively to society, then they are obligated to do so. In the specific context of engineering, it can be argued that engineering graduates ought to use their talents as a common asset to benefit society, and in particular the least fortunate.

As Walker and McLean (2013) point out, we need to revisit the idea of what we mean by 'public services' in order to revive the understanding that a service is 'public', not because it is publicly funded, but rather when it is seen to serve the public – that is, when citizens have legitimate claims on state resources that can expand their capabilities (i.e. opportunities for legal aid, health care, social welfare, urban infrastructure, clean water and so forth). Therefore, the burden and challenges of social transformation should not fall entirely on professionals in the public sector, leaving those in the private sector free of obligations for positive change. This is of particular importance within the realm of professional engineering, where many qualified engineers opt to work in the private sector. In addition, both Sen and Nussbaum's conceptualizations of the capability approach are specifically concerned with the poor, vulnerable and disadvantaged. As such, capabilities-based professionalism requires professionals to attend to these lives, whatever else they might choose to do and be as professionals (Walker & McLean, 2013). Walker and McLean (2013) emphasize that a version of professionalism that inflects towards justice, empowerment and capability enhancement aligns with the perspective that service should be judged and balanced against a larger public good. This implies that practitioners have a duty to judge what they do in light of that larger good, and to do so not as passive servants but active agents (Walker & McLean, 2013). Building on this line of argument, professionals ought to be educated in the direction of holding public-good values and committing to helping underprivileged communities. This is important for any unequal society, but most especially for developing countries like South Africa where there is a massive gap between rich and poor. Similarly, it is important for any profession, but most especially for (engineering) professionals whose work entails using technical knowledge and skills to convert natural resources into artefacts that can promote human well-being.

As Walker and McLean (2013) explain, capability-based professional ethics and practical engagement to bring about social change requires the translation of normative ideas about justice into strategies and targeted interventions. This would constitute strategic interventions to embed higher, university and engineering education in particular, within a framework of social justice. Doing so would allow universities to take their place as institutions that cultivate 'engineers for social justice'. Therefore, a key criterion for quality in engineering education in universities ought to be how professional engineers are educated to use their knowledge and skills to enlarge the range of capability sets valued by poor and marginalized communities. Another important criterion would be how engineers can be educated to contribute to public policies and actions that enhance valuable functionings that are essential for freedom.

Drawing from this discussion of the concepts that shape my understanding of development and its sustainability, I defend the claim that engineering education should be *for* sustainable human development. That is, engineering education should

- enlarge the professional capabilities and functionings of engineering graduates;
- provide them with meaningful opportunities to develop, demonstrate and deepen their commitment to the cause of poverty eradication; and
- enhance their ability to exercise agency to promote sustainable human development as a public good.

Such a model of engineering education has the potential to nurture engineering professionals who contribute to reducing injustice through their actions. Furthermore, if engineers are educated with the knowledge and skills that enable them to function as agents of justice, they have the obligation to do so. However, how can engineers be educated to work for sustainable human development? At the same time, how can we enable engineers to make appropriate judgements concerning innovations and technological advancements worth pursuing to achieve sustainable human development? Thinking about these kinds of questions has informed the aim and objectives of this book, which are described in the next section.

Sustainable human development

The capability approach, while conceptually rich in its normative account of development, says little about how to maintain or sustain the freedoms that we might achieve for people. This point is made strongly by Wolff and De-Shalit (2007) in their emphasis on 'secure functionings'. It is important to note that Sen's (1999) capability approach acknowledges human diversity to the point that it does not prescribe a fixed set of beings and doings that individuals should strive for to achieve well-being. Instead, it identifies freedom as the most indispensable condition to achieving well-being. This makes it difficult for the capability approach to describe, specifically, what the future should be like for people; it places that responsibility in the hands of people themselves to define this through processes of public deliberation (Sen, 2003). In other words, the approach does not predefine what people will value being and doing in the future.

The ontological basis of the capability approach encourages the assumption that effective *freedoms* to choose and pursue valued beings and doings will always matter to all people. For this reason, Sen (1999) argues for the importance of public participation, dialogue and deliberation in arriving at valued capabilities for specific situations and contexts. He argues that all members of any collective or society 'should be able to be active in the decisions regarding what to preserve and what to let go' (Sen, 1999: 242). The process of public discussion should enable individuals to be active contributors to change; citizens whose voices count (Walker, 2006). Sen (1999) is thus critical of the idea that 'pure theory' can substitute for the reach of democracy, or that a list of capabilities (or SDGs and MDGs) can be produced irrespective of what the public understands and values.

On the contrary, Nussbaum (2000) is a proponent of a universal, cross-cultural list of central capabilities and she argues that we need to have some idea of the kind of freedoms we are striving towards, and agree on them. Nussbaum (2000) therefore gives specific content to capabilities, disagreeing with Sen's reluctance to make commitments about what capabilities a society should primarily pursue. The lack of commitment to specific valued capabilities means limited guidance in thinking about social justice (Nussbaum, 2000). Nussbaum's tentative and revisable list of ten central human capabilities are: (1) life; (2) bodily health; (3) bodily integrity; (4) sense, imagination, and thought; (5) emotions; (6) practical reason; (7) affiliation; (8) other species (namely, living with a concern for); (9) play; and (10) control over one's political and material environment (Nussbaum, 2000: 78). Nussbaum (2000) asserts that these capabilities are the core requirements for a decent life and that they represent a minimal agreement on social justice. Furthermore, a society that does not guarantee the active cultivation and stimulation of such key freedoms cannot be considered a just society, whatever its level of affluence (Nussbaum, 2000). Therefore, while Sen's capability approach does not suggest what people will value being and doing in the future (aside from being free to do and to be what they deem valuable), Nussbaum's capability list provides a starting point for deliberating about general capabilities worth pursuing and hence worth sustaining. Furthermore, capabilities (8) and (10) on Nussbaum's list (the capability to live with concern for other species and the capability to have control over one's environment) are clearly relevant to considerations of the relationship between human beings and non-human life, which is an important element of sustainable development and hence important for our thinking about sustainable human development.

As Anand and Sen (1996) point out, there is no basic difficulty in broadening the concept of human development as outlined in the HDRs, to accommodate claims of future generations and the urgency of environmental protection, as done in the WCED's definition of sustainable development. Anand and Sen (1996) suggest that the human development paradigm translates readily into a critical and overdue recognition of the need for active international efforts to preserve the quality of the environment in which we live. That is, we can evaluate how the human developments we have achieved in the past, and what we are trying to achieve at present, can be sustained in the future (and further extended) rather than being threatened by cumulative pollution, exhaustion of natural resources, and other deteriorations of global and local environments (Anand & Sen, 1996). At the same time however, safeguarding future capabilities has to be done in a way that does not compromise current efforts towards eliminating the widespread deprivation of basic human capabilities that characterizes the unequal and unjust world in which we live (Anand & Sen, 1996).

While it is clear that the WCED's definition of sustainable development does not unpack the notion of development per se, it does focus attention on questions surrounding the temporal dimensions of development and how desirable living conditions that have been achieved can and should be maintained. This temporal focus, which brings our attention to what ought to happen (now as well as in the future), enriches the capability approach because it prompts considerations about the future in a way that the capability approach has not done exhaustively in its normative conceptualization of development – that is, by not clarifying which capabilities will matter to this end in the future. Additionally, the capability approach is weaker on its emphasis of the importance of non-human life, specifically in relation to human beings relationship with the natural environment. By 'natural environment', I refer to all vegetation, microbes, soil, rocks, atmosphere and natural phenomena that occur within their boundaries. Also included under the term natural environment are all universal natural resources and physical phenomena that lack clear-cut boundaries, such as air, water, energy, radiation, electric charge and magnetism, not originating from human activity.

A concern for the broader natural environment is implied in Nussbaum's (2006) concern with animals, many of which depend on a delicate interaction with the natural environment to survive. Nussbaum (2006) emphasizes that human beings share the world and its scarce resources with other intelligent creatures that inspire sympathy and moral concern, and deserve a dignified existence. However, the focus of her argument about the importance of non-human life is not necessarily on the well-being of the natural environment itself. Nussbaum (2006) states that when we think about the concept of global justice, we typically think of extending our theories of justice geographically (to include more of the human beings on the Earth's surface) or temporally (to take account of the interests of future people). What comes to mind less often, Nussbaum argues, is the need to extend our theories of justice outside the realm of the human, to address issues of justice involving non-human *animals* (Nussbaum, 2006).

From her discussion of 'species membership' (see Nussbaum, 2006: 21–22) it is clear that Nussbaum's primary concern is about the lack of consideration for non-human life, particularly non-human animals, in our conceptions of social justice. That is, Nussbaum does not explicitly argue for the need to extend theories of justice to include the physical natural environment. In contrast, the theory of justice brought forward through the WCED's concept of sustainable development is specifically concerned with human beings' relationship with the physical environment, and it is much more prescriptive about what this relationship should look like in the future. As affirmed by Pelenc et al. (2013) the capability approach is much less explicit about ecological constraints (on human flourishing). It does not adequately emphasize the fundamentality of environmental sustainability or opportunities for the natural environment to thrive, as a prerequisite for human development.

Pelenc et al. (2013) argue that the current conceptualization of the capability approach makes it a difficult instrument for assessing the sustainability of human well-being. This weakness can be overcome by a stronger acknowledgement of the intrinsic and instrumental values of nature, thereby adding an ecological or environmental dimension to the approach (Pelenc et al., 2013). Another recommendation made by Pelenc et al. (2013) is that the ex-ante dimension of responsibility be integrated into the capability approach, as opposed to considering responsibility from a consequentialist viewpoint (i.e. ex-post responsibility). That is, instead of viewing responsibility as something that emerges once a person exercises their freedom to act; it should be seen as existing even prior to taking action. For example, engineers do not become responsible for the environment because of their past actions (e.g. helping to create nuclear energy); they are responsible for the environment by virtue of possessing capacities for moral judgement, in the form of knowledge, skills and effective power and freedom to do so. By fully integrating the ecological dimension of well-being into an extended vision of the capability approach, a new definition of an agentic engineer arises: a responsible individual acting so as to 'generate sustainable human development for future persons' (Pelenc et al., 2013: 77).

Pelenc et al. (2013) also argue that descriptions about the relationship between the individual and collective experiences of well-being achievement should be strengthened by the idea of 'collective agency'. Scholars of the capability approach have sought to define collective capabilities (or group capabilities) and collective agency in several ways. While Stewart (2005) defines collective capabilities as the average of all selected individuals in a group; Comim and Kuklys (2002) view collective capabilities as more than the aggregation of individual capabilities. Instead, collective capabilities are described as the freedoms that can only be achieved because of social interaction (Comim & Kuklys, 2002). In this view, individual capabilities are governed by collective capabilities, because the act of choosing the life that one has reason to value might be a collective rather than an individual act (Ibrahim, 2006).

Sen (2002) on the other hand, rejects the concept of 'collective capabilities'. He argues that capabilities resulting from collective action still remain 'socially dependent individual capabilities' (Ibrahim, 2006). For Sen, only those capabilities related to humanity at large, such as drastic reductions in poverty, can be considered collective capabilities (Ibrahim, 2006; Sen, 2002). In emphasizing the importance of collective capabilities, it is necessary to introduce the concept of collective agency. Collective or group freedom is the freedom of a group of individual agents to perform a set of distinct actions in combination; they constitute the new range of choices that individuals (as a group) gain as a result of collective action (Ibrahim, 2006).

In order to expand their collective freedoms and capabilities, individuals need to exercise agency. Acts of agency are mainly affected by prevailing communal values and social structures; therefore, agents are constituted by and constitute structures (Ibrahim, 2006). That is, individual agency brings about change not only through individual deeds, but through formal and informal collective action (Deneulin & Stewart, 2002). In contrast to individual agency where a person 'individually' pursues their own perception of the good, through acts of collective agency, the individual can pursue this perception of the good collectively by joining or participating in a group with similar goals (Ibrahim, 2006). For example, individual engineers seeking to enhance human development for poor communities can join groups such as Engineers without Borders.

Collective agency is thus not only instrumentally valuable for generating new capabilities, but also intrinsically important in shaping and pursuing the individual's perception of the good (Ibrahim, 2006). As Ibrahim (2006) asserts, it is indisputable that human beings can bring about changes in their societies through both individual and collective actions. The important question is, which way is more effective? (Ibrahim, 2006). Ibrahim agrees with Fukuda-Parr (2003) that collective action is a vital force that can pressure changes in policies and bring about political change. Collective agency is therefore crucial for people to influence the social structures in which they live (Ibrahim, 2006). In the case of engineers, collective agency is crucial for them to be able to influence engineering work structures or pressure changes in industry so that poverty reduction might feature more strongly in companies' policy imperatives.

As mentioned earlier, engineering activities are central to the creation of social artefacts and systems (roads, railways, wastewater systems, etc.) that have generally been seen as manifestations of development. This is because such artefacts represent the transformation of natural resources into infrastructure, which serves universal human needs and the global economy. Considering that engineers are major contributors and often pioneers of technological advancements that are created to contribute to development, they have to make moral judgements about the technologies, products and processes that are worth pursuing to achieve sustainability. Through the lens of the capability approach and human development paradigm, if engineering outcomes do not increase possibilities for current and future generations globally to live the kind of lives they have reason to value or achieve valued functionings, then they are not necessarily examples of sustainable development. To summarize:

> [S]ustainability is a matter of *distributional equity* in a very broad sense, that is, of sharing the capacity for well-being between present people and future people in an acceptable way – that is in a way which neither the present generation nor the future generations can readily *reject*.
>
> (Anand & Sen, 2000: 2038, original emphases)

If we think about sustainable development from a capabilities perspective, the main implication for engineering education is that it should provide students with opportunities to develop, demonstrate and deepen their commitment to enhancing the capabilities of the poor, and the capacity of the environment.

While one can argue that many students in engineering programmes have opportunities to learn about ways in which they can contribute to reducing carbon dioxide emissions through their work, thereby redressing environmental pollution, it is more difficult to claim that the same students have chances to learn how they might meaningfully redress extreme poverty through their work. There are many examples of curriculum reform in engineering education across the world, which reflects institutional responses to global action plans aligned with ESD (for example, see Mulder & Jansen, 2006; Von Blottnitz, Case & Fraser, 2015). Unfortunately, most courses that teach 'sustainable development' generally interpret the purpose of ESD narrowly, primarily seeing ESD as a means to ensure that students learn about environmental sustainability (Karatzoglou, 2013). This is unfortunate because, as mentioned earlier, the two key concepts of sustainable development are human needs, particularly those of the poor to which overriding priority should be given; *and* the limitations of the environment to cater for current and future human and non-human life. These key concepts suggest that restoring environmental balance and eliminating poverty are *both* amongst the bottom-line objectives of sustainable development. Moreover, eliminating poverty can also be considered as the bottom-line objective of the SDGs and MDGs. It is therefore a cause that deserves much more attention in engineering programmes and courses that address sustainable development. If sustainable development is to become the leitmotiv of engineering education, it can be argued that the primary concern of sustainability courses should be addressing questions related to how engineers can and should direct their knowledge, expertise and effective power towards conserving the environment *and* eliminating poverty.

Looked at from a capabilities perspective, if development is characterized by enhanced capabilities and functionings, and the outcome of engineering activities is development, then it can be argued that the main objective of engineering should be to create opportunities for people living in poverty or leading vulnerable lives to do and be what they have reason to value. In both cases, the implication is that engineering graduates ought to have opportunities to develop concern for, and commit to, alleviating poverty through their professional functionings. Failure to create these opportunities in engineering curricula and pedagogy is problematic for public-good professionalism (see Kulacki, 1999; Walker, 2012; Walker & McLean, 2013).

Aims and structure of the book

This book aims to provide a conceptualization of the notion of quality in university engineering education through the lenses of the capability approach and human development paradigm. As such, the book aims to demonstrate the usefulness of the capability approach as a normative lens through which to conceptualize the ends of engineering education. The book's theoretical ambitions are also to show how the capability approach can be informed by, and informs the concept of, 'sustainable development', and to illustrate what pedagogical and curricula implications this may have on ESD particularly in engineering. In this way, the book is strategically located between two directions in higher education research. It builds on the work of scholars of engineering education and of university education on the nexus of development and sustainability. At the same time, this work takes up theoretical impulses set out by scholars who have applied the capability approach and human development paradigm in higher education and engineering education studies.

The book will contribute to higher education literature on the capabilities approach, engineering education, and ESD by:

1   demonstrating how the theoretical concepts of the capabilities approach can be operationalized and empirically applied in the context of engineering education;
2   presenting the perspectives of engineering employers, educators and students on capabilities and functionings that are enlarged through engineering education, and theorizing on their implications for pro-poor engineering;
3   providing a capabilities-inspired, empirically informed framework for public-good engineering; and
4   describing how engineering education can enable graduates, through their work, to function as agents of sustainable human development.

This is done across three parts into which this book is divided. Part I comprises Chapters 1 and 2. While the present chapter provides the background and an introduction to the book's thesis and the theoretical framework that underpins it, Chapter 2 presents a capabilities lens on researching engineering education and describes the research context and methods used to gather the empirical data from which this book draws.

Part II is made up of Chapters 3, 4 and 5, where perspectives on engineering and engineering education are discussed based on students', employers' and educators' perspectives respectively. Chapter 3 reports on students' views on becoming an engineer, with a particular focus on valued educational capabilities and functionings that are relevant for advancing sustainable human development. Chapter 4 discusses lecturers' perspectives on teaching for public-good engineering, while Chapter 5 provides views from employers on the type of skills they perceive as necessary for public-good professionalism.

Part III of this book comprises Chapters 6 and 7 and describes transitions towards engineering for the public good. Chapter 6 outlines what universities can do to advance sustainable human development through engineering education, while the concluding chapter discusses the findings from interviews conducted with students and reflects on the extent to which they are able to be public-good engineers and practise socially just engineering in their current employment.

The three parts lend themselves differently to specific readers. Engineering employers, educators and students might find Parts II and III of particular interest, while Part I will likely appeal most to sustainability and social justice activists, capability scholars and researchers conducting studies in the areas of engineering education and ESD. These are groups for whom the book is mainly intended, as it does not provide comprehensive pragmatic advice for institutional implementation of policy or procedures that might translate a framework for public-good engineering education into reality. Rather, it is hoped that this book will provide inspiration and ideas for anyone who is interested in exploring how we might orient technical knowledge and transversal skills towards the public good.

Notes

1 See also Sustainable Development Timeline (IISD, 2012).
2 Human Development Reports are produced by the United Nations Development Programme (UNDP). The first report was published in 1990 (see UNDP, 1990) and subsequent issues seek to bring the human development perspective to bear on a range of contemporary societal issues (for example see UNDP, 2015).
3 Biogas is a mixture of different gases produced by the anaerobic digestion of organic matter. It can be produced from raw materials such as agricultural waste, manure, municipal and food waste, plant material, sewage, etc.
4 Project-based learning refers to teaching approaches that use multifaceted projects as a central organizing strategy for educating students. Students are typically assigned a project that requires them to use diverse skills (researching, writing, interviewing, collaborating, etc.) to produce various work products (research papers, scientific studies, etc.).
5 Problem-based learning is a student centred pedagogy that entails group work to solve complex and real-life problems and helps develop students' content knowledge and their problem-solving, reasoning, communication and self-assessment skills.
6 Back-casting refers to developing normative scenarios and exploring their feasibility and implications. In ESD, it is as a tool for connecting desirable long-term future scenarios with present situations by means of a participatory process.
7 In this book, the term 'capabilities' or 'capability' is used to refer to effective and valued freedoms, opportunities, possibilities and/or choices as defined in Sen's (1999) capability approach. It is therefore not to be confused with the general definition of capability as 'ability' or a measure of one's aptitude.
8 The HDI is a composite measurement of life expectancy, education and income per capita indicators that are used to rank countries into four tiers of human development, thereby assessing human well-being from a broad perspective that goes beyond income.
9 The MPI uses multiple factors to measure acute poverty internationally at the household level. It complements traditional income-based poverty measures by capturing how deprivation in education, health and living standards overlaps, thus providing vital information on who is poor and *how* they are poor.

References

Ahern, A., O'Connor, T., McRuairc, G., McNamara, M. & O'Donnell, D. (2012). Critical thinking in the university curriculum – the impact on engineering education. *European Journal of Engineering Education, 37*(2), 125–132.

Alkire, S. (2002). Dimensions of human development. *World Development, 30*(2), 181–205.

Alkire, S., & Deneulin, S. (2010). The human development and capability approach. In S. Alkire, & S. Deneulin (eds), *An introduction to the human development and capability approach.* London: Earthscan.

Alkire, S., Jindra, C., Aguilar, G. R., Seth, S. & Vaz, A. (2015). *Global Multidimensional Poverty Index 2015* (Research Brief). Oxford Poverty & Human Development Initiative (OPHI). Accessed 1 September 2017 from www.ophi.org.uk/wp-content/uploads/Global-MPI-8-pager_10_15.pdf.

Anand, S., & Sen, A. (1996). *Sustainable Human Development: Concepts and Priorities* (paper written in preparation for the 1994 Human Development Report). UNDP Human Development Report Office. Accessed 1 September 2017 from http://hdr.undp.org/sites/default/files/anand_sudhir_-_sustainable_human_development-_concepts_and_priorities.pdf.

Anand, S., & Sen, A. (2000). Human development and economic sustainability. *World Development, 28*(12), 2029–2049.

Boni, A., McDonald, P. & Peris, J. (2012). Cultivating engineers' humanity: Fostering cosmopolitanism in a technical university. *International Journal of Educational Development, 32*(1), 179–186.

Boni, A., & Walker, M. (2013). Human development, capabilities, and universities of the twenty-first century. In A. Boni and M. Walker (eds), *Human development and capabilities: Reimagining the university of the twenty-first century.* London and New York: Routledge.

Comim, F., & Kuklys, W. (2002). Is poverty about poor individuals? Presented at the 27th General Conference of the International Association for Research in Income and Wealth, Djurham (Stockholm Archipelago), Sweden. Retrieved from file:///C:/Users/HoppenerM/Downloads/Is_Poverty_About_Poor_Individuals_.pdf.

Connor, A. M., Karmokar, S., Whittington, C. & Walker, C. (2014). Full STEAM ahead: A manifesto for integrating arts pedagogics into STEM education. In *IEEE*, Wellington, New Zealand. Accessed 1 September 2017 from http://dx.doi.org/10.1109/TALE.2014.7062556.

Crabtree, A. (2013). Sustainable development: Does the capability approach have anything to offer? Outlining a legitimate freedom approach. *Journal of Human Development and Capabilities, 4*(1), 40–57.

Crocker, D. A., & Robeyns, I. (2010). Capability and agency. In C. Morris (ed.), *Amartya Sen* (1st edn). New York: Cambridge University Press.

De la Harpe, B., & Thomas, I. (2009). Curriculum change in universities: Conditions that facilitate education for sustainable development. *Journal of Education for Sustainable Development, 3*(1), 75–85.

DEAT. (2008). *People – Planet – Prosperity: A national framework for sustainable development in South Africa.* Department of Environmental Affairs and Tourism.

Deneulin, S., & Stewart, F. (2002). Amartya Sen's contribution to development thinking. *Studies in Comparative International Development, 37*(2), 63–70.

Fadeeva, Z., & Galkute, L. (2012). Looking for synergies: Education for sustainable development and the Bologna Process. *Journal of Education for Sustainable Development, 6*(1), 91–100.

Fernandes, S., Flores, M. A. & Lima, R. M. (2012). Students' views of assessment in project-led engineering education: Findings from a case study in Portugal. *Assessment & Evaluation in Higher Education, 37*(2), 163–178.

Fernandes, S., Mesquita, D., Flores, M. A. & Lima, R. M. (2014). Engaging students in learning: Findings from a study of project-led education. *European Journal of Engineering Education, 39*(1), 55–67. Accessed 1 September 2017 from https://doi.org/10.1 080/03043797.2013.833170.

Fernández-Baldor, Á., Boni, A., Lillo, P. & Hueso, A. (2014). Are technological projects reducing social inequalities and improving people's well-being? A capability approach analysis of renewable energy based electrification projects in Cajamarca, Peru. *Journal of Human Development and Capabilities: A Multi-Disciplinary Journal for People-Centered Development, 15*(1), 13–27. Accessed 1 September 2017 from https://doi.org /10.1080/19452829.2013.837035.

Fukuda-Parr, S. (2003). The human development paradigm: Operationalizing Sen's ideas on capabilities. *Feminist Economics, 9*(2–3), 301–317. Accessed 1 September 2017 from https://doi.org/10.1080/1354570022000077980.

Hopkins, C. (2012). Reflections on 20+ years of ESD. *Journal of Education for Sustainable Development, 6*(1), 21–35.

Ibrahim, S. (2006). From individual to collective capabilities: The capability approach as a conceptual framework for self-help. *Journal of Human Development, 7*(3), 397–416.

International Institute for Sustainable Development. (2012). *Sustainable Development Timeline.* Accessed 9 December 2014 from www.iisd.org/pdf/2012/sd_timeline_ 2012.pdf.

IUCN. (1980). *World conservation strategy.* IUCN-UNEP-WWF.

Jones, P., Trier, C. J. & Richards, J. P. (2008). Embedding education for sustainable development in higher education: A case study examining common challenges and opportunities for undergraduate programmes. *International Journal of Educational Research, 47*(6), 341–350.

Karatzoglou, B. (2013). An in-depth literature review of the evolving roles and contributions of universities to education for sustainable development. *Journal of Cleaner Production, 49*, 44–53. Accessed 1 September 2017 from http://dx.doi.org/10.1016/j. jclepro.2012.07.043.

Kulacki, F. A. (1999). Engineering, engineers and the public good. *William Mitchell Law Review, 25*(1), 157–179.

Lélé, S. M. (1991). Sustainable development: A critical review. *World Development, 19*(6), 607–621.

Lessmann, O., & Rauschmayer, F. (2013). Re-conceptualizing sustainable development on the basis of the capability approach: A model and its difficulties. *Journal of Human Development and Capabilities, 14*(1), 95–114.

Lozano, R. (ed.) (2013). Advancing higher education for sustainable development: International insights and critical reflections. *Journal of Cleaner Production, 48*, 3–9. Accessed 1 September 2017 from http://dx.doi.org/10.1016/j.jclepro.2013.03.034.

Lucena, J., & Schneider, J. (2008). Engineers, development, and engineering education: From national to sustainable community development. *European Journal of Engineering Education, 33*(3), 247–257.

Mebratu, D. (1998). Sustainability and sustainable development: Historical and conceptual review. *Environmental Impact Assessment Review, 18*(493–520). Accessed 1 September 2017 from http://citeseerx.ist.psu.edu/viewdoc/download;jsessionid=2954BD7 DAF9D6719BD51AB2B6CC0B495?doi=10.1.1.474.8171&rep=rep1&type=pdf.

Mulder, K., & Jansen, L. (2006). Integrating sustainable development in engineering education – reshaping university education by organizational learning. In J. Holmberg, & B. E. Samuelsson (eds), *Drivers and barriers for implementing sustainable development in higher education: Education for sustainable development in action* (Technical Paper no. 3), Paris: UNESCO, pp. 69–74,

Nussbaum, M. C. (2000). *Women and human development: The capabilities approach.* Cambridge: Cambridge University Press.

Nussbaum, M. C. (2006). *Frontiers of justice: Disability, nationality, species membership.* Cambridge, MA: Harvard University Press.

Paden, M. (2007). Strategy for ESD in sub-Saharan Africa. *Journal of Education for Sustainable Development, 1*(1), 127–132.

Peeters, W., Dirix, J. & Sterckx, S. (2013). Putting sustainability into sustainable human development. *Journal of Human Development and Capabilities, 14*(2), 58–76.

Pelenc, J., Lompo, M., K., Ballet, J. & Dubois, J.-L. (2013). Sustainable human development and the capability approach: Integrating environment, responsibility and collective agency. *Journal of Human Development and Capabilities, 14*(1), 77–94.

Petersen, R. P. (2013). The potential role of design in a sustainable engineering profile. In *EESD13*. Cambridge, UK. Accessed 1 September 2017 from www-csd.eng.cam.ac.uk/proceedings-of-the-eesd13-conference-cambridge-2013-v-2/eesd13-published-papers/premer-petersen-r.pdf/at_download/file.

Ramos, T. B., Caeiro, S., Hoof, B. van, Lozano, R. & Huisingh, D. (2015). Experiences from the implementation of sustainable development in higher education institutions: Environmental management for sustainable universities. *Journal of Cleaner Production,* (106), 3–10. Accessed 1 September 2017 from https://doi.org/doi:10.1016/j.jclepro.2015.05.110.

Repetto, R. (1986). *World enough and time.* New Haven, CT: Yale University Press.

Rist, G. (2008). *The history of development: From western origins to global faith.* London & New York: Zed Books.

Robert, K. W., Parris, T. M. & Leiserowitz, A. A. (2005). What is sustainable development? Goals, indicators, values, and practice. *Environment: Science and Policy for Sustainable Development, 47*(3), 8–21. Accessed 1 September 2017 from https://sites.hks.harvard.edu/sustsci/ists/docs/whatisSD_env_kates_0504.pdf.

Schneider, J., Leydens, J. A. & Lucena, J. (2008). Where is 'community'? Engineering education and sustainable community development. *European Journal of Engineering Education, 33*(3), 307–319.

Segalás, J., Ferrer-Balas, D. & Mulder, K. F. (2010). What do engineering students learn in sustainability courses? The effect of the pedagogical approach. *Journal of Cleaner Production, 18*, 275–284. Accessed 1 September 2017 from https://doi.org/10.1016/j.jclepro.2009.09.012.

Sen, A. (1985). Well-being, agency and freedom. *Journal of Philosophy, 82*(4), 169–221.

Sen, A. (1999). *Development as freedom.* Oxford: Oxford University Press.

Sen, A. K. (1992). *Inequality re-examined.* Oxford: Clarendon Press.

Sen, A. K. (2002). Response to commentaries. *Studies in Comparative International Development, 37*(2), 78–86.

Sen, A. K. (2003). Development as capability expansion. In S. Fukuda-Parr (ed.), *Readings in human development.* Oxford University Press.

Sen, A. (2009). *The idea of justice.* Cambridge, MA: The Belknap Press of Harvard University Press.

Stewart, F. (2005). Groups and capabilities. *Journal of Human Development, 6*(2), 185–204. Accessed 1 September 2017 from https://doi.org/10.1080/14649880500120517.

Tilbury, D., & Mula, I. (2009). A United Nations Decade of Education for Sustainable Development (2005–14): What difference will it make? *Journal of Education for Sustainable Development, 3*(1), 87–97.

Trevelyan, J. (2007). Technical coordination in engineering practice. *Journal of Engineering Education, 96*(3), 191–204. Accessed 1 September 2017 from https://doi.org/10.1002/j.2168-9830.2007.tb00929.x.

ul Haq, M. (1995). *Reflections on human development*. New York: Oxford University Press.

UN. (1972). *Report of the United Nations conference on the human environment*. Stockholm: United Nations.

UN. (2012). *Realizing the future we want for all* (Report to the Secretary-General). New York: United Nations System Task Team.

UN DESA. (2015). *Global sustainable development report*. United Nations Department of Economic and Social Affairs. Accessed 1 September 2017 from https://sustainabledevelopment.un.org/content/documents/1758GSDR%202015%20Advance%20Unedited%20Version.pdf.

UNCED. (1992). *AGENDA 21*. Rio de Janeiro, Brazil: United Nations Conference on Environment & Development. Accessed 1 September 2017 from https://sustainabledevelopment.un.org/content/documents/Agenda21.pdf.

UNDP. (1990). *Human development report 1990*. New York and Oxford: Oxford University Press. Accessed 19 June 2013 from http://hdr.undp.org/sites/default/files/reports/219/hdr_1990_en_complete_nostats.pdf.

UNDP. (2015). *Human development report 2015: work for human development*. New York: United Nations Development Programme. Accessed 26 July 2016 from http://hdr.undp.org/sites/default/files/2015_human_development_report.pdf.

von Blottnitz, H., Case, J. M. & Fraser, D. M. (2015). Sustainable development at the core of undergraduate engineering curriculum reform: A new introductory course in chemical engineering. *Journal of Cleaner Production, 106*, 300–307. Accessed 1 September 2017 from https://doi.org/10.1016/j.jclepro.2015.01.063.

Walby, S. (2011). Sen and the measurement of justice and capabilities: A problem in theory and practice. *Theory Culture and Society, 29*(1), 99–118.

Walker, M. (2006). Towards a capability-based theory of social justice for education policy-making. *Journal of Education Policy, 21*, 163–185.

Walker, M. (2012). Universities, professional capabilities and contributions to the public good in South Africa. *Compare: A Journal of Comparative and International Education, 42*(6), 819–838. Accessed 1 September 2017 from https://doi.org/10.1080/03057925.2012.685584.

Walker, M., & McLean, M. (2013). *Professional education, capabilities and the public good: The role of universities in promoting human development*. New York: Routledge.

WCED. (1987). *Our common future* (World Commission on Environment and Development). New York: Oxford University Press. Accessed 1 September 2017 from www.un-documents.net/ocf-02.htm.

Wolff, J., & De-Shalit, A. (2007). *Disadvantage*. Oxford: Oxford University Press.

WSSD. (2002). *The World Summit on Sustainable Development*. Johannesburg, South Africa. Accessed 1 September 2017 from www.un.org/events/wssd/summaries/.

2 A capabilities lens on researching engineering education

As outlined in Chapter 1, the way we view education is challenged when we look at development primarily in terms of capabilities expansion, instead of primarily in economic terms (Ribeiro, 2015) – that is, when the human being is placed at the centre of concerns, and sustainable and human development is presented in terms of enlarging individuals' choices (UNDP, 1990). However, the capability approach is clear in depicting education as having both intrinsic value for individuals *and* social value for communities (Sen, 1999). In addition, the capability approach is a theory of human nature that is not merely focused on individuals, but is evaluative and ethical from the onset (Nussbaum, 2000). For example, questions that can stimulate our thinking about the type of world we want to live in include: 'Among the many things human beings might develop the capacity to do, which ones are the valuable ones? Which are the ones that a minimally just society will endeavour to nurture and support?' (Nussbaum, 2011: 28). Applied to engineering education, we might then ask:

> Amongst the many things that future engineers might develop the capacity to do, which are the important ones for public-good engineering? Which are the most relevant for sustainable development? Moreover, which are the ones that engineering education should endeavour to nurture and support?'

A capabilities view on engineering education inspires the judgement of educational practices according to whether and how they enhance individual well-being for each student, whether the classroom community is a context for mutual well-being (Wood & Deprez, 2012), and whether individual students' capabilities can be used to widen capabilities in society. That is, from a capabilities perspective, engineering education should strive to widen opportunities 'to be and to do' for students, 'both in the spirit of individual enhancement and its impact on and influence of social enhancement' (Wood & Deprez, 2012: 477). In this sense, educational capabilities create: (1) the opportunity for individuals to participate in education; (2) the effective freedoms gained through education for the individual (Vaughan, 2007); and, (3) the effective freedoms gained through education for wider society. This implies that the responsibility of professional educators is correspondingly threefold: (1) to ensure that students can fully participate in learning experiences; (2) to ensure that students have opportunities to discern what they need to realize their valued functionings (Wood & Deprez, 2012); and (3) to help ensure that students' valued functionings are reasonably aligned with the objective of enhancing valuable capabilities in wider society.

Thus conceived, education is a capability in itself and it is foundational to other capabilities (Sen, 2002; Terzi, 2007; Unterhalter, 2002). The following section expands on the idea of education as a capability, and considers what other dimensions of education one might argue provide a foundation for educational capabilities that engineers need in order to promote sustainable human development.

Dimensions of education for public-good engineering

Education as a capability

According to Sen (2002), Terzi (2007) and Unterhalter (2002), the capability to be educated is basic in the sense of being a fundamental freedom, and foundational to other freedoms as well as future ones. Terzi (2007) provides the example of the opportunity to learn mathematics. She argues that formally learning mathematics not only expands the individual's various functionings related to mathematical reasoning and problem solving, but it also widens the individual's sets of opportunities (Terzi, 2007). On the one hand, Terzi (2007) agues, more complex capabilities are enabled (for example, applying mathematical knowledge to algebra, geometry or calculus). On the other hand, better prospects for opportunities in life are enabled (Terzi, 2007) (for example, having broader career options in mathematics-related occupations such as accounting, actuarial sciences and engineering).

Therefore, the broadening of capabilities enabled by education extends to the advancement of complex capabilities, by promoting reflection, understanding, information and awareness of one's capabilities (Terzi, 2007). At the same time, education promotes opportunities to formulate a range of beings and doings that individuals have reason to value (Terzi, 2007; also see Saito, 2003). Furthermore, the expansion of capabilities entailed by education extends to varieties of occupations and certain levels of social, civic and political participation (Terzi, 2007). As such, providing access to education and promoting a concrete set of basic learning outcomes, such as reading and writing (Unterhalter, 2002), creates opportunities for other, more sophisticated beings and doings such as being knowledgeable about the challenges of sustainable development.

However, from a capabilities viewpoint, it can be argued that learning that stops at only basic reading and writing is insufficient to advance sustainable development in its full sense (Ribeiro, 2015). In the case of engineers, it can similarly be argued that education that stops at providing technical expertise and a basic understanding of the concept of sustainable development is inadequate to advance sustainable human development to the fullest extent possible. That is, engineering education should manifest as an opportunity for students to learn how they can advance sustainable human development. In order for this happen, engineering students need not only to learn engineering expertise, but also to learn to value principles of social justice and recognize the inherent potential of engineering to contribute to development that is more just.

Education as an instrument of social justice

According to Oosterlaken (2009), adopting the capability approach immediately seems to be strongly compatible with recognizing and improving the contribution to development of technology and engineering products. After all, Oosterlaken asks, what is technology for, if not for increasing human capabilities (Oosterlaken, 2009)? Just as the invention of the wheel enhanced our opportunities to transport heavy loads, more recently, the computer enhanced our capacity to make complex calculations efficiently (Oosterlaken, 2009). This is an example of how technologies have grown more complex over time, and how they are (in an increasingly complex way) intertwined with society, institutions, laws and procedures (Oosterlaken, 2009). Additionally, technological advancement intends to add to our capabilities to survive (such as in the case of medical equipment), or to participate in public deliberation (such as in the case of internet applications that facilitate political discussion) (Oosterlaken, 2009). As obvious as making this connection between technology and capabilities may seem, philosophers working on the capability approach so far do not seem to have thoroughly realized the relevance of technology, engineering and design for capability expansion (Oosterlaken, 2009).

It is important to note that philosophers and sociologists of technology have argued in past decades that engineering products are far from being neutral tools to be used at will for either good or bad (Oosterlaken, 2009). Rather, they are value-laden and thus inherently normative (Oosterlaken, 2009). Based on this point of view, sustainable human development and social justice have great potential to be realized through technology, if professional engineering functionings are unequivocally aligned with them. This means that the 'details of design are morally significant' (Oosterlaken, 2009: 95). Therefore, if technologies are value-laden, engineers should be mindful of this and design technologies in such a way that incorporates their moral values, and not too easily assume that a certain product or technology will do well in expanding people's capabilities (Oosterlaken, 2009). As such, if the capability approach is applied to the design of new technologies and products, the most important objective for engineering might be to use 'capability-sensitive design' (Oosterlaken, 2009: 96) and engineering knowledge to advance social justice.

As Oosterlaken states, capability-sensitive design is not something completely new or entirely different from what Nieusma (2004) calls 'alternative design scholarship'; there are significant synergies as is evident from the explanation that follows. Design scholars from diverse fields have attempted to assist marginalized social groups by redirecting design thinking towards their needs

(Nieusma, 2004). By offering different options to dominant design activities, alternative design scholarship seeks to understand how unequal power relations are embodied in, and result from, conventional design practice and products (Nieusma, 2004). That is, alternative design scholars analyse how technologies and other engineered artefacts are implicated in larger social problems such as rampant consumerism, ecological abuse, and restricted access to the built environment (Nieusma, 2004). Alternative design scholarship offers designers and engineers (and other professional groups at the forefront of development work) an opportunity to rethink how their work might be applied as wisely and as fairly as possible (Nieusma, 2004).

In agreement with Oosterlaken (2009), there is a clear link between capability-sensitive design, universal design (see Goldsmith, 2000) and partici-patory design methodologies (see Bratteteig & Wagner, 2014 or Schuler & Namioka, 1993). Universal design is founded on the assumption that it is pos-sible to design objects and spaces so that they are usable (and will be used) by a vast range of the population, including but not limited to people with disabilities (Connell & Sanford, 1999; Goldsmith, 2000; Nieusma, 2004). Universal design theorists prompt designers to think systematically about inclusion and to broaden their notions about who the users are (Nieusma, 2004). For example, some out-comes of engineering (like luxury cars) expand capabilities for the rich, instead of broadening capabilities for poor and marginalized communities. By virtue of the steep price attached to such products, poor and marginalized groups in society are often systematically, but unnecessarily, impeded in their access to certain means of transport. Thus conceived, some engineering outcomes, by design, further alienate poor and marginalized communities from certain cap-abilities. This notion is discussed by Lucena (2013), who describes how students in a sustainable engineering design class ought to be guided to analyse the social justice dimensions of a public transportation project in a neighbourhood with people living below the poverty line. This approach serves as an example of the importance of interdisciplinary collaborations in creating opportunities to enhance the potential of engineering education to function as an instrument of social justice. It also shows an example of how universities might create a com-munity service activity close to home where the social justice dimensions are more visible, relevant and connected to students (Lucena, 2013).

Universal design insights have been influential in challenging such narrow approaches to product design by contributing to analyses of social power in design by: (1) identifying groups of people whose needs systematically go unmet, and (2) advocating that the design community consider the needs of these groups much more seriously (Nieusma, 2004).

From its inception, participatory design scholarship has sought to cope with differences of perspective and goals in an explicit, productive and fair way (Brat-teteig & Wagner, 2014; Nieusma, 2004). Instead of ignoring the fact that con-flicting interests underlie many important design decisions, participatory designers attempt to leverage such differences to arrive at outcomes suitable to diverse interests (Nieusma, 2004). Participatory design scholars call attention to underlying inequalities, and provide two core reasons for working against them: participatory decision making is fairer and it is more intelligent than non-participatory processes (Nieusma, 2004). It is fairer because people who are affected by a decision or event should have an opportunity to influence it, and it is more intelligent because broad participation informed by multiple interests is more likely to result in widely agreeable solutions to shared problems (Nieusma, 2004).

It is thus clear that principles embedded in universal and participatory design are consistent with ideals of social justice. While universal design is concerned with widening the use and accessibility of social artefacts and the built environment to marginalized populations, participatory design aims at making design processes more inclusive and hence beneficial to the end user. In this way, participatory design is aligned with the concept of public deliberation, the importance of which is emphasized in the capability approach. Capability-sensitive design can therefore be described as an extension of these objectives, because it prompts questions surrounding the effective opportunities and functionings enlarged by design outcomes. More specifically, it advocates for more attention to be paid to the capabilities of people living in poverty. This indicates that capability-sensitive design is able to integrate lessons from existing fields of scholarship in a more comprehensive approach that offers a clear philosophical foundation for the ultimate ends of design (Oosterlaken, 2009). Most importantly, capability-sensitive design can provide engineers with the inspiration to orient engineering design towards social justice.

Once engineering students are equipped with knowledge that enables critical awareness of the interconnectedness of engineering, design and the broader objectives of social justice, they need to be encouraged to take action that advances it. That is, once engineering students recognize that engineering knowledge can be placed at the service of social justice, they need to develop the autonomy and agency to translate this possibility into reality, through their professional functionings (both individually and collectively). Therefore, engineering education ought to develop and heighten students' agency and resilience. This is particularly important because of existing economic, political and environmental constraints (or conversion factors) that make engineering activities complex and challenging.

Education as a foundation for agency

According to Lozano, Bonni, Peris and Hueso (2012), the concept of agency (discussed in Chapter 1) is particularly relevant for reflecting on education as it implies three levels of claims, namely the claims that it is possible to:

1   educate people to apply reason to personal decisions and preferences;
2   enhance people's capacities to reflect critically on the world and to envisage desirable changes; and
3   cultivate the capacities to accomplish such changes in practice.

That is, for the capability approach, the goal of education is also to expand people's agency: to enable them to be the authors of their own lives (Lozano et al., 2012). Therefore, without an authentic opportunity to be educated or the means to avail themselves of that opportunity, many people may be limited to constrained agency and freedom (Wood & Deprez, 2012). If higher education experiences are to aid students in being and acting in ways that they value, they ought to create opportunities for authentic autonomy and choice in terms of how and what students learn, and in terms of how they demonstrate their learning (Wood & Deprez, 2012). Moreover, students need opportunities to develop 'authentic and expressive voices' (Wood & Deprez, 2012: 479). In addition, in order to exercise their voices and choices well, students need to develop critical capacities in order to recognize how conventional cultural assumptions have shaped their perceptions, attitudes and values (Wood & Deprez, 2012). Ideally, in the process of encountering relevant topics (such as sustainable development in engineering education), lecture halls should be spaces that are conducive for critical, dialogic and inquiring exchanges (Wood & Deprez, 2012). Wood and Deprez (2012: 479) refer here to a context that: provokes students' views on a variety of course topics; 'scaffolds their reasoning and reflection as they sift through differing opinions and arguments', and promotes balanced judgement of opposing points of view or respectful critiques. Furthermore, because student agency is a fundamental dimension of human well-being (see Walker & Unterhalter, 2007), higher education needs to provide the conditions for it to develop (Wood & Deprez, 2012).

As asserted by Walker (2006), a lack of agency or constrained agency equates to disadvantage, and it is therefore essential to decide what capabilities support agency development in higher education (Walker, 2006). In the case of cultivating public-good engineers, we therefore need to consider the ways in which engineering education as an opportunity and as a process develops agency in learners. Drawing from Walker's discussion on the assessment of pedagogic quality in higher education from a capabilities perspective, we could argue that if agency is being disabled in engineering education, then engineering education is diminished and its quality undermined. This is because failing to develop agentic engineers is failing to maximize the potential for engineering knowledge to be used *for* social justice. If this is the case, then the potential to develop engineers who are agents of sustainable human development is lessened.

Education as a basis for sustainable human development

To enhance development as expressed in the capability approach, education must move towards specifically addressing the needs and aspirations of individual students, their ability to think, reason and build up self-respect, as well as respect for others (Ribeiro, 2015). According to Ribeiro, the importance of such mental power (i.e. cognitive, emotional and social abilities) is making its way into education policies often under the name of 'life skills'. Life skills education has gradually come to be seen as a comprehensive approach to a good-quality education. Specific teaching methodologies for mental skills development based on participation, interaction and the use of learning-friendly environments have been developed and used extensively for teaching and learning life skills (Ribeiro, 2015). By focusing on the methodology, the approach can be adapted specifically to address multiple values, attitudes and behaviours regarding a number of different topics, including environmental protection, gender issues, human rights approaches and the promotion of tolerance and peace building (Ribeiro, 2015).

Ribeiro convincingly argues that an educational framework for life skills can be seen as a basis for ESD. She grounds her proposal in the life skills framework for 'teaching, learning, and human development' recommended in the report to UNESCO by the International Commission on Education for the 21st Century (see UNESCO, 2014). According to Ribeiro (2015), the framework consists of four pillars of learning that combine life skills and technical skills in a teaching and learning situation. These four pillars are: (1) learning to know, (2) learning to be, (3) learning to live together and (4) learning to do:

- Learning to know refers to the understanding and use of knowledge, where related abilities include critical thinking, problem solving and decision-making life skills that are fundamental to informed action.
- Learning to be concerns the concept of agency, which includes life skills for coping, self-awareness, self-esteem and self-confidence, while aiming at building an identity, valuing oneself, setting goals, etc.
- Learning to live together implies feeling affiliated to a group, a category, a society, or culture and understanding and respecting differences. Related interpersonal abilities include communication and negotiation life skills that are essential to define a person as a social being in constant interaction with the world.
- Learning to do is linked to the mastering of cultural tools (i.e. patterns of behaviour) in order to act. Related abilities are associated with the practical or technical application of what is learned (Ribeiro, 2015).

This account of life skills underscores that actions are influenced not only by knowledge but by perceptions, values and attitudes that affect one's decision to act (one's agency) in particular ways. As Ribeiro explains, learning to be and to live together underlines the importance of interaction between internal and external factors. Internal factors refer to the assumption that reality for each person is defined by him or herself, which is directly linked to the notion of agency in the capability approach (Ribeiro, 2015). Amongst other things, this involves seeing oneself as the main actor in defining a specific outcome, be that outcome negative or positive. External factors refer to the need to recognize the impact of external pressure, the need for continuous social support, and the viewing of collective well-being as a prerequisite to individual well-being (Ribeiro, 2015). This is not dissimilar from Nussbaum's (2000) notion of internal, external and combined capabilities, with the last being what we should aim for, even though Nussbaum offers no definite concept of agency, seeing agency as subsumed into well-being (see Nussbaum, 2011).

Ribeiro therefore argues that education for sustainable human development must be an education that aims to help people of all ages understand better the world in which they live, and to act better on this understanding. It needs to address the complexity and interconnectedness of problems such as poverty, environmental degradation, human rights, etc. (Ribeiro, 2015). And these topics should be addressed by providing not only information, but also the abilities needed to understand and use this information to establish agency and inspire action that leads to sustainable development (UNESCO, 2005). In other words, engineering education should be of such quality that it leads to particular learning outcomes in the form of valuable capabilities. But how do we know which capabilities will be valued by future engineers? How can we determine which capabilities ought to be valued? That is, how do we determine which of their valued capabilities are relevant for sustainable human development? Like Nussbaum (2000), who argues that the lack of commitment to specific valued capabilities means limited guidance in thinking about social justice, I suggest that a lack of commitment to the specific capabilities that engineers should value results in limited guidance in thinking about sustainable human development. A starting point in addressing the aforementioned questions therefore lies in theoretically determining the educational capabilities that are enhanced through an education in engineering, which are also foundational to the engineering functionings that are geared towards social justice.

Towards a theoretical framework for public-good engineering

Given the aim of theoretically determining categories of the capabilities fundamental to public-good engineering, a certain ideal, general level of specification is necessary. This necessitates the development of an 'ideal-theoretical list' of educational capabilities (Walker, 2006; Wilson-Strydom, 2014). As Walker asserts, such a list need not be generated strictly through public participation (and is limited in this respect), but making it public is to invite participatory dialogue (Walker, 2006). In her argument that there is a valid case for ideal-theoretical lists of educational capabilities, Walker states that such lists should be for a particular purpose, evaluation or critique. They also should not be fixed, canonical or hierarchically ordered, and they should include participation and dialogue in some way (Walker, 2006). The idea, Walker argues, is for higher education communities to produce their own flexible, revisable and general list in a participatory manner, but not one definite list of higher education capabilities for all contexts. Also, the selection of capabilities ought to be multidimensional, the dimensions should be incommensurable, and one dimension should not be reduced to any of the others (Alkire, 2002, 2010; Nussbaum, 2003; Robeyns, 2005; Walker, 2006). This is important to note because each dimension supports the others, and all are important (Walker, 2006). Walker also asserts that a working list provides content to what we count as 'higher education' and it addresses the case for a theoretical understanding of the human good.

However, putting specific content into capabilities (by developing a list) is a complex task. Robeyns (2003: 70–71) suggests five useful criteria for the selection of capabilities:

1   'Explicit formulation' – the idea that any list should be 'explicit, discussed and defended'.
2   'Methodological justification' – clarifying and scrutinizing the method that has generated the list and justifying its appropriateness.
3   'Sensitivity to context' – taking into account audience and situation, speaking 'the language of the debate', and avoiding 'jargon' that might alienate prospective groups. In some contexts therefore, the list might be more abstract or theory-laden than in others.
4   'Different levels of generality' – drawing up a list in two stages, where the first stage involves an 'ideal' list and the second a more 'pragmatic', second-best list, taking actual constraints into account.
5   'Exhaustion and non-reduction' – including all the important elements and ensuring that each is not reducible to any other (although there may be some overlap).

These criteria for selecting relevant functionings and capabilities (in education in this case) provide a methodological basis upon which to proceed with one of the tasks of this book: determining what subsets of enabling conditions are fundamental to capabilities for public-good engineering. Drawing from questions asked about the relationship between capabilities and higher education (see Walker, 2006), what we need to ask in the case of engineering education for sustainable human development (or public-good engineering) is:

•   Does anything count as engineering education? If not, how do we judge which students in engineering education are lacking capabilities central to public-good engineering? And how do we make judgements about the quality of engineering education?
•   Should we then produce a list, or lists, in order to indicate the content to a norm of social justice in engineering education?
•   In addition, should we try to work out what such engineering education might look like, and then consider how practice and reality are congruent with ideas of justice?

These questions illustrate that if we are concerned about engineering education and its contribution to sustainable human development, we need some idea of what we take to count as 'engineering education'. While at some abstract philosophical or theoretical level one might argue that all capabilities valued by engineers matter, it can also be argued that there are some capabilities that matter more than others do because of their relevance to sustainable human development. Considering this, what capabilities matter most for public-good engineering?

Both the first and second chapters of this book have indicated that engineering education can be considered as being in alignment with sustainable human development if it:

1   enhances students' valued capabilities;
2   develops their technical expertise;
3   provides effective opportunities for students to develop reasons to value social justice; and
4   promotes students' agency, and inspires them to use engineering knowledge and design for the public good.

This chapter has also shown that a shift towards viewing sustainable human development as the ends of engineering education requires the identification of appropriate educational capabilities. The process of formulating a provisional list of educational capabilities for public-good engineering entailed the following:

1   Considering Robeyns' (2003) criteria as guidelines for sifting through potential capabilities, and distilling the most important ones.
2   Drawing from a normative account of engineering education outcomes, a review of literatures on engineering ESD and the dimensions of education identified as relevant for public-good engineering.
3   Analysing how other scholars (i.e. Terzi, 2007; Walker, 2006; Wilson-Strydom, 2015) have gone about developing ideal-theoretical lists for educational capabilities.

As discussed in Chapter 1, the doings and beings that characterize agentic engineers are: the pursuit of goals aligned with principles of social justice (such as poverty reduction); the application of effective power through individual and collective agency; the pursuit of objectives that are conducive to individual and societal well-being; and being responsible for engineering outcomes. These characteristics – the corresponding normative account of engineering education, and the dimensions of education relevant for public-good engineering – are abstract and theory-laden. Empirical applications in Chapters 3 to 5 elicit the views of practising engineers, engineering educators and students in order to substantiate these ideas. This is of methodological importance for developing an ideal-theoretical list of educational capabilities because it not only reflects adherence to the criterion of 'sensitivity to context', but also allows qualified contributions to this theorizing, which ensures a more comprehensive list of incommensurable capabilities that are actually valued by engineers. The methodological significance of this process of developing an ideal-theoretical list of educational capabilities lies in the fact that the normative ideas put forward in the first two chapters are supplemented with empirical data that comprise a combination of diverse perspectives on engineering education. The shortcoming of this method is the lack of deep public participation, other than through the selected dissemination of these ideas to academic peers (at conferences). Nevertheless, supplementing the proposed framework with empirical data creates a dialogic process in an effort to develop a list, because it allows the participants' perspectives to inform and enrich these conceptualizations. A similar argument is made by Wilson-Strydom (2014) in her development of a capabilities list for equitable transitions to university. She describes a two-step process that entails the combination of a top-down (theory driven), and a bottom-up (empirical) approach to develop her list (Wilson-Strydom, 2014). The proposed framework (see Table 2.1) links the normative objectives of engineering education (discussed in Chapter 1) with the four dimensions of education identified as relevant for public-good engineering (discussed in the previous section), and it shows the dimensions of learning (also discussed in the previous section) that can respectively be associated with them.

This framework offers a normative critique of engineering education outcomes based on Amartya Sen's capability approach and points to multidimensional freedoms and functionings – particularly those of the poor – as proxies of quality in engineering education and socially just engineering.

Data and research context

This book draws on empirical data that was collected between 2013 and 2017. The purpose of the study on which this book draws was to use the capability approach as a normative framework to define higher education's contribution to

Table 2.1 A normative framework for engineering education

Normative objectives of engineering education	Dimensions of education relevant for public-good engineering	Dimensions of learning
Enlarge valued capabilities and functionings of engineering graduates	Education as a capability	Learning to know
Provide opportunities for students to develop, demonstrate and deepen commitment to poverty eradication	Education as a means to social justice	Learning to care
Enhance graduates' ability to acknowledge and exercise their agency	Education as a foundation for agency	Learning to be and learning to do
Promote sustainable human development as a global public-good	Education as sustainable human development	Learning to live together

Source: Author's own.

human development by exploring, describing and combining diverse perspectives on engineering education in universities and its contribution to sustainable human development.

The research questions that guided the study were:

1   How can the capability approach offer a normative critique of engineering education in universities?
2   What capabilities and functionings are enlarged through engineering education? In addition, what implications do they have for pro-poor, public-good engineering?
3   How can engineering education enable graduates, through their work, to function as agents of sustainable human development?
4   How can engineering education also improve graduates' capability for employment?

Qualitative research methods (interviews and focus group discussions) were used to gather thick descriptions, which were aimed not at comparing or generalizing findings but to help broaden our understanding of what it means to be an engineer in the modern world from the perspective of people who teach, are learning to become engineers or are practising engineering.

Data was therefore gathered from engineering educators, engineering students and engineers or engineering employers. The universities from which students and lecturers were recruited (University of Cape Town (UCT), South Africa and Universität Bremen (UB), Germany) were selected on the basis of their exemplary engineering curricula in terms of addressing sustainable development and/ or infusing the humanities in their curricula and pedagogies.

Professional engineers with extensive work experience in any engineering field who have worked with or led engineering teams were interviewed. Another selection criterion was employment in companies that either explicitly endorse engineering practices that promote energy efficiency, or are involved in renewable energies or community development programmes, either as part of their corporate social responsibility programmes or as reflections of their support of initiatives that are pro-sustainable development. Below is a timeline of the data collection process:

July 2013: ten employers are interviewed from across seven medium to large companies that operate in diverse engineering disciplines in Germany and South Africa (see summary of company profiles in Table 2.2).

March–August 2014: 18 students participate in four separate focus group discussions. The students are enrolled across four disciplines, either at Universität Bremen (UB) in Germany or the University of Cape Town (UCT) in South Africa (see summary in Table 2.3). At the time the focus group discussions were held, all students were enrolled in their first or second year of a master's degree in an engineering programme that substantially engages with 'sustainable development' in its curriculum.

March–August 2014: ten engineering lecturers are interviewed from UCT, UB, Stellenbosch University in South Africa and the Technische Universität Clausthal in Germany, across six engineering faculties (see summary in Table 2.4).

December 2016–June 2017: 15[1] of the 18 students who participated in the focus group discussions in 2014 were interviewed. They are now either seeking employment, or are employed and/or pursuing PhD studies in South Africa, Zimbabwe, Australia, Germany or the United Kingdom (see profiles in Table 2.5).

The four stages in the cycle of analysis consistent with grounded theory that were applied to the transcripts are coding, conceptualizing, categorizing and theorizing (Glaser, 1978; Glaser & Strauss, 1967). The step-by-step procedure followed in analysing the interviews and focus group discussion was as follows:

1　coding, which entails reviewing the transcripts sentence by sentence to identify anchors (words or phrases) that allow the key points of the data to come forward;
2　conceptualizing, which means grouping codes with similar content (where new concepts are core parameters of the data and codes can be seen as dimensions of these concepts);
3　categorizing, which is about developing categories that broadly group the concepts and constitute the basic elements to be generated into a hypothesis or a theory; and
4　theorizing, which is the process of constructing a system of explanations for the main concerns of the subject of the research.

Table 2.2 Engineering employer profiles

Interviewee	Company	Qualification/background
From Germany		
Mr Klemp	MT Energie	MSc Physics
Mr Braun	MT Energie	Mechanical engineering
Mr Lehman	MT Biomethan	Process and industrial engineering
Dr Klein	EWE NETZ	PhD Process engineering
Dr Weiss	ProcessQ	PhD Process engineering
From South Africa		
Ms White	Sasol	Chemical engineer
Mr Kumar	Sasol	Electrical engineer
Mr Schrader	STEAG Energy	Process engineer
Mr Chambers	Group Five	Civil engineer
Dr Shaw	Group Five	PhD Organizational behaviour
Total: 10 employers (note: 8 male, 2 female)		

Source: Author's own.

Table 2.3 Student profiles

Student	Study programme (all MSc)	University	Nationality	Gender
Focus group 1				
Anna	Industrial Engineering	UB	German	Female
Lisa	Industrial Engineering	UB	German	Female
Phillip	Production Engineering	UB	German	Male
Focus group 2				
Arnold	Process Engineering	UB	German	Male
Kurt	Process Engineering	UB	German	Male
Markus	Process Engineering	UB	German	Male
Rupert	Process Engineering	UB	German	Male
Focus group 3				
Anesu	Chemical Engineering	UCT	Zimbabwean	Male
Vimbai	Chemical Engineering	UCT	Zimbabwean	Female
Mufaro	Chemical Engineering	UCT	Zimbabwean	Female
Anashe	Chemical Engineering	UCT	Zimbabwean	Female
Focus group 4				
Mayita	Chemical Engineering	UCT	Zimbabwean	Female
Kopano	Chemical Engineering	UCT	South African	Male
Mandy	Chemical Engineering	UCT	South African	Female
Tendayi	Chemical Engineering	UCT	Zimbabwean	Male
Thandi	Chemical Engineering	UCT	Zimbabwean	Female
Valerie	Chemical Engineering	UCT	South African	Female
Interview				
Tinashe	Chemical Engineering	UCT	Zimbabwean	Male

Total: 18 students, 4 focus groups, 1 interview

Source: Author's own.

Table 2.4 Lecturer profiles

Interviewee	Faculty/department	University
From Germany		
Prof. Bremer	Applied Mechanics	TUC
Prof. Kleid	Production Engineering	UB
Prof. Marco	Production Engineering	UB
Prof. Schneider	Physics and Electrical Engineering	UB
Prof. Schwartz	Production Engineering	UB
From South Africa		
Prof. Block	Engineering and the Built Environment	UCT
Prof. Grant	Chemistry and Polymer Science	SU
Prof. Hunter	Engineering and the Built Environment	UCT
Dr Jones	Engineering and the Built Environment	UCT
Prof. Smith	Engineering and the Built Environment	UCT

Total: 10 lecturers (note: 7 male, 3 female)

Source: Author's own.

Table 2.5 Student destinations post-graduation

Student	Current employment/job status	Company/institution	Current location
Anna	Operations manager	nextbike GmbH	Germany
Phillip	PhD candidate/research assistant	UB	Germany
Arnold	PhD candidate/research assistant	UB	Germany
Rupert	PhD candidate/research assistant	UB	Germany
Anesu	Product development engineer	Axis House	South Africa
Vimbai	Management consultant and business analyst	EIU Canback	South Africa
Mufaro	Water sector analyst	GreenCape	South Africa
Anashe	Graduate engineer	Oil and gas extraction company	South Africa
Mayita	PhD candidate	Leibniz Institute for Functionalized Polymers	Germany
Kopano	PhD candidate	University of Queensland	Australia
Mandy	PhD candidate/research assistant	UCT and Southampton University	South Africa and United Kingdom
Tendayi	Unemployed freelance engineer	N/A	Zimbabwe
Thandi	Proposal engineer	WEC Projects	South Africa
Valerie	Production engineer	Unilever	South Africa
Tinashe	Researcher	SU	South Africa

Source: Author's own.

Rather than constructing a system of explanations for the perceptions held by the participants, the aim was to propose a framework of engineering education for sustainable human development. It is also important to note that the intention was not to carry out a grounded theory study. Rather the aim was to make use of the procedure outlined in grounded theory as a means to guide the analysis of the qualitative data gathered – that is, not to employ grounded theory as a methodology, but to apply some techniques consistent with grounded theory as an aid to the process of analysis.

In all chapters that follow, excerpts from the interview (indented) and focus group transcripts are used extensively, and are interjected by summaries of interpretive text in order to foreground the empirical data but also give context to the engineering employers', educators' and students' perspectives.

Why perspectives from Germany and South Africa?

Most literature on higher education and engineering education in particular, is based on data gathered from the global North, written from global North perspectives. Comparatively few studies focus on normative accounts of ESD based on data from developing countries, and written from global South perspectives. While there is value in exploring views from different contexts separately, what is original and significant about the work of this book is the examination of these perspectives together, combining a normative approach with original empirical work, and recognizing that they are different outlooks on the same issue: how engineering education in universities contributes to sustainable human development. Instead of dichotomizing global North/South perspectives, the book combines the views of individuals who are affiliated with engineering education in different ways, within different socio-economic, political, geographical and cultural contexts in the global North (Germany) and global South (South Africa) for its empirical base. Specifically, the viewpoints of 18 masters' students and ten lecturers from engineering faculties at UB (Germany) and the UCT (South Africa), as well as ten engineering employers from both countries, were explored using qualitative methods (semi-structured interviews and focus group discussions).

These diverse perspectives offer contrasting and critical views on the assumption that society is in pursuit of an agenda for 'sustainability' that is valuable for all, and of future engineers' roles in determining such an agenda. The findings also show that the participants perceive degrees of ambiguity about the extent to which engineers are educated to use their skills, knowledge and effective power as professionals who contribute to solving human development and sustainability challenges in a just way – that is, in a way that explicitly prioritizes poverty reduction or expanding freedoms for people living in poverty as a means of advancing social justice. Reflecting on these perspectives from Germany and South Africa, the rest of the book considers what justice-based, capability-inspired engineering education might look like, if it is to enhance future engineers' opportunities to use their agency to practice public-good engineering for sustainable human development.

Any pair or group of countries that one might consider as being at different stages of development can similarly offer diverse perspectives. The reasons that Germany and South Africa make particularly interesting case study contexts for exploring perspectives on engineering education lie in the stark differences and delicate similarities between the two countries. For example, Germany and South Africa are both economically dominant and energy-intensive industrial powerhouses in their respective continents (Tyler, 2012). However, Germany is a wealthy, developed country ranking fourth on the UN's HDI,[2] while South Africa is a medium income developing country, with high levels of poverty and inequality and it is ranked 119th on the HDI.

As Campt (2005) asks with regard to context: how and why do we situate the stories we want to tell in the ways we do? What information needs to be known so that our stories make sense? Against what backgrounds and in what frameworks do we want our stories to be understood? What other stories do our tales cite or reference, and what differentiates our stories from those of others? In agreement with Campt (2005), the contexts (both discursive and socio-historical) are the possibility of existence and intelligibility of people's perspectives. Context also creates the boundaries of looking at and understanding perspectives (Campt, 2005). In this book, describing the socio-historical context of higher education in Germany and South Africa is to delineate the space in which engineering education in universities can be understood.

A brief socio-historical description of higher education in South Africa and Germany

During the late 1940s under apartheid rule, the state in South Africa was redesigned to organize civil society more firmly along the lines of 'race'[3] and ethnicity (Reddy, 2004). This translated into an administrative practice where all social services were provided separately and unequally (Reddy, 2004). The programme of racially determining social relations allowed the state to centralize, administer and uniformly impose its ideology on educational policy in line with its apartheid project (Reddy, 2004). By so doing, the National Party government introduced an interventionist character into relations between state and civil society, as it related to the terrain of higher education (Reddy, 2004).

The ideological functions of educational policy under apartheid were to stratify and segregate South Africa socially. Therefore, educational resources were distributed unequally on the basis of race, resulting in a differentiated higher education landscape (Reddy, 2004). As a result, a particular higher education system was inherited from apartheid: one that was internally divided and isolated from the international community of scholars (CHE, 2004). It was highly fragmented in structural and governance terms, and was far from being a coherently coordinated system (CHE, 2004). The higher education system under apartheid law was inherently inequitable and it was designed to 'reproduce white and male privilege, and black and female subordination in all spheres of society' (Badat, 2003: 13). Accordingly, black people, as the largest South African demographic group, had the lowest participation rate in higher education (CHE, 2004). The effects of a disjointed system were observable at an institutional level, and higher education institutions themselves became implicated (willingly or not) in perpetuating the apartheid system of 'privilege and penalty, of opportunity and stricture, of advantage and disadvantage' (CHE, 2004: 230).

Higher education in Germany has also been characterized by a differentiated and segregated system. From 1933–1945 under totalitarian leadership by the Nazi Party, apolitical scholarship was not allowed, and the Nazi regime insisted that university activities be pursued in accordance with its official political principles and aims (Hearnden, 1976). During this period, higher education in Germany was highly centralized. However, not long after the end of World War II and the fall of Nazism, the country became geographically (as well as politically, socially and culturally) divided into East (Democratic Republic) and West (Federal Republic) Germany by the erection of the Berlin Wall in 1961 (Hearnden, 1976). Despite their common roots, universities and higher education in East and West Germany took very different paths after the end of World War II (Mitter, 1990; Nugent, 2004). The systems were differentiated on almost all levels, including secondary schools, access, research and teaching (Nugent, 2004). The higher education systems were also differentiated according to their goals and value orientation, legal order and curricula (Mitter, 1990).

In the East, the school system was more unified than in the West (Nugent, 2004). Furthermore, since the end of the 1960s, the German Democratic Republic had instituted a strong separation of research and teaching in the realm of higher education and training (Nugent, 2004). According to Nugent, academic research in East Germany was carried out by academies of science, and universities were reduced to teaching institutions with curricula strongly tied to the ideals of the ruling Communist Party, the Sozialistische Partei Deutschlands. As a result, the structural and administrative nature of university study in the East was controlled and 'school-like' (Nugent, 2004) – that is, in East Germany the establishment of a 'socialist' regime was followed by the 'consistent adjustment of the education system to the uniform political and ideological power structure and, manifested by an articulate, gradually achieved, retreat from what was called the 'bourgeois' past' (Mitter, 1990: 333). On the other hand, in West Germany, policy makers and educationalists largely adhered to the *Grundgesetz* (Basic Law) and the constitutions of the *Länder* (States) that lay the foundation for 'teachers and educators to preserve and spread a core of democratic, liberal and social values' (Mitter, 1990: 333).

During the early stages of reintegrating the German Democratic Republic into the system of the Federal Republic of Germany, the entire educational system in the East was re-evaluated from primary schools to advanced scientific research (Nugent, 2004). Although the main academic concern was the reconstruction of universities, the leitmotif behind the push for university reform was modernization (Mitter, 1990). Moreover, although the main idea behind modernization was economic, the concept of modernization also meant the establishment of equal opportunity for groups that, up to that point, had been hindered from participating in higher education based on the perception of their rights as citizens (children of the working class, Catholics, some members of the provincial population and women) (Mitter, 1990).

In 1990 the German Democratic Republic joined the Federal Republic of Germany to form the reunited nation of Germany, after more than four decades of forced division.

In South Africa, in 1994, a new constitution that enfranchised racial groups who were previously disadvantaged through the apartheid system took effect and the first democratic elections in the same year led to a coalition government and marked the official end of the apartheid system. As South Africa entered a process of social, economic and political reconstruction in 1994, it was clear that merely reforming limited aspects of higher education would be insufficient to meet the challenges of a democratic country aiming to take its place in the world (CHE, 2004). Rather, a comprehensive transformation of higher education was required, marking a fundamental departure from the socio-political foundations of the apartheid regime (CHE, 2004). Redress of past inequalities in higher education was a central issue in policy debates from the early 1990s, and was identified as a policy goal in the White Paper and National Plan (CHE, 2004). The first period of policy activity from 1990–1994 was primarily associated with 'symbolic' policy making, where the intention was to declare a break with the past and signal a new direction, and the second period from 1994–1998 focused on framework development (CHE, 2004). A third period of policy making began in 1999, as efforts turned to policy implementation (CHE, 2004). This was a period in which there were calls for more targeted, differentiated, information-rich policy interaction between government, higher education institutions and society (CHE, 2004).

Since 1994, there have been numerous changes to the university terrain. Smaller universities and 'technikons' (polytechnics) were incorporated into larger institutions to form comprehensive universities. South Africa currently has 26 public universities. These comprise 11 traditional universities, six comprehensive universities[4] (DHET, 2013) and eight universities of technology (two of which only began operating in 2014). There are also two institutes of higher education, which serve as administrative hubs coordinating higher education provision through partnerships with universities (DHET, 2013). The 2011 student headcount for the 23 operational universities at the time was 937,455 (which includes full-time and part-time enrolments). This represents nearly a doubling from 1994, when the headcount was 495,356 (DHET, 2013).

Since the end of World War II, the number of people in university has more than tripled in Germany (Winkel, 2010). Nevertheless, university attendance is lower than that of many other European nations. This is partly because of the dual education system, with its strong emphasis on apprenticeships, and because many jobs that do require a degree in other countries (like nursing) require a qualification from a higher education institution such as a *Krankenschwestern-schule* or Nursing School (which is not regarded as a university). In contrast with the 26 universities in South Africa, there are currently 331 universities in Germany,[5] with a combined student population of approximately 2.4 million

(HRK, 2013). Of these, 110 are traditional universities (or similar institutions) and 221 are universities of applied sciences or *Fachhochschulen* (HRK, 2013).

Germany and South Africa are countries with many significant differences (see Table 2.6 for examples of some development indicators). However, they have faced similar challenges in terms of having to reform their universities and rebuild their societies after periods of forced separation and separate development, so that they may be more socially just nations in which *all* their citizens can live and learn where and how they have reason to value. Looking at the role of universities during periods of transformation it is clear that governments grapple with what Nugent (2004) refers to as 'seemingly opposing and contradictory ideologies within traditional and novel structural frameworks'. Over time, the goals towards which higher education policies are aimed change according to the political and socio-political conditions of the time. Although one cannot make a straightforward comparison of the role played by the state, engineering or higher education in the reconstruction and development of Germany and South Africa post democratization in South Africa and reunification in Germany, some parallels can be drawn between the development agenda that the two countries pursued in the early 1990s.

Specifically, it is clear that education and engineering lie at the centre of government's plans for development. This is made clear in government planning documents such as:

- the South African National Development Plan (NDP);
- the South African National Strategy for Sustainable Development and Action Plan (NSSD1); and
- the German National Sustainable Development Strategy (NSDS).

These all emphasize the vital role that education plays in achieving national and (global) sustainable and millennium development goals (see DST, 2013; DST &

Table 2.6 Selected development indicators for Germany and South Africa

	Germany	*South Africa*
Population	80,722,792	54,300,704
HDI ranking	4 (very high)	119 (medium)
Labour force participation rate		
(as % aged 15 and older)	60.3	53.0
Total unemployment rate		
(as % of labour force)	4.6	26
Youth not in school or employment		
(% ages 15–24)	6.4	31.3
Gross domestic product (GDP), total	3,586.5	680.9
(2011 PPP $ billions)		
Gross enrolment ratio, tertiary		
(as % of tertiary school-age population)	65	20
Number of universities	331	26

Source: Author's own.

BMBF, 2013; NPC, 2011; NSDS, 2012; NSSD1, 2011; RNE, 2005). The theoretical underpinnings for this assumption lie in the human capital model (see Becker, 1962; Schultz, 1961), according to which investments in human capital should improve the productivity of the labour force, increase the innovative capacity of the economy and facilitate the transmission of new knowledge and technologies.

Importantly, even if countries at different stages of development should prioritize national objectives according to their respective urgent needs, the ideal and challenge to create a more socially just world transcends the borders of nation states. As such, both global North and global South countries need to take necessary action to ensure that education enables people, not only today but also in the future, to 'live in a world in which economic prosperity for all goes hand in hand with social cohesion and the protection of natural resources' (NSDS, 2012: 17): that is, in a world that recognizes a commitment to intergenerational equity and the peaceful coexistence of *all* people (NSDS, 2012).

Therefore, while there is value in conducting comparative research, one of the things that make this book unique is the exploration of German and South African perspectives together. Instead of comparing these views, they are combined in the hope that this will result in rich data that can enhance the normative conceptualizations of engineering education proposed in this book. Furthermore, diverse and multiple perspectives have the potential to create nuanced understandings of the issue at the heart of this work. This book recognizes that German and South African perspectives can offer particularly interesting views on the same issue: how engineering education in universities contributes to sustainable human development. After all, sustainable human development is not a concern that matters more or less in the global North or South. It is a universal concern.

Author positioning

I am neither an engineer, nor an engineering educator. This means that my knowledge and understanding of the engineering profession and engineering education is theoretical, not practical. My decision to focus on the education of engineers therefore does not stem from any sort of affiliation with engineering, but rather it was based on the belief that the work engineers do is more intertwined with 'development' than that of any other profession.

I consider my positionality as a non-engineer advantageous for the research undertaken as I have been able to bring attention to aspects of engineering work that engineers themselves often take for granted. Therefore, although I do not bring expert engineering knowledge to this project, my interaction and discussions with people who do function as students, teachers and practitioners of engineering enrich my understanding and perspective of what it means to practise engineering, or to be an engineer. While I could gain insight and broaden my perceptions about teaching, learning and the values associated with engineering education, the research participants had the opportunity to reflect on the greater significance of their professional functionings; together, their perspectives and reflections, embedded in and reflecting both theory and practice, have enriched this work.

Notes

1 Three students who studied at UB, Kurt, Lisa and Markus, could not be located at the time this chapter was written.
2 To see the latest HDI rankings visit: http://hdr.undp.org/en/countries (accessed 1 September 2017).
3 While I do not subscribe to racial classification, I make use of the terms 'race' or 'black' and 'white', commonly used in South Africa, because the long legacy of apartheid necessitates the (careful) use of these categories when discussing social injustices that happen(ed) in and through higher education.
4 Comprehensive universities combine the functions of traditional universities and universities of technology.
5 These differences should be considered in relation to each country's population numbers. The 2015 mid-year population estimate for South Africa is 54.96 million (Statistics South Africa, 2015), while Germany's stands at 81.30 million (Federal Statistical Office of Germany, 2015).

References

Alkire, S. (2002). Dimensions of human development. *World Development, 30*(2), 181–205.

Alkire, S. (2010). *Human development: definitions, critiques, and related concepts* (background paper for the 2010 Human Development Report). Oxford Poverty & Human Development Initiative, Oxford Department of International Development, Queen Elizabeth House, University of Oxford. Accessed 1 September 2017 from www.ophi.org. uk/human-development-definitions-critiques-and-related-concepts/.

Badat, S. (2003). Transforming South African higher education, 1990–2003: Goals, policy initiatives and critical challenges and issues. In N. Cloete, P. Pillay, S. Badat & Teboho Moja (eds), *National Policy and a Regional Response in South African Higher Education*. Pretoria: Partnership for Higher Education in Africa.

Becker, G. S. (1962). Investment in human capital: A theoretical analysis. *Journal of Political Economy, 70*(5), 9–49.

Bratteteig, T., & Wagner, I. (2014). *Disentangling participation power and decision-making in participatory design*. Heidelberg, New York, Dordrecht, London: Springer.

Campt, T. (2005). *Other Germans: Black Germans and the politics of race, gender, and memory in the Third Reich*. Ann Arbor, MI: University of Michigan Press.

CHE. (2004). *South African higher education in the first decade of democracy*. Pretoria: Council on Higher Education (CHE).

Connell, B. R., & Sanford, J. A. (1999). Research implications of universal design. In E. Steinfeld & G. Scott Danford (eds), *Enabling environments: Measuring the impact of environment on disability and rehabilitation* (pp. 35–57). New York: Kluwer Academic Publishers.

DHET. (2013). *2014 White Paper for post school education and training*. Pretoria: Department of Higher Education and Training (DHET).

DST. (2013). *Enhancing science partnerships for innovation and sustainable development*. Accessed 1 September 2017 from www.germansouthafrican-scienceyear.co.za/

news/latest-news/germany-and-south-africa-look-to-more-advanced-partnerships-in-science-and-technology.html.

DST & BMBF. (2013). *German–South African cooperation on science, technology and innovation for sustainable development*. South African Department of Science and Technology (DST) in collaboration with the German Federal Ministry of Education and Research (BMBF).

Federal Statistical Office of Germany. (2015). *Statistisches Jahrbuch 2015*. Statistisches Bundesamt. Accessed 1 September 2017 from www.destatis.de/EN/FactsFigures/SocietyState/Population/CurrentPopulation/CurrentPopulation.html.

Glaser, B. (1978). *Theoretical sensitivity*. Mill Valley, CA: Sociology Press.

Glaser, B. G. & Strauss, A. L. (1967). *Discovery of grounded theory: Strategies for qualitative research*. Mill Valley, CA: Sociology Press.

Goldsmith, S. (2000). *Universal design: a manual of practical guidance for architects*. Oxford: Architectural Press.

Hearnden, A. (1976). *Education, culture and politics in West Germany*. Oxford, New York, Toronto, Sydney, Paris, Frankfurt: Pergamon Press.

HRK. (2013). *Recommendation of the 15th General Meeting of the German Rectors' Conference (HRK)*. Karlsruhe: German Rectors' Conference (HRK). The Voice of the Universities. Accessed 1 September 2017 from www.hrk.de/uploads/tx_szconvention/HRK_MV_15_Empfehlung_Europaeische_Studienreform_EN_01.pdf.

Lozano, J. F., Bonni, A., Peris, J. & Hueso, A. (2012). Competencies in higher education: A critical analysis from the capabilities approach. *Journal of Philosophy of Education, 46*(1), 132–147.

Lucena, J. (ed.). (2013). *Engineering education for social justice: Critical explorations and opportunities* (Vol. 10). Dordrecht, Heidelberg, New York, London: Springer.

Mitter, W. (1990). Educational reform in West and East Germany in European perspective. *Oxford Review of Education, 16*(3), 333–341.

Nieusma, D. (2004). Alternative design scholarship: Working toward appropriate design. *Massachusetts Institute of Technology Design Issues, 20*(3), 13–24.

NPC. (2011). *National development plan 2030. Our future – make it work* (executive summary). Pretoria: National Planning Commission, Office of the President, South Africa. Accessed 10 September 2013 from www.poa.gov.za/news/Documents/NPC%20National%20Development%20Plan%20Vision%202030%20-lo-res.pdf.

NSDS. (2012). *National sustainable development strategy* (Progress Report). German Federal Government.

NSSD1. (2011). *National strategy for sustainable development and action plan 2011–2014*. Department of Environmental Affairs. Accessed 1 September 2017 from www.search.gov.za/info/search.jsp.

Nugent, M. A. (2004). *The transformation of the student career: University Study in Germany, the Netherlands, and Sweden*. London and New York: Routledge/Falmer.

Nussbaum, M. C. (2000). *Women and human development: The capabilities approach*. Cambridge: Cambridge University Press.

Nussbaum, M. C. (2003). Capabilities as fundamental entitlements: Sen and social justice. *Feminist Economics, 9*(2–3), 33–59. Accessed 1 September 2017 from https://doi.org/10.1080/1354570022000077926.

Nussbaum, M. C. (2011). *Creating capabilities: the human development approach*. Cambridge, MA and London: The Belknap Press of Harvard University Press.

Oosterlaken, I. (2009). Design for development: A capability approach. *Design Issues, 25*(4), 91–102.

Reddy, T. (2004). *Higher education and social transformation: South Africa case study* (CHE Commissioned Paper). Pretoria: Council on Higher Education (CHE).

Ribeiro, A. S. (2015). A normative framework or an emerging theory? The capability approach in higher education research. In J. Huisman & M. Tight (eds), *Theory and method in higher education research* (Vol. 1, pp. 277–294). Bingley: Emerald Group Publishing.

RNE. (2005). *BRICS+G Sustainability and Growth: Brazil, Russia, India, China, South Africa and Germany in dialogue on sustainability strategies.* Berlin: Deutsche Gesellschaft für Technische Zusammenarbeit (GTZ) GmbH and the German Council for Sustainable Development. Accessed 1 September 2017 from www.nachhaltigkeitsrat.de/fileadmin/user_upload/dokumente/publikationen/broschueren/bricsplusg_booklet.pdf.

Robeyns, I. (2003). Sen's capability approach and gender inequality: Selecting relevant capabilities. *Feminist Economics, 9*(2–3), 61–91.

Robeyns, I. (2005). Three models of education: Rights, capabilities and human capital. *Theory and Research in Education, 4*(1), 69–84.

Saito, M. (2003). Amartya Sen's capability approach to education: A critical exploration. *Journal of Philosophy of Education, 37*(1): 17–34.

Schuler, D., & Namioka, A. (1993). *Participatory design: Principles and practices.* New Jersey: Lawrence Erlbaum.

Schultz, T. W. (1961). Investment in human capital. *American Economic Review, 51*(1), 1–17.

Sen, A. (1999). *Development as freedom.* Oxford: Oxford University Press.

Sen, A. K. (2002). Response to commentaries. *Studies in Comparative International Development, 37*(2), 78–86.

Statistics South Africa. (2015). *Mid-year population estimates 2015* (Statistical release No. P0302). Accessed 1 September 2017 from www.statssa.gov.za/publications/P0302/P03022015.pdf.

Terzi, L. (2007). Capability and educational equality: The just distribution of resources to Students with disabilities and special educational needs. *Journal of Philosophy of Education, 41*(4), 757–773.

Tyler, E. (2012). *Germany's transition to renewable energy: A model for South Africa?* (pp. 1–14). Cape Town: Heinrich Böll Foundation.

UNDP. (1990). *Human development report.* New York: Oxford University Press.

UNESCO. (2005). *International conference: Globalisation and education for sustainable development. Sustaining the future.* Nagoya, Japan: UNESCO Publishing.

UNESCO. (2014). *Roadmap for implementing the Global Action Programme on Education for Sustainable Development.* France: United Nations Educational, Scientific and Cultural Organization.

Unterhalter, E. (2002). The capabilities approach and gendered education: An examination of South African complexities. *Theory and Research in Education, 1*(1), 7–22.

Vaughan, R. (2007). Measuring capabilities: An example from girls' schooling. In M. Walker & E. Unterhalter (eds), *Amartya Sen's capability approach and social justice in education* (pp. 109–130). New York: Palgrave Macmillan.

Walker, M. (2006). *Higher education pedagogies.* Berkshire and New York: Society for Research into Higher Education and Open University Press.

Walker, M., & Unterhalter, E. (eds). (2007). *Amartya Sen's capability approach and social justice in education.* New York: Palgrave Macmillan.

Wilson-Strydom, M. (2014). A capabilities list for equitable transitions to university: A top-down and bottom-up approach. *Journal of Human Development and Capabilities: A Multi-Disciplinary Journal for People-Centered Development, 7*(2): 145–160.

Wilson-Strydom, M. (2015). *University access and success: Capabilities, diversity and social justice*. New York: Routledge.

Winkel, O. (2010). Higher education reform in Germany. *International Journal of Educational Management, 24*(4), 303–313.

Wood, D., & Deprez, L. S. (2012). Teaching for human well-being: Curricular implications for the capability approach. *Journal of Human Development and Capabilities: A Multi-Disciplinary Journal for People-Centered Development, 13*(3), 471–493. Accessed 1 September 2017 from https://doi.org/10.1080/19452829.2012.679651.

Part II

3 Becoming a public-good engineer
Students' perspectives

This chapter explores engineering students' aspirations, valued capabilities and functionings. In doing so, it reveals the motivation behind students' decisions to pursue careers in engineering and explores students' views on their perceived roles in society as future engineers. The chapter draws substantially on the voices of students. This means throughout the chapter, summaries of my interpretation of the data are broken up with excerpts of students' responses. The chapter also looks at how the students evaluate their decisions to study engineering. There is then a discussion on students' valued functionings. To conclude, the chapter reflects on the implications of these findings for becoming a public-good engineer.

As described in Chapter 2 (and summarized in Table 2.3), at the time data was collected the students from UCT were enrolled in their first or second year of a master's programme in chemical engineering. Of the 11 participants, seven were Zimbabwean and four were South African. The students from UB were enrolled in their first or second year of industrial, production or process engineering master's degrees; all are German nationals. For orientation purposes, all the excerpts from students' responses are denoted 'ZIM', for Zimbabwe, 'SA' for South Africa and 'GER' for Germany. Although the students from UCT have different nationalities, both Zimbabwean and South African views offer global South perspectives and all the students' undergraduate and postgraduate engineering studies took place at the same university.

Why become an engineer?

It is not surprising that all students cited the aspiration to be employed. When asked about the future or where they would like to see themselves and how they imagined their lives, most of them gave responses that focused primarily on the kinds of jobs they would like to have. What is interesting are the dissimilar factors that influenced different groups of students to select engineering as a preferred career. These factors are discussed first in order to highlight the conversion factors that shape students' aspirations as well as their motivations for studying engineering. Thereafter the chapter considers what these motivations and aspirations might mean for public-good engineering.

Motivations for studying engineering

Tendayi (ZIM) explains how his decision to study engineering was made difficult because of pressure from his parents, who preferred that he study medicine. He insisted on his choice to study engineering despite the disappointment shown by his parents. This response shows that his decision was well thought through, and that he was challenged to exercise his agency by being persistent about pursuing a career he valued:

> [when] you are coming from a family where you have parents who have been paying school fees for you, when it comes to that plan whereby you're telling them that 'I'm going to study engineering' [and] there's this thing like 'I want my son to be a doctor' You know? But it's not who you are – It's always a problem for them to understand (…). They would always feel that you made the wrong choice, but as an individual you'll see this is me. This is what I want. This is what I identify myself with. They [parents] will get to a point to understand that it's your decision. Because a career is about enjoying it, not just the money. But anyway I think (…) I'm comfortable, I'm happy with the career I chose.

Similarly, Vimbai (ZIM) explains that her parents also wanted her to study medicine. Unlike Tendayi (ZIM) she was willing to fulfil her parents' wishes but the possibility to study medicine was not an option for her due to constraints associated with her legal status, i.e. being a foreign student and hence not allowed to enrol for medicine in South Africa. Her response also shows that she 'genders' engineering disciplines and that she has specific ideas about what constitutes engineering that is suitable for men and women:

> Growing up, you know how it is when parents instil a career in you? I'd always wanted to be a doctor because my parents had said so. And then when I moved to South Africa the only thing I could apply for at UCT was engineering because they don't take international students for medicine. So of the engineering programmes that were available, chemical [engineering] sounded more 'feminine' kind of.

And while there was interest expressed in selecting a study programme that was challenging, it appears that some students had a distorted understanding of the profession based on the information available to them.

Studying medicine is also mentioned as a preferred option by Mayita (ZIM). She says:

> I got the wrong impression what chemical engineering was. I initially wanted to be in medicine, which you find a lot of chemical engineers wanted to do, and you kind of just picked up what the next hardest thing was based on you being good at chemistry. And then you come here and realize it

(chemical engineering) has almost nothing to do with chemistry and then you're in the system and you try to learn about it. So that was my motivation for being in engineering.

Unlike Mayita (ZIM), Tendayi (ZIM) seems to have had a good understanding of engineering programmes and the capabilities for employment that would be available to him if he studied engineering. He mentions his talent for subjects in the natural sciences, which he cites as factors that made it easy for him to choose engineering:

I (…) understand the benefits of studying engineering. Engineering covers everything; [different] sectors. If you want to go into the financial sector you can do that. So it was more of the diversity that the engineering discipline comes with which could also enhance the probability of getting a job; yes. So that's another point and especially in engineering as a person who was more gifted in the sciences, it was also easy for me to be in engineering.

A noteworthy difference in the students' motivations to study engineering is easily observable. Consider the following responses from German students about the reasons they chose to study engineering. Phillip (GER) notes:

I wanted to study mathematics first because I was very good at it in high school and then I realized in the first semester that mathematics wasn't for me after all because it was too theoretical and parallel to my mathematics course I was already attending mechanics lectures that were offered by Faculty 4. So that's where I realized that was the right thing for me and so I moved to Mechanical Engineering and I already found technology fascinating from early on – I grew up on a farm around tractors and stuff like that so I found it cool and quite interesting to see how things are operated and so when this option was open to me-yeah, so that's why [I decided to study engineering].

Lisa's (GER) statement is quite similar and it is clear that she has a long-standing interest in mechanics and technology:

I chose engineering in particular because I've been interested in technology since I was a child (…) and started pretty early with helping my dad repair engines and stuff.

Rupert (GER) explains that his good performance in mathematics and science in high school signalled he might do well to continue with a degree that is founded on natural sciences. Interestingly, he also indicates that he pursued engineering studies in particular, rather than choosing a degree in physics, for example, because he perceived physics students as 'nerdy':

I was always I think a little better in mathematics and science classes in school so yeah I wanted to study something that had to do with science and mathematics and this stuff and yeah I didn't want to study physics because I saw these guys sitting there and they were so like – nerds – just my perspective, and yeah I went to study engineering.

So, while most German students' responses indicated an intrinsic motivation to study engineering, the Zimbabwean and South African students were motivated to study engineering by dynamics that are more complex. The German students seem to have made their decision to study engineering based on interest in the natural sciences as the main motivating factor. In addition, even when a compromise was made to change or opt for an alternative course of study, the students' personal interests seem to remain the top priority in making study/career decisions. Anna's (GER) description of her thought process in deciding to study industrial engineering reveals fear of failure in pursuing a traditional engineering programme. She describes how she negotiated between her initial or preferred course of study and the course she felt confident enough to succeed in:

I actually wanted to study business management first but that was monotonous for me so I thought I'd rather combine that, with my existing interest in technology and I didn't want to study straight mechanical engineering because I thought it might be too mathematics-oriented and that maybe I wouldn't cope with that.

Anna (GER) is the only student who mentions concern of not being able to 'cope' with traditional engineering studies. All other students seemed to appreciate the challenging engineering programmes rather than being intimidated by them.

Not surprisingly, some students mention the prospects of a good salary as a motivation for becoming engineers. It is noteworthy that only South African and Zimbabwean students provide this type of response when asked to talk about the reasons behind their decision to study engineering. This reinforces the idea proposed in the next chapter (Chapter 4) that South African lecturers (and students) tend to focus on the monetary aspects and/or benefits of education ahead of any of its other values. Zimbabwean students have similar views, which could be attributed to the fact that prevailing socio-economic conditions in Zimbabwe (and some other developing countries) are even more unfavourable than in South Africa, therefore prompting Zimbabwean students to think first and foremost about their financial future when considering prospective careers.

Anesu (ZIM) is candid about the reasons for his choice of study, explaining that his decision boiled down to competitiveness amongst friends to earn a top salary or get a job that was highly esteemed:

For me I think it was more of the money because like looking at what engineers do and what they get [paid] out of it; it was sort of – it created sort of a motivation. Also considering where I grew up, like there was always a competition from my friends saying like: 'who's going to get the best job ever?' so being an engineer was sought of something high up there. So it was a motivation to get there. That was one of the driving forces to get into engineering.

Kopano (SA) similarly considers the prospect of earning a good salary as a motivator for studying engineering. His words indicate that he shortlisted engineering as a study option, based mainly on the prospect of earning a good salary:

I just googled 'top starting salary'.

Of the remaining three South African students, Mandy and Thandi cited bursary offers, and Valerie cited the advice of her high school teacher:

I just listened to my high school teacher.

It therefore appears that the most important factor for South African students' decisions to study engineering had more to do with their perceived opportunity for employment, rather than an intrinsic motivation to become engineers. On the contrary, most Zimbabwean students' responses indicate that they would have preferred to be medical doctors.

In summary, the factors that emerged from the data as most influential on students' decision to study engineering are: a lack of opportunity to study medicine (for Zimbabwean students), an affinity for natural sciences or interest in science and technology (for German students), and earning a good salary (for South African students).

Career aspirations

Some students found it difficult to articulate their aspirations. A particularly interesting example of this is provided in Mayita's (ZIM) response to what her aspirations are. She explains that she has had to alter her ambitions due to various constraints that made it nearly impossible for her to do or be what she has reason to value. She therefore feels that she is not in a position to say what she would like to do because of the uncertainty surrounding the feasible options available to her. What Mayita says below is a comment she made after Mandy (SA) said she would look for a job upon completion of her master's degree:

Can we get those jobs? That's the question. I mean a lot of us, or well I know I'm here because I couldn't find a job. It wasn't a choice to do master's, and even now with a little bit more, like a master's degree and that backing you, you still can't find a job. So you can't even, you may have had a five year, ten year plan but if you can't get to some form of market it's – I don't know – I don't know where I'm gonna be in five years.

To get a sense of what her aspirations were before she realized some of the constraints that prohibit her from achieving her vision, Mayita was asked what she would have liked to be if these constraints were non-existent. Although completely hypothetical in its nature, this question helped her to articulate what she wanted, by allowing her to imagine the best-case scenario, and not consider the real barriers to her aspirations. Her response suggests she simply would like to get a job, and later start her own business. She says:

> [I] just [want] to get a bit of [work] experience and then after that, assess businesses, and start my own. So maybe five years from now, in that starting phase of thinking of starting my business. [That] is where I would like to be.

Mayita is not the only student who considers starting up their own business. Tinashe (ZIM) expresses the same wish, but hers is unique compared to all other students as she is the only student who wants to add a commerce-based master's degree to her qualifications. Her response also indicates that she has a keen interest in and appreciation of entrepreneurship:

> I'm hoping to go into business after this but I do first want to do two years in the petrochemical industry hopefully, and after that I want to do an MBA in finance.

A typical example of the type of responses that came from the German students regarding their aspirations is provided below. Arnold (GER), who would like to apply his engineering knowledge in research that advances options for energy efficiency, answered as follows:

> I think I will stick to research, not necessarily at the university but some research. And right now I would say I would like to do research about efficiency and sustainability and something like that.

Similarly, Markus (GER) explains that he would also like to do work that is related to sustainable development. His response shows that he has thought critically about ways in which engineers can contribute to sustainable development across various industries:

> I think that I will go into industry but it doesn't mean that I have to go into some green peace company to work on the efficiency of processes because if you go to car manufacturer you can still increase the efficiency of the engine or something and you still do something for sustainability and the environment even though you're not working for a green company, so I think it doesn't really matter, – it's not that easy to say you work for a green company or another one, it's more complicated, [by] which fields you are working [in] and what you try to improve. I think that's the main thing

engineers want to do they always want to improve something. And if you can combine the improvement of things with sustainability or energy savings then it doesn't matter where you – or which kind of company [you work in].

While some students seemed sure of the career path they would like to follow, others were less decisive. Rupert (GER) says he has not yet decided whether he will pursue an academic or a corporate career, and it is interesting to note that his response implies that his employment is solely dependent on his decision to be employed:

> I haven't decided if I want to stay and do some research at university, or go into industry but I think a lot of engineering is lot about optimization as he just said, so yeah always about optimization of price and yeah, ecological things, yeah so I think I would like to work on optimization in some way and always keep that sustainability thinking in mind.

Similarly, Kurt (GER) says:

> Yeah, I want to work in industry but I don't know exactly, haven't decided.

On the contrary, Anashe (ZIM) has quite clear ideas about what she aspires to be. She would like to pursue a corporate career and she hopes to work in engineering design. Her response indicates that she is aware that what she aspires to might be characterized by stressful work situations. Nevertheless, she weighs this possibility against the odds of achieving happiness or fulfilling the desire to travel and her statement suggests she would consider this a fair trade-off for a demanding job:

> What I would really like to do is to be a practising engineer, but on the design side, like to be a consultant and I'd like to work on like different pro-jects, even with hectic deadlines – I know it could be stressful but at the end of the day it would be like something that you can look back at and be happy about. And yeah I want to travel overseas.

Similarly, Vimbai (ZIM) would like to work in industry as opposed to working in academia, and she has a specific picture of herself in mind. Below she explains that she finds engineering tasks that necessitate her presence at a plant or construction site quite undesirable. Instead, she would like to work as a consultant:

> I find it so difficult to picture myself at a plant. Like having that life of always wearing PPE [personal protection equipment] every day, I just don't think I'd be happy in that situation. (...) I see myself more in the consulting side, either engineering consulting or some other consulting but then some-thing that I can work [at] from the office and still apply the skills that I've acquired during my six long years at varsity.

For Vimbai (ZIM) the idea of studying for six long years in order to end up in overalls and a helmet is not an attractive thought. On the contrary, Anesu (ZIM) describes this as exactly what he would like to do:

> I see myself as (…) like – heading like the process engineering [department] in mining and stuff – wearing the PPE and stuff – I think that's basically where I see myself – sometime soon.

To summarize, these students aspire towards different career paths. While some students would like to continue with conducting research within universities, others are keen to begin their corporate careers in the engineering sector or would eventually like to become engineering consultants. Also, while some have decided that they would like to work in companies that are explicitly pro-sustainable development, others feel that they can do positive work in companies that are not primarily geared towards sustainable engineering, a few students are undecided about where they would like to work, and one sees herself venturing into entrepreneurship.

There are interesting differences in the way the students spoke about their employment. First, it seems that the Zimbabwean students are primarily concerned about their employability, whereas the South African and German students seem less worried about the possibility that they might be unemployed once they have completed their studies. In addition, most Zimbabwean students appear to have continued their postgraduate studies out of failure to find employment after their undergraduate studies.

When looking at the students' motivations for studying engineering there are also some clear differences. Most Zimbabwean students were primarily uninterested in engineering but pursued engineering studies as a second option to studying medicine. According to the students, they could not study medicine, not because they did not qualify to do so but because international students are not allowed to enrol in medical degrees in any South African university.

Through the lens of the capability approach (Sen, 1999) and human development paradigm (ul Haq, 1995), if we are to consider education as a means of development or achieving well-being, we need to ask how each and every student is enabled to flourish in and through education (Walker, 2003). This means, if the curricula, pedagogies and institutional arrangements that characterize higher education do not result in graduates' opportunities to be and do what they have reason to value, education cannot be considered as being for human development. Taking a close look at how the students who participated in this study are enabled to flourish shows different interplays of local and international students' aspirations, capabilities and conversion factors that ultimately shape their functionings. As the summary in Table 3.1 shows, all (local and international) students had the same educational functioning i.e. they were all studying engineering. However, they had dissimilar educational aspirations, and the educational capabilities and conversion factors that underlie their decisions to become engineers vary.

Table 3.1 Interplay of students' aspirations, capabilities, and functionings

Educational aspirations	Effective opportunities	Conversion factors	Functioning
Zimbabwean students			
To study medicine	Opportunity to enrol in any programme student qualifies for	Prohibited from studying medicine	Studying engineering
South African students			
To study something that guarantees a good salary	Opportunity to enrol in any programme student qualifies for	Ability to choose preferred degree	Studying engineering
German students			
To study something that student is good at/passionate about	Opportunity to enrol in any programme student qualifies for	Ability to choose preferred degree	Studying engineering

Source: Author's own.

From Table 3.1 it is clear that while all the students were studying to become engineers, not all of them *wanted* to be engineers. This means that there are students who are fundamentally uninterested in becoming engineers but are opting to do so (right up to master's level) because of limited options to become what they have reason to value. One has to consider the implications of becoming an engineer when students only have extrinsic reasons to do so. Arguably, students who become engineers but do not develop appropriate engineering identities may not care to direct their efforts to public-good engineering. That is, if engineering is only looked at as a mere technical job and a means to a good income, it will not be carried out with the compassion required for public-good engineering or engineering that is pro-poor and geared towards sustainable human development. The following section discusses what the students value most about studying engineering. The discussion shows that all the students speak positively about their educational experiences and that even those who were not initially keen to study engineering nonetheless developed a significant appreciation for the engineering profession.

Valued capabilities and functionings

The range of capabilities and functionings discussed in this section reflect what the students described as things they appreciate most about their studies; such functionings may not necessarily be directly oriented to the public good. While some students spoke about their appreciation of engineering knowledge, and how it broadens their understanding of other aspects in life, others spoke about feeling resilient and that their ability to cope with general life challenges has improved. For example, Kurt (GER) appreciates enhancing his understanding of the technical composition and functionality of artefacts used in daily life:

I think I really appreciate it when I understand things I didn't know before, just like things you see every day but you can't really say how it works and you get to learn about them and understand them, yeah I think that's one of the parts that I enjoy just like yeah, getting to know how it works.

Knowing how things work is closely related to opportunities for using that understanding to solve various problems. The students often said that they feel they can solve any problem, and generally attribute this not only to engineering knowledge but also to the resilience they have developed during the course of their studies. For instance, Mufaro (ZIM) explains that she is no longer intimidated or afraid when she is presented with a problem but is instead confident in her ability to solve problems, and attributes this to the problem-solving approaches that she has learned from her studies:

The way I tackle problems I think it's something I didn't have when I was starting my degree, but then now it's like I have it. And I'm not as, like, scared of, like, technical jargon or whatever you know? Even if I don't understand I can still approach and try to understand. So I think maybe the confidence and the way I solve problems [is what I appreciate the most].

Similarly, Mufaro (ZIM) says her analytical skills have improved, and that the way she approached problems when she started her undergraduate studies is very different from the way she views problems now that she is a master's student. She also speaks of her personal development and elaborates on this aspect of her experience at university when she explains that by the time one gets to the end of the fourth year of study, failure would be a familiar experience. Asked to give examples of what failure she was talking about, her focus group members gave examples of failing tests or exams that they then had to resit. The end of Mufaro's (ZIM) response triggered her focus group members to talk about overcoming hurdles and learning to keep going after failure. Similar notions are reflected in some lecturers' responses (discussed in the next chapter). As Mufaro (ZIM) asserts:

When I see a problem now I feel like, challenged to find a solution, I want to get to the bottom of almost everything – I think that's what I've gained from my past four years. And also I've realized that if you fail at anything you can still get up.

Likewise, Vimbai (ZIM) talks about overcoming life's challenges and asserts that persistence and hard work result in positive outcomes.

The most valuable thing I've gained from – okay first from the four years right? is that life can be challenging, but then if you work hard you can still overcome all the hurdles and as long as you work consistently, things will work out.

Anashe's (ZIM) explanation suggests that being aware of the failure of others creates a sense of affiliation amongst the students, and that a valuable outcome from this failure is the development of resilience:

> By the time you get to your final year [you] start understanding that failure is not, like, something that's 'out there' like, it's part of life. And the most important thing is how you recover from that and move on. Because, now once you've fallen down and you've risen – you're not going to make the same mistake.

Going through the process of failing challenging modules and completing the same module a second time with a favourable grade appears to be one of the factors that instils a sense of confidence in the students' perceived abilities to solve problems, including 'non-engineering' problems. It is clear that the development of resilience and confidence contributes to students' general sense of empowerment and 'can do' mentality. Anesu's (ZIM) words indicate this well:

> I feel like I can attempt almost anything, even things that are outside engineering. I feel like my mind is more open and I actually enjoy like looking at other problems as well. Like non-engineering (…) problems.

The feeling that one 'can do anything' is linked to the dissipation of fear, which can be attributed to successfully completing a challenging university qualification such as an engineering degree. Mufaro's (ZIM) response illustrates this well and shows that her higher education experience has challenged her to cope with different fears that she associated particularly with engineering studies:

> I think it takes away your fear as well. Like, I think getting through undergrad you go through a lot to get through it and you just – the fear of hard subjects has gone away – my fear of trying new things has gone away – my fear of fiddling with things has gone away, like in a lab or wherever.

The difficulties experienced during their studies can be described as one of the factors that made the students appreciate the completion of their undergraduate degrees even more. Students also spoke of how they felt their 'smartness' was validated by remarks from people who are impressed that they not only completed an engineering degree but are now enrolled in a master's programme. Vimbai (ZIM) says:

> People [think] you're like this super smart person like 'oh you're even doing master's in engineering!'

Comments such as this, which students said they sometimes receive from strangers, and the positive reaction of family members on graduation day, are some of the examples provided of situations that reinforced the feeling that the challenges and failures experienced in their studies have been worthwhile. Anesu's (ZIM) words reflect this well, and they also indicate that he values making his parents proud:

> (…) in the end it makes you appreciate your degree more when you look at that paper you're like 'wow!' (…) And even at graduation you see that they [his parents] are happy, you know? Like, they have brought up an engineer!

Students also reflected on the breadth of engineering application in industry, citing sectors such as food, mining, transportation and energy as potential areas of employment. Their responses clearly indicate that they appreciate the opportunity to find employment in diverse fields of work. Mayita (ZIM) says knowing this gives her the reassurance that she will ultimately find a job because the set of skills that she has acquired from her degree opens up many options that will become available to her upon completion of her studies. She believes that a master's degree in chemical engineering:

> [G]ives us the skill set to be able to do anything. Particularly in engineering you can go out into the bank[,] you can go into consultancy, we learn how to problem solve it's not specific to engineering (…) the skill set we get after that is quite diverse.

Mayita's (ZIM) statement contradicts the view of employers who think that engineering students do not have a wide understanding of the work areas in which engineering knowledge can be applied. Her words clearly show that she is aware that the knowledge and skills gained from an engineering degree are not limited in their application to the engineering industry. Some students spoke about the lessons and values they now have as a result of their broader higher education experiences. Rather than highlighting how their employment opportunities have been enhanced by studying engineering, some students' responses indicate that they appreciate more the opportunity for personal development. As Anna (GER) explains, studying at a university:

> also has an effect on the personal side, but I think that is generally the case when you study; not limited to studying engineering but in general. When you study, you grow.

Similarly, Phillip (GER) talks about the value of university learning quite broadly, citing being independent and taking responsibility for one's well-being and personal development as valuable outcomes. His words also show that, in reflecting about his higher education experience, he considers what happens outside the classroom as a space of learning and growth too:

> I think one also learns to be independent (…) you have your own place where you have to take care of the household and things like that. You also

learn to be responsible for yourself and it helps in your personal development. (…) I would definitely say that it doesn't only lead to progress in one's career.

To summarize, students value a range of beings and doings that are enabled by their higher education experiences and engineering education more specifically. In general, students appreciate opportunities for growth and personal development through learning how to be responsible for themselves, be more confident and be resilient and fearless. Students' responses also indicate that experiencing failure contributed to the development of their resilience because it forced them to deal with disappointment in their abilities to pass each exam at the first attempt. At the same time, failure was described as one the worst feelings one can experience as a student. However, feelings of disappointment fuelled by failure dissipated as soon as the students communicated with fellow students and realized that failure was not a condition unique to themselves, but rather a common phenomenon amongst engineering undergraduate students and common in the life experiences of people in general. Being aware of the fact that failure is a common experience creates a sense of normality and affiliation amongst students.

In relation to engineering knowledge, students appreciate deepening their understanding about the technical functionality of how things work, and enhancing their problem-solving approaches and techniques. Therefore, based on the interpretation of the findings presented in this section, the students' valued educational capabilities can be summarized as follows:

- learning how things work;
- learning how to solve problems;
- opportunities to work in diverse fields;
- opportunities for personal development;
- being resilient;
- being confident and feeling empowered;
- being perceived as 'smart'; and
- having a sense of affiliation.

Because these capabilities have to be considered in relation to their relevance for public-good engineering, it was important to distil this list accordingly. Doing so required consideration of the goals of engineering education based on a lecturer's perspectives (discussed next in Chapter 4) as well as the dimensions of public-good engineering (discussed thereafter in Chapter 5). This resulted in the following capabilities being identified as those that are arguably most important for engineers to function as agents of sustainable human development:

- solving problems;
- being confident and feeling empowered;
- being resilient and having a sense of affiliation; and
- working in diverse fields.

From the above capabilities, and in conjunction with the theoretical framework provided in the previous chapter, respective functionings can be extrapolated. That is, through the lens of the capability approach, one can argue that the potential to become a public-good engineer rests on engineering students' valuing the following doings and beings:

- applying engineering knowledge to help *solve problems* and challenges associated with sustainable human development;
- developing one's sense of *confidence and being empowered* to exercise individual and collective agency to advance social justice;
- developing a *sense of belonging* with fellow engineers, and learning to *persevere* in the face of individual failure; and
- *being employable* and having opportunities to apply professional engineering expertise in a wide range of contexts, industries and job positions for the sake of the public good.

Each capability and its corresponding functioning can be read as 'if–then' statements that represent a series of hypotheses about the kinds of beings and doings that can and ought to be achieved through engineering education for sustainable human development.

For example, looking at the first capability on the list i.e. solving problems, the following statement would apply:

> *If* engineering education provides students with opportunities to learn how to solve problems, *then* engineering graduates should be able to apply engineering knowledge to help solve problems and challenges associated with sustainable human development.

Using the second capability on the list as another example, i.e. being confident and feeling empowered, one could argue:

> *If* engineering education empowers students and develops their confidence, *then* engineering graduates should be confident to use their individual and collective agency to advance social justice.

The same principle applies to the remaining capabilities.

It is interesting to note that although this summary of valued capabilities and functionings is presented as one cohesive list, these categories were not evenly distributed across the data. That is, transcripts from focus groups with South African and Zimbabwean students were more often coded with the terms 'confidence', 'resilience', 'empowerment' compared with the transcripts of the focus group discussions with German students. On the other hand, 'problem solving' was equally prominent across the data, while 'personal development' was more common in the German data.

Because the intention is not to dichotomize perspectives but combine them, the identified capabilities and functionings are summarized together (see Table 3.2) and illustrate the value of combining diverse perspectives on engineering education. If the data had comprised only global North perspectives, functionings such as being resilient and having a sense of affiliation would not feature in these findings. Similarly, had only global South perspectives been considered, the findings would lean more heavily towards concerns about employment and employability. Considering both perspectives clearly provides a fuller and more nuanced understanding of the various reasons that students might decide to pursue engineering, what they are able to gain from engineering education and how this is linked to their potential to become public-good engineers.

The next section looks at students' perceptions of the role of engineers in society, and reflects on the connections between these perceptions and the students' aspirations, motivations, capabilities and functionings discussed previously.

Students' views on their roles in society as future engineers

To facilitate thinking about the contributions the students would like to make to society, students were given the example that one could sum up one function of medical doctors as that of 'saving lives'. The students were then asked to complete the same sentence for what they think engineers do. Most responses fell within the scope of describing engineers as 'problem solvers' and people who 'fix things' or even 'run lives'. When they elaborated on their answers, students often gave examples of different areas where engineering knowledge can be used to solve problems or improve the human condition. For example, Mayita (ZIM) says:

Table 3.2 Educational capabilities and functionings for public-good engineering

Capabilities	Functionings
Solving problems	Applying engineering knowledge to help solve problems and challenges associated with sustainable human development
Being confident and feeling empowered	Developing one's sense of confidence and exercising individual and collective agency to advance social justice
Being resilient and having a sense of affiliation	Developing a sense of belonging with fellow engineers and learning to persevere in the face of individual failure
Working in diverse fields	Being employable and having opportunities to apply professional engineering expertise in a wide range of contexts, industries and job positions for the sake of the public good

Source: Author's own.

We're involved in making everything that everyone uses on a daily basis; from the soap in the morning to what you eat, to the clothes you put on. There's a chemical engineer in that process – down to the diamond on your finger.

With this statement, Mayita (ZIM) emphasizes the different sectors in which chemical engineers are employed (e.g. manufacturing, food production and mining) and various human needs (e.g. sanitation, food and clothing) that are serviced with the aid of chemical engineers. In other words, Mayita's statement points to the involvement of engineers in catering for both fundamental human needs: 'what you eat', and also luxurious desires: 'the diamond on your finger'. Many responses also represent the view that engineers help improve people's standard of living, quality of life or the efficiency with which they are able to live their lives. For example, Markus (GER) says:

Maybe you could add like the standard of living, I mean getting more sophisticated products means also increasing your own life [quality] like having a nicer phone, or whatever people think is important to them, involves often, engineering techniques so…

Phrased in capabilities language, this means that engineers do work that is concerned with creating or enhancing valued human capabilities, or in Markus' words, 'whatever people think is important to them'.

This articulation of engineers' role in society implies that engineers are more involved in providing solutions to problems as society defines or sees them, rather than according to how engineers may perceive human problems. This idea is closely related to what Professor Schneider (GER) (in the next chapter) refers to as a problem in engineering education, namely that engineering students are taught that 'technology is value-free' and that engineering is practised objectively.

In many ways the students' responses suggest that they indeed view engineering as work that should be carried out objectively to fix problems in '[m]ore of a technical way, not like a social way', as Markus explains, or simply deal with 'Facts, facts, facts', in Rupert's words. For example Phillip (GER) states:

Engineers make life – through technology – help to make life more efficient, I'll say.

The emphasis on how engineers contribute to society is usually on technology or scientific methods. As Rupert (GER) explains:

We learn to solve problems in a particular way, but it's not like it's better, but in a very – in a scientific way.

Markus (GER) similarly explains that engineers solve problems in:

More of a technical way, not like a social way.

At this point in the discussion, Arnold (GER) explains some differences in problem-solving approaches between engineers and other professional groups:

> I think there is a big difference because [in engineering] you just look at the parameters and then you think about how to change them, how to affect them and it has nothing to do with like social understanding between people[,] it's just like the technical – and it's always facts, so you always know the numbers....

Rupert (GER) interjects:

> Facts, facts, facts....

Despite this emphasis on the importance of technical engineering knowledge being the key to solving problems, some students' responses suggest that they do recognize how engineering outcomes are closely linked to human capabilities. Kurt (GER) says:

> I think there is a social role because what the engineer is doing most of the time, it affects the social life as well. So you are responsible as an engineer to maybe reduce the CO_2 from your plant or whatever, so there is some kind of social responsibility when you work on some problems.

On the other hand, some responses suggest that engineers can and should do more than solve technical problems. Tendayi's (ZIM) view suggests that engineers also have the knowledge to protect society from harm and therefore have the responsibility to do so:

> I think as engineers we're also there to protect the society because we know what's good and what's bad for the society.

Mufaro's (ZIM) understands the functions of engineering in society as design, creation and innovation:

> When I think of engineers I think of like more of this creativity and design and you know? Just – new things into the society. So I think that's what engineers' role in society is.

Similarly, Vimbai's (ZIM) view is that:

> Engineers are more, you know? Innovative; than being sort of the guys who-like scientists and stuff. I think for us, I think it's more of applying what we have learnt (...) to solve the day to day problems that we might be facing in society.

On the other hand, Mayita's (ZIM) opinion is that a major part of engineers' roles has more to do with maintaining the innovation, products or processes already implemented in society, as opposed to creating what is 'new'. She acknowledges that a general goal of engineering is to improve things, but she pays equal attention to the fact that engineers' work is often about keeping things in place that have already been implemented. She says engineering is about:

> Improving and maintaining. A lot of engineering is maintaining what's already there.

Likewise, some students' responses suggest that a major role of engineers is to correct, adjust or realign past engineering solutions. Mufaro's (ZIM) view indicates her acknowledgement that engineers are responsible for taking part in creating processes or products that pollute the environment. She also refers to '*our* engineering actions' as opposed to simply saying 'engineering actions', which indicates that she identifies with engineering professionals and that she is expressing a sense of shared responsibility:

> I think there's still a lot to of, if I can say damage control, like if we look at emissions and try to normalize things again (...) because of the consequences of our engineering actions, yeah.

Towards the end of one of the focus group discussions, Arnold, Markus, Rupert and Kurt (GER) joke about how engineers destroy the world, only to save it. I commented on the irony of their joke, to which Arnold replied:

> Well, yeah, it is [ironic]. I mean, many problems we are facing today are at least influenced by engineers I mean maybe they didn't know better, maybe they are not as open minded as we are now but I mean carbon emission is often done by industries and industries are done by engineers so sometimes I think we have to solve problems other engineers initiated before.

Likewise, Mayita (ZIM) states that she has often come across information or heard it said that much environmental damage has resulted from engineering:

> What I've heard often from the older generation is chemical engineers are responsible for a lot of degradation right now – a lot of stuff that's gone wrong in the world; so we think we're helping, but are we really helping?

Mayita's powerful question shows that she is critical of the notion that what engineers do, necessarily helps or 'fixes things' or 'solves problems'.

Both Mayita's (ZIM) and Arnold's (GER) views show that the students are able to pose questions that challenge some assumptions about the role of engineers in society. Their views show that although they value possessing knowledge that enables them to solve problems, they do not take it for granted that engineering outcomes always achieve this. This is important because:

> separately, the fields of engineering and social justice are about hope because those of us who enact, teach and/or benefit from them hope that their manifestations in the world, in the form of technologies or social policies, will bring some kind of social good and make the world a more compassionate, just place.
>
> (Lucena, 2013: 3)

As the students' critical reflections show, these two fields of practice and sources of hope have rarely come together, let alone become integrated; and when they do it is often via clashing organizational, pedagogical, practical or technical manifestations, which often result in the opposite of what we might hope for – exacerbated social inequalities and injustices (Lucena, 2013).

To summarize, students generally perceive engineers as efficient problem solvers, who through technology and science are able to apply specific technical knowledge to attend to a variety of basic human needs, desires or pressing challenges in creative and innovative ways. The role and function of engineers in society was described with phrases ranging from 'fixing things' to 'protecting society', which shows that the students recognize that engineers can apply their knowledge to non-living 'things' to affect changes in human life. With regard to protecting society, emphasis is placed on the issue of negative impacts on the environment. There is a keen awareness amongst the students that some engineering outcomes cause damage to the environment, thus creating new problems from the very solutions they implement.

Summative discussion

The findings presented in this chapter have dealt with students' aspirations, their motivations for studying engineering, and what they value most about the process and its outcomes. It is important to note that there were no obvious differences between student responses across the various engineering disciplines (i.e. industrial and production engineering, and process and chemical engineering). Not surprisingly, the capability for employment emerged as the most common valuable outcome of engineering education across the data, but the students aspire to very different career paths. While some students would like to continue conducting research within universities, others are keen to begin their corporate careers in the engineering sector or would eventually like to become engineering consultants. In addition, while some have decided that they would like to work in companies that are explicitly in favour of sustainable development, others feel that they can do positive work in companies that are not primarily geared towards sustainable development.

The discussion on students' motivations for choosing to study engineering highlighted the importance of asking questions about students' educational capabilities instead of simply looking at their functionings, if one seeks to understand how higher education is enabling them to thrive. Questions related to students' motivations behind studying engineering were important in order to try to establish the extent to which their study choices were intrinsically motivated as this information could be used as indicators of valued educational capabilities. The findings revealed that some students' decisions were made in a manner that seems somewhat arbitrary. For example, some students wanted to study something that was rooted in mathematics and science because they performed well in these subjects in high school. At the same time, they did not want to be perceived as 'nerds' so they opted for engineering studies instead of a degree in physics, for example. On the other hand, a few students were primarily concerned with shortlisting jobs with high salaries, with one student saying that he just 'googled' 'top starting salary' to review his career options. A number of students initially wanted to study medicine, and ultimately decided on engineering because their preferred choice was not available at their university. The most important indication from these findings is that only one of the students went into engineering studies primarily out of direct interest in the engineering profession per se. The potential problems this poses for developing public-good engineers were discussed and it was argued that engineering education should provide students with opportunities to develop appropriate engineering identities and dispositions towards technology.

Having discussed students' motivations for studying engineering, the discussion moved to students' aspirations, where it was revealed that valued functionings include being confident, resilient and fearless, as well as being problem solvers. Based on the interpretation of students' articulation about what they appreciate most from their studies, it appears that some of the capabilities that underlie valued functionings include the opportunities to learn 'how things work' and how to solve problems, as well as opportunities for personal development and the prospect of working in diverse industries. These capabilities and functionings represent what future engineers' contributions to society might be.

The last section of this chapter considered how students perceive the role of engineers in society and it shows that students generally see engineers as problem solvers. Also, students perceive engineers as contributors to positive change in and valuable benefits to society. However, there are mixed views on the value of engineering solutions to society because of the negative impacts of engineering activities on the environment. While many engineers think that engineering should have nothing to do with social justice because they are bound to an ideology of depoliticization in engineering that leads them to draw a boundary around the technical content and leave non-technical issues out of engineering (Lucena, 2013), it is clear that some students' rationality surrounding this matter shows critical thinking and reflexivity in action. But this is not the case for all engineering students, and it should be. Importantly, students whose views are reported on in this book attended universities that foster transversal skills like critical thinking. Regardless of where future engineers might be educated, engineering curricula and pedagogies should offer each student opportunities to reflect on questions such as: Who benefits from the problems that engineers solve?

Connecting apparently abstract and apolitical concepts with questions about power and inequality can, in effect, encourage students to critique dominant economic and cultural values and to consider that there might be meaningful, and more just, alternatives (Lucena, 2013).

The next chapter discusses in more detail, approaches for inspiring this kind of thinking in engineering classrooms.

References

Lucena, J. (ed.). (2013). *Engineering education for social justice: Critical explorations and opportunities* (Vol. 10). Dordrecht, Heidelberg, New York, London: Springer.

Sen, A. (1999). *Development as Freedom*. Oxford: Oxford University Press.

ul Haq, M. (1995). *Reflections on human development*. New York: Oxford University Press.

Walker, M. (2003). Framing social justice in education: What does the 'capabilities' approach offer? *British Journal of Educational Studies, 51*(2), 168–187.

4 Teaching for public-good engineering

Lecturers' perspectives

The results reported in this chapter are based on findings from ten semi-structured interviews conducted with lecturers from UCT and UB. Like the presentation of the findings in the previous chapter, the discussion draws substantially on the voices of the lecturers, with their answers interjected by summaries of the interpretation of their responses. These summaries also link the selected interview excerpts by contextualizing the quoted words in order to make clearer the connection between the interview data and the conclusions that can be drawn from their analysis. This chapter also weaves relevant secondary literature through the empirical data. This approach works to highlight the alignment of the lecturers' perspectives, with recommendations from international literature on engineering education reform. Starting by reintroducing the interview participants, the chapter then discusses the value and purpose of engineering education, before unpacking the different types of knowledge or ways of knowing that can be considered as indispensable to engineering education. Thereafter findings are presented on what the lecturers thought they could do to teach non-technical skills. This is followed by the summative discussion that concludes the chapter.

At the time of the interviews, most interviewees were senior academics within the Faculty of Production Engineering at UB or the Faculty of Engineering and the Built Environment at UCT. As the following individual profile summaries show, all interviewees also serve/served as head of an engineering department or research group at their respective universities:

From Germany

1   *Professor (emeritus) Doktor Ingenieurwesens (Dr Ing.)* [Doctor of Engineering] *Bremer* is an honorary professor of Applied Mechanics. His career in teaching and research spans across institutions such the University of Karlsruhe, the Technical University of Berlin and the Technische Universität Clausthal where he taught in the areas of Fluid Mechanics, Thermodynamics, Systems Engineering and Technology Assessment.

2   *Professor Dr Ing. Kleid* heads the Department for Integrated Product Development at the Faculty of Production Engineering at UB. The courses he

offers include Introduction to Engineering Design, Applying and Comparing Creativity Techniques, Computer-Aided Design Management and Virtual Product Development, and Production Systems.

3   *Professor Dr Ing. Marco* is dean at the Faculty of Production Engineering at UB and heads the Hybrid Materials Interfaces Research Group within the Department of Process Engineering. The courses he teaches include Foundation of Materials Sciences, Photovoltaics and Biology for Engineers.

4   *Professor Dr Schneider* is an honorary professor leading the Vocational Education and Training Research Group at the Faculty of Physics and Electrical Engineering at the UB. An expert in the field of vocational training research, his current projects also include extensive comparative education research involving Germany and South Africa.

5   *Professor Dr Ing. Schwartz* is a director of the Bremen Institute for Mechanical Engineering, within the Faculty of Production Engineering at UB. Heading the department of Design and Process Technology, she teaches courses such as Assembly Technology and Systems, Process Planning and Assembly Logistics.

From South Africa

1   *Professor Block* is associate professor at the Faculty of Engineering and the Built Environment in the Department of Chemical Engineering at UCT. He is a senior lecturer in Chemical Engineering and head of research in Environmental and Process Systems Engineering.

2   *Professor Grant* is a senior lecturer at the Faculty of Science in the Department of Chemistry and Polymer Science at Stellenbosch University. She runs a multidisciplinary research group with interests in Medicinal Chemistry, Chemistry Education and the Philosophy of Science, Education and Chemistry.

3   *Professor (emeritus) Hunter* served as Head of the Department of Chemical Engineering, Dean of the Faculty of Engineering and the Built Environment and Acting Deputy Vice-Chancellor at UCT before his retirement in 2009.

4   *Dr Jones*, of the Faculty of Engineering and the Built Environment at the department of chemical engineering at UCT, is director of the Centre for Catalysis Research.

5   *Professor Smith* is also from the Faculty of Engineering and the Built Environment at the Department of Chemical Engineering at UCT. She teaches chemistry to undergraduate engineering students. She is also a student advisor to first-year chemical engineering students.

During the interviews, these lecturers shared their views on issues ranging from the purposes of engineering education to the pedagogical practices they employ to encourage critical thinking. They were also asked about the extent to which they felt students understand the complexity and interconnection of trends influenced by technological innovations and how the engineering curricula at their respective universities are addressing sustainable development concerns. The following section presents the corresponding findings, presented thematically.

The purposes of engineering education

The goals of engineering education are described in various ways, ranging from the purpose of equipping graduates with knowledge and competencies for work, to the purpose of helping students realize their potential in any area of life. Whereas some lecturers describe the purposes of engineering education broadly and speak of outcomes that are related to enhancing students' autonomy, decision-making abilities and self-determinism, others use 'toolbox' analogies to refer to skills that students need for employment.

Professor Schwarz's (GER) explanation of teaching and learning in engineering is that lecturers do not 'teach engineering'. Rather, she purports that lecturers teach students one of many subjects that they can build upon and connect with other subjects to result in the practice known as 'engineering'. She describes this as a practice that changes continuously and is developed throughout one's academic and/or professional career and she asserts that universities are also responsible for developing students' bravery to use engineering knowledge throughout their lifetimes:

> People who invented laser technology, who built up the laser machines, the first ones [engineers] never learned about lasers during their studies. They learned about physics, about mechanics, control theory – they learned about design. And then someone had an idea and they were able to transform their basic knowledge into a new field. And that is what we are heading for in university; to give the students the ability to deal with the first job and then five years later to deal with the second job, and the third job and then we have to make them fit for the next fifty years of technological improvements. To deal [with], to understand, to develop and to further enhance. So that's what we give them. What I think – what I expect them to take. Yeah? The knowledge, the methodology and also the courage to use it.

Professor Schwartz (GER) describes the goal of engineering education using similes and metaphors, sometimes even extrapolating moral lessons from films to bring her views across. Using a scene from the science-fiction adventure movie, *Indiana Jones and the Temple of Doom*, she describes what engineering students are being prepared for by universities. Referring to the film's main character, she compares Indiana Jones' challenge[1] to traverse unsteady terrain, to challenges engineering graduates will face as professional engineers. In doing so, she indicates that engineers often have to make decisions under difficult and uncertain circumstances and she argues that university education aims to prepare students for similar situations that they are likely to encounter at work (and in life). From her perspective, the purpose of engineering education is to develop students' capacities to make decisions autonomously and develop innovative approaches and methods to solution seeking that are founded on engineering knowledge:

> When he (Indiana Jones) is in the temple in Petra, then he has all the tiles [in front of him] and some of them break down and some of them are stable. All of our students have to go, during their career, through such a field and you never know in advance which way is the right one for each of them. And what we're doing in the student time is that we build up these tiles so that we give them the opportunity to build up on them, to build new houses on these tiles, and to be able to decide which tiles to use and to be able to make up new things from the common ground. To build up new things, new ideas, new products, new processes from what they know basically. And we give them both the knowledge and the methodology to deal with the problems.

Similarly, Professor Kleid (GER) describes the goals of engineering education broadly. He is disinclined to name specific goals of engineering education. Instead, he describes the aims of engineering faculties as preparing students for the world of work and for life. He does however emphasize the importance of keeping engineering production 'a German thing', which suggests the pride he has in the quality of German engineers. It also indicates that he acknowledges how doing so also supports national development imperatives. He sees this way of identifying with the profession as being an important element to the development of German engineers. He says:

> We at this faculty do not have specifically formulated goals per se, and this is something which is continuously being discussed by us. We are called Produktionstechnik[2] and I would say the overarching aim of all my colleagues or of the faculty, is to educate young people during their time at the university so that they in the end are capable for employment, capable for the future, on one side. But one goal that is also always present is that we keep production in Germany. And that is the overriding aim. One could break it up into subsections but it's about educating excellent engineers who uphold this strength even in international comparison; helping to further develop them.

Professor Kleid (GER) also argues that, as a result of their higher education experiences, graduates should develop a sense of freedom about who or what they want to be in the world. His view suggests that he finds it important that engineering education (and education in general) develops students' sense of independence to determine their futures:

> In my view they should, at the end of their studies, and this is one of the major goals of education – and you won't achieve this for all students because it's also a societal problem – we must manage to give as many

students as possible the feeling that they can determine their own position. And we have to strive for that – [so that] students see their position. And that, they must know for themselves.

Professor Kleid (GER) elaborates this view about the goals of engineering education, and his response is powerful because it focuses not on predetermining what students should be or do once they complete their studies, but rather on the *opportunities* that should be created through university leaning. This view resonates with a capabilities view of development, where development is defined as freedom, i.e. a freedom to do and be what one has reason to value. He also stresses the outcome of stimulating students' curiosity. This implies that he assumes students enter universities with a desire for knowledge and with inquisitive, questioning minds. He argues that university education should stimulate this curiosity and help students recognize opportunities where they can successfully apply what they learn – that is, it should help students imagine new areas where their engineering knowledge can be used:

> I believe (…) we have to offer more options where young people can be successful. And we have to show them what they can do, not what is impossible. Rather show: 'here, you can do this' – 'and that'. I think it's much more about awakening curiosity. – I think it's also educators who have to change, right? In the long run university should awaken student's curiosity, and provide an environment where that can also be served, or satisfied. And that is in my view one of the biggest challenges.

As mentioned earlier, not all lecturers' views on the purposes of engineering education were broad and abstract. For example, Professor Marco (GER) describes these goals as threefold. First, to provide foundational theoretical natural sciences and engineering knowledge, through subjects such as mathematics, physics, chemistry, etc. Second, to teach students the practical application of that knowledge at its more advanced stages, which is achieved through compulsory *Praktika* or internships (locally or abroad). Third, to advance research that is carried out across various departments in the engineering faculty, where students have the opportunity to do a *Forschungspraktikum* or research-based internship. To summarize, he sees research-based learning as an umbrella concept for the three main goals of engineering education and as the means by which engineering students are prepared to become qualified engineers:

> The concept of 'forschendes Lernen' is quite big here at Universität Bremen: you learn through research. So you have these three aspects: the fundamental sciences, the research and you have the practical applications. And all three contribute then to your qualification.

Some lecturers at UB mentioned that breaking up the previously offered Diplom five-year programmes into a three-plus-two-year cycle structure is not desirable.

These concerns are raised due to the idea that at the end of the three year period students have completed the foundation phase of their path towards becoming engineers, but are still far from having the capacity to perform engineering activities independently in professional settings. Professor Kleid (GER) says:

> I am not particularly for the bachelor master system. Many German engineers aren't. (…) I am against the idea of someone coming to the university and leaving with a bachelor degree (…). Even if someone goes somewhere else, we try to advise them to go to another university, don't go straight into work – well if one really wants to then they should – but the advice goes more in the direction that one should study further to get a higher degree.

Professor Hunter's (SA) view similarly focuses on what students need to be able to do before they qualify as engineers. However, his terminology is quite different to that of Professor Marco (GER). At this point it is interesting to note that words such as 'toolkit', 'toolbox' and 'tools' are used almost only by the South African lecturers. The words toolbox and toolkit generally refer to sets of graduate attributes (engineering education outcomes) and the tools would therefore be a particular skill (e.g. the ability to calculate complex mathematical equations). For example, Professor Hunter (SA) says the goals of engineering education are:

> To provide a student with all the necessary tools so when the student leaves university they've got the toolbox to start out becoming an engineer.

Professor Grant (SA) also says:

> Engineering education is about giving students the toolkit they need for employment.

These responses resemble the kind of language one might associate with utilitarian views on education, where education is primarily defined in instrumental terms according to the competencies (skills) a student can acquire through education, for the sole purpose of employment. Also emphasizing the tools that students need for employment, Professor Jones (SA) gives an example of what university learning ought to prepare students to do. However, his response focuses more on developing students' potential to take responsibility and be accountable for engineering outcomes:

> Engineering education should prepare the students for taking over responsibility in a plant environment and responsibility for the people working there and for the products that the company produces for world markets.

Some lecturers also emphasize that what graduates take with them from university is just enough knowledge to *begin* understanding the broader spectrum of the engineering profession, which allows them to gain relevant work to register with the necessary professional bodies (the Engineering Council of South Africa (ECSA) for example).

Professor Smith (SA) says the following about engineering education in universities:

> I think it's important to say that it's the one stage towards your becoming the engineering professional.

The stages to becoming a professional engineer are described at length by Professor Hunter (SA), who emphasizes that upon graduation students haven't become engineers yet, but are at the stage where they have what it takes to grow into being an engineer:

> It takes seven years to produce an engineer, four years at university then they get the thing called a degree which is a starter pack and then three years as a candidate engineer in industry. [They get] registered with ECSA then they are ready to start practising as an independent engineer. So that is why I feel very strongly when consulting companies come around the engineering faculties and try to recruit our very clever students into becoming consultants the day after they graduate; that's a crime because they haven't become engineers. They've got a toolbox. And I'm worried that the modern current thinking on engineering education is failing to remember to give the student a good toolbox.

What emerges clearly from the data is that German and South African lecturers talk differently about the purposes of engineering education. When looking across the data, it is easily observable that the German lecturers speak about the goals of engineering education quite broadly. Based on their views, engineering education seeks to:

- develop students' capacities to make decisions autonomously and create innovative approaches and methods to solution seeking, which are founded on engineering knowledge;
- enhance students' sense of determination to be and do what they have reason to value in life as well as determine their roles in society;
- stimulate students' desire for knowledge and help them recognize opportunities where they can successfully apply what they learn, in their work and in their lives; and
- provide students with opportunities for research-based learning.

These four goals reflect and are consistent with skills like critical thinking and open-mindedness, which emerge from the data on employers' views (discussed in the next chapter).

On the other hand, South African lecturers speak more narrowly about the goals of engineering education. Based on their views, engineering education seeks to:

- provide students with the necessary knowledge and skills that they need to become engineers and be employable; and
- develop students' potential to take responsibility for running engineering organizations and be accountable for the engineering outcomes produced by them.

Having anticipated that some lecturers' responses might focus specifically on the goals of engineering education in relation to graduate employability, there was a question in the interview schedule that was directed at finding out what lecturers thought about the value of engineering education beyond preparation for employment. In this question each interviewee was asked to comment on a statement that draws substantially from Boni and Walker's (2013) view that universities ought to advance equalities and contribute to sustainable and democratic societies. The statement read:

> Education institutions should also promote social goods, through enhancing personal development, contributions to society, fair participation in the economy, well-being, participation and empowerment, equity and diversity, sustainability, world citizenship, imaginative understanding and freedom.
>
> (Boni & Walker, 2013)

South African lecturers' responses to this comment illustrate that their views on the goals of engineering education are not far from those of the German lecturers. On the contrary, they seem to share similar ideas about the broader contributions higher education should make to students' development. However, they seem more concerned with the structural, economic, temporal and institutional constraints that make it difficult for universities to achieve the goals noted above. For example, Professor Jones (SA) says:

> I think that is a true statement for the original idea of the university, for what is called in Germany at least the Humboldt ideal of the university. University is the place where people study, as opposed to being taught, right? Where they are so directed in their study that they have mentors that guide them in their study and as a result of the process of studying they come out as complete persons, personalities. All of that really epitomizes what you just described. There's a lot of political terminology in that sentence but in essence what it means is the ideal citizen is described by those qualities that you just read to me. And I do subscribe to that ideal. In the actual study environment it is met with realities of the sheer mass of students and the limited resources in terms of infrastructure and financing and skilled educators – to actually allow this to happen.

Professor Jones (SA) continues and expresses concern about the extent and reach of universities to impart values and attributes mentioned in the Boni and Walker (2013) quote:

I don't know whether that challenge is easily addressed at a university pro-gramme level, I'm not sure. I think we can do a lot more to sensitize stu-dents to the need to take on their personal responsibilities for the things that you mentioned there and it is a challenge for the profession. Sometimes I worry that the (engineering) profession doesn't have the profile that it ought to have in society.

Professor Jones' (SA) views clearly indicate that he has similar ideas about the purposes of engineering education to those of his German counterparts, and his opinion is typical of the South African lecturers' views. One might then wonder why South African and German lecturers articulated the goals of engi-neering education in very different ways, since their views are fundamentally similar.

The most likely reasons are linked to the context in which education, employ-ment and life in general take place. As indicated in Chapter 2, South Africa has high levels of unemployment, so it is logical that employability concerns are at the forefront of conversations about education outcomes. It is also possible that the lecturers are aware that many students encounter barriers to accessing higher education because of high university tuition fees and the fact that many students come from low- or middle-income households that struggle to pay these fees. Because of the high price tag attached to university degrees, South African lec-turers might focus primarily on whether or not the knowledge imparted by universities actually leads to employment, as being employed probably means a brighter future in terms of having more economic freedom (which is beneficial not only to the individual graduate, but to their family too).

On the other hand, zero university tuition fees in Germany and more favour-able economic conditions means that lecturers (and students) are probably more concerned with broader educational outcomes, as opposed to being worried about 'getting their money's worth' out of university education. This is reflected in the findings from the focus group discussions with students (discussed in Chapter 3) where South African students similarly raise concerns about their employability when talking about their education, whereas the German students do not.

As such, it appears that South African lecturers and students *talk* about the purposes of engineering education differently to German lecturers, but this does not necessarily mean that they *see* the goals of engineering education dif-ferently. Rather, it appears that less favourable socio-economic conditions in South Africa influence the emphasis placed on the issue of employment when talking about higher education outcomes. On the other hand, more stable socio-economic conditions in Germany might make it easier for lecturers and students to focus more of their attention on broader outcomes when talking about higher education.

Although universities ought to enhance engineering graduates' capability for employment by ensuring that students learn appropriate technical skills to be employable, this should not be done at the expense of enhancing students' opportunities to learn how to: make decisions autonomously, determine their roles in society or recognize broader opportunities for intrinsically meaningful employment. In addition, engineering students should have opportunities to learn how to think critically, become more open-minded as well as communicate and collaborate effectively with diverse teams (this is discussed fully in the next chapter). As argued by Nieusma and Riley, by placing technical functionality at the centre of development work, engineering-for-development projects and engineering activities in general tend to obscure non-technical dimensions of development work that are pivotal to achieving social justice goals (Nieusma & Riley, 2010).

Therefore, an overemphasis on the importance of technical skills for employability in engineering education is not in the best interest of developing public-good engineers. That is, engineers who not only have a sound base of technical engineering knowledge but are also critical thinkers who can apply this knowledge appropriately in practice while being fully conscious of their roles in society and willing to use their agency to promote social justice and advance sustainable human development as a public good.

Developing engineering identities

Professor Schneider (GER) argues that engineering knowledge can go a long way in affecting graduates' occupational identity and commitment to the engineering profession, explaining that this is dependent on developing deep and meaningful understanding of what they are effectively doing:

> Professional identity (…) is for personal development, extremely important – and in so far the quality of occupations are very important for the personal development and of course for commitment. If a person understands what he is doing, he's not only a robot doing what the boss says.

Correspondingly, Professor Schwarz (GER) explains the value of engineering knowledge by describing the role of engineers in society and explains what it might mean to identify oneself as an engineer. Using an analogy about different levels of participation in a societal cause, she reasons that engineers' assignment in society is to be proactive agents of positive change:

> I say we have different roles in society, there are people who climb the trees to say save the trees, and that's one role. And the engineer can say what can I invent that I do not need them [trees] anymore for my product? So I wanted to be the one who thinks about the better solution, the best solution instead of just saying I'm against it. Of course it's important that people say I'm against [something] but that's not enough. That's just the beginning. It doesn't help us to be against everything. We've got to be for something. So the question is what is it for? And that's from my point of view the engineering subject. To be *for* something.

Professor Schneider's (GER) perspective is that engineers and other professional groups that contribute to the creation and design of development projects fail to make appropriate ethical judgements because of their education. In particular, he talks about the failure of universities to impart engineering knowledge that encompasses an understanding of the reasons behind the necessity for technology. He calls this the 'purpose–means relationship', defining technology as a 'realization of human needs':

> Every technology is ultimately the articulation of a societal purpose, otherwise it would not exist. Every technology is the materialization of a purpose, backed by interests, which are backed by needs and dreams. Needs and dreams are translated into interest by the people. There is a balancing of interests, then there is a purpose. Out of it engineers create specifications and these specifications become products and processes which are bound by the feasibility allowed by technology and science.

Professor Schneider (GER) also argues that the problem with technical subject matter is that it is taught as an objective science, rather than as knowledge that has its own set of pre-existing values. He goes on to explain that leaving it up to the state to decide on the appropriateness of technologies for society is problematic because this results in a top-down approach that causes engineers to function as objective technical experts whose knowledge enables them to contribute to innovation, but whose value judgements are not meaningfully considered or required in the process:

> They [engineers] are taught in the university: technology is value-free. And they have no responsibility for why and they have no responsibility for the follow up, they leave the politicians to think about that; (…) this is wrong. It's basically wrong because every technology is the articulation of a societal purpose, and if you don't understand the purpose and where it comes from then you have no understanding of technology, that is the problem. And engineers normally, especially in universities, have no understanding of technology, they don't understand it. Really they don't understand it. They have knowledge of how it functions. But not why is technology this shape, and its effects –no idea. In so far they are connected to possibilities, but not to the needs and purposes.

This argument aligns with empirical research that shows how engineered systems, in the form of public transportation systems hide biases against marginalized groups (see Lucena, 2013). Such research challenges the assumption that engineered systems are value-neutral to illustrate how engineers, and their political clients, often express visions of social justice but at the same time might be blind to hidden unjust assumptions in their modelling that eventually lead to injustices and inequalities (Lucena, 2013).

In the excerpt below Professor Schneider (GER) shares his thoughts on why he believes engineers have a precarious understanding of technology that may lead to them unknowingly contributing to unjust ends. He also states that the biggest problem lies in engineering curricula that are reduced to modules emphasizing the 'how' of technical knowledge and technology at the expense of knowing 'why' certain technologies are more worth creating than others, if the goal is accomplishing sustainable human development. He believes that it is therefore easy to use engineers for unjust ends. He says:

> If there is a dictator who says do this or do that they [engineers] would do it. Because their implicit education is a problem, they don't understand technology. They only understand how it works, how to produce, how to do research – And they believe it's value-free – unbelievable!

A helpful way to get engineering students to make inferential sense of propositional and procedural knowledge (Muller, 2015; Winch, 2014) is suggested by Professor Hunter (SA), who says that giving engineering students examples of the context in which their knowledge might be used in the world of work is a good starting point:

> A nice pedagogical approach for me is that any lecturer the first lecture or two of a course should be the context. I'm going to teach you reaction kinetics, I'm going to teach you – I'm a mechanical engineer I'm gonna teach you fluid flow. I'm an electrical engineering lecturer and I'm going to teach you semi-conductors – so the first thing you must help a student understand: why do I need to know about this if I want to be an electrical engineer? So it's critical for me that the lecturer should put the course into context. Now sometimes curriculum changes are such in nature that we think too much about the psychology and teaching and all that good stuff but it's just simple stuff and that's coming back to my toolbox. I'm going to give you a toolbox and I want to make sure when you leave UCT or Pretoria university or whatever you're coming from you've got a reasonably good toolbox and you roughly know which tools you've got in there and what they are there for.

Asked if he thought students are able to make connections between engineering outcomes and broader issues such as the ideal of social justice, Professor Block (SA) answers:

> I would say generally not; but there will be individual students who have a deeper interest and who do a lot of reading in addition to their studies who might make some sense of these things; but they are not equipped with any tools in particular to then translate that broader interest in innovation and technology and society and responses to global warming or whatever, [and how] to take that broader thinking into their engineering practice.

Likewise, Professor Hunter (SA) emphasizes the importance of understanding the necessity of engineering subjects to help students realize the relevance of certain courses that may otherwise be perceived as irrelevant to them. He argues that students should be able to ask themselves the following kinds of questions and generate answers to them too:

> So why do I need to know fluid flow? I'm gonna be a civil engineer, do I need to know about water? [Yes] because civil engineers design sewage pipes. So that's why I have that tool in my toolbox!' Whether you're gonna use that tool later on depends on a lot of things you may never use that tool again because you may go off into some sector in industry and mechanical engineers may go into aeronautical engineering and not use some of [that knowledge]. So I think lecturers need to be thinking about what competences they want their students to have when they finish the course and why. How does it fit in to the discipline?

Professor Schwartz (GER) explains that her interest in mechanical engineering was based on what she knew about the profession and what she thought of the possible application of that knowledge. She argues that engineering knowledge is more widely applicable than knowledge gained from economics or commerce-based subjects, and she asserts that more people with this kind of knowledge should be in leadership positions of companies as they have more potential to advance positive change in society because of their knowledge:

> So I ended up in mechanical engineering because I thought that is something where we can change things, [where] we can also change things in economics because we understand something in economics much more than economics people understand from technical science. And that's what my experience was, that we need more people also in leadership who understand the details and also the connections. Who see how all the processes are interlinked between humans and things; between different disciplines. Everything is interconnected and that was my personal reason why I was in the subject because I saw that's the subject where I can change things, really change, not talk about – but do, and I think that we can do.

Teaching non-technical skills

As discussed in Chapter 1, engineering education programmes around the world are increasingly undergoing reform to incorporate humanities and 'sustainability' courses in their curricula. These changes reflect examples of efforts in higher education (especially in universities) to balance technical skills with non-technical skills, in order to ensure that future engineers are 'whole' engineers. This section discusses how engineering lecturers perceive the teaching of non-technical skills. First, their views on how this can be achieved through curriculum reform is outlined and thereafter their views on the kinds of pedagogies that are helpful in enhancing students' non-technical skills are described. To conclude, the chapter considers the implications of these perspectives on teaching and learning in engineering through a capabilities lens.

Appropriate curricula

Like the recommendations provided in engineering education literature (Ahern, O'Connor, McRuairc, McNamara & O'Donnell, 2012; Anteliz, Thorpe & Danaher, 2015; Bailey, 2009; Fernandes, Flores & Lima, 2012; Fernandes, Mesquita, Flores & Lima, 2014; Male & Bennett, 2015; Von Blottnitz, Case & Fraser, 2015), most lecturers stressed the role of curriculum in imparting non-technical skills. For example, Professor Smith (SA) speaks of a reformed chemical programme at UCT that is characterized by project-based learning and sustainable development as a concurrent theme throughout the curriculum. The new curriculum, she explains, seeks to engage more explicitly with sustainable development challenges by incorporating 'sustainability' theory and principles into technical courses. Doing so, she argues, results in opportunities for students to think more broadly about the results of engineering activities, which creates opportunities for students to think more critically about what they do as engineers:

> For critical thinking specifically there I would speak particularly to the new curriculum (...) which has project work throughout and I think particularly having sustainable development now as a strand of what is taught in first year chemical engineering, alongside with – how do you work with chemical equations and calculations – that opens things up quite dramatically.

The notion of embedding or integrating non-technical skills in engineering curricula is popular amongst all lecturers, as it is in the literature. A good example is the proposal to integrate the humanities into engineering education. Bissel and Bennett (1997) convincingly argue for incorporating history into the engineering curriculum. They call for deeper engagement with history about the nature of technology and its complex interrelation with society, politics and economics, arguing that the historical chronologies of inventions and inventors sometimes found in engineering textbooks tend to present an over-simplified 'master narrative' of historical development. Bissel and Bennet (1997) posit that such a perspective on the history of technology is counter-productive for future engineers, who will need to deal with complex contexts in their professional lives. They also state that it is problematic to teach the kind of history of technology in which the progress of technology from early times to its present magnificence is presented from the standpoint of the present, omitting any examination of false starts or alternative traditions. Therefore, a holistic study of the history of technology can offer insight into the nature of technological change, examples of the complex relationship between technology and society, and different and valuable perspectives of the subject matter for both learner and teacher (Bissel & Bennett, 1997).

Bissel and Bennett (1997) posit that in contrast to mathematics and science, where the history of the disciplines has long found a place in university curricula, the history of technology does not feature in many European engineering degrees. In their paper, the authors consider the pedagogical potential of courses offered at a British university of technology on the history of technology, demonstrating how historical material can enhance the teaching of various topics within the engineering curriculum. For example, the study of 'devices that failed' are included in the course 'Science, Technology & Everyday Life', which gives students the opportunity to learn about the history of technology, which encourages students to think more critically and adopt unfamiliar perspectives in the learning process (Bissel & Bennett, 1997).

However, some lecturers are hesitant to promote ideas about deep curriculum reform. For example, Professor Block (SA) explains the difficulty of the balancing act that goes on in deciding what should change in the curriculum and what should stay as it is. He concludes that adding new courses to already congested curricula is problematic, but acknowledges that desirable skills for engineering practice change over time, and that this necessitates re-evaluating the content of engineering curricula:

> But yeah how do you reform a curriculum? How deep do you go? (...) You know? People don't want to throw out what was there because that was good; they just want to add and add and that just can't be you know? So, we only have four years with the students – so how do you reform that curriculum? What matters to a generation that has calculators on phones? – and powerful ones too! So, you know? Do you need to be able to prove theorems if you want to engineer? Or do you need to know how to store your data on a cloud? (...) what are the skills that are needed these days?

Similarly, Professor Kleid (GER) is concerned about what might be lost due to making too many changes to a fundamentally good engineering curriculum. He indicates that 'curriculum reform' often manifests in elective courses being added to the curriculum, which results in overcrowded study programmes:

> In the past I also did a lot of study advising, and then I also spent some time on the examination board, and I find it shocking how tightly structured many programmes are. (...) And in the past, especially in the engineering sciences, we didn't have things like that [elective humanities courses]. I'm not saying that everything in the engineering sciences was good, no that's not what I'm saying at all, there is always something to adjust, especially along with changes in society, but one could have done some things differently without endangering that which actually functioned well.

Professor Smith (SA) also acknowledges the complexities and challenges of curriculum reform measures. Although she is a proponent of adjusting engineering curricula so that they might enhance students' non-technical skills, she emphasizes that engineering curricula ought to remain dominated by technical subject matter. That is, priority should not be given to having courses that develop students' transversal skills, at the expense of teaching courses that are indispensable to the technical aspects of engineering practice:

> Look it's a challenge because you have a programme where also you have to remember there's a lot of detailed technical work students have to do. You cannot get away from that. They're not going to be the professionals who can tackle these problems if they don't have that technical base as well, so the integration and balance of those elements. I think that's the challenge going forward.

According to Nieusma and Blue (2012) a facet of engineering knowledge that matches militarism and cultures of warfare is the pervasive distinction made between the 'technical core' of engineering expertise and competency in all things 'social' together with that which is political. A capabilities lens on engineering education offers analytic grounds for rejecting the division between so-called impartial technical knowledge and characteristically biased 'social' knowledge, because it highlights that even the most undisputed factual knowledge has social underpinnings, both by virtue of it being *human* knowledge and by virtue of the fact it is the outcome of human social activity (Nieusma & Blue, 2012). I agree with Nieusma and Blue that reliance on the distinction between technical and social knowledge in engineering is almost exclusively strategic – used to promote the status of particular attitudes and worldviews, but having limited epistemological usefulness in engineers' (technical) problem-solving activities, which are always necessarily situated in social (organizational, political and economic) contexts (Nieusma & Blue, 2012).

The question of the role and importance of ethics for engineers and engineering activities is also addressed in the work of Keulartz, Schermer, Korthals and Swierstra (2004). Keulartz et al. (2004) argue that the vocabulary rooted in neither traditional philosophy nor applied ethics can adequately cope with the dynamic character of modern technological culture because there is insufficient insight into the moral significance of technological artefacts and systems. According to Keulartz et al. (2004), technology studies (STS) can contribute to the ethical evaluation of technological development and that pragmatism can be a very useful tool in developing an ethical approach better equipped to deal with technology than applied ethics. In their paper, Keulartz et al. (2004) sought to develop a new perspective of engineering ontologies by bringing together insights from applied ethics, STS and pragmatist philosophy. The value of the argument brought forward in this work lies in the elucidation of the responsibility and accountability associated with technological advancements and innovations to which engineers contribute.

While most lecturers' responses brought attention to issues of curriculum reform, others spoke more about pedagogies that they thought might be helpful to enhance students' non-technical skills. Examples are discussed in the next subsection.

Helpful pedagogies

Like the literature on engineering education that encourages pedagogical reform (for example see Acharry, 2013; Connor, Karmokar, Whittington & Walker, 2014; Dym, Agogino, Eris, Frey & Leifer, 2005; Kotta, 2011; Markauskaite & Goodyear, 2017; Petersen, 2013), lecturers' responses that centre on engineering pedagogies cite project-based learning, teamwork and facilitating open discussions or debates as a good methods of teaching critical thinking. As Professor Schwarz (GER) explains:

> That's one thing I do in my classes. So we have discussions. Even if there are one hundred and fifty students in the class – we have discussions. Open discussions. For me it's important, so I try to do that. One point. Second, I'm teaching design. And we do practical exercises in groups along the whole semester, and the groups have to present four times in the semester. Everyone in the course has to be at least once at the front to present. And they are not presenting to me. They are presenting to the other [students]. So I normally only ask one question maybe just to be a little bit polite. What I force the guys [to do] is to present to the group, and the group is asked to understand and then they start this dialogue. And over the semester you can see how they learn to think about people – other people's solutions, to ask the right questions, to answer these questions, to reflect on what they are doing-sometimes I jump in just to give a little bit of process help – so I like to ask the question: do you know what's happening here now?

Similar approaches are identified by Lucena (2013) who provides an example of a first-year engineering course at the University of Western Australia entitled 'Global Challenges in Engineering'. The course is designed to encourage students to question basic taxonomies of knowledge and there are no lectures; students attend workshops where they are expected to debate about different meanings attached to concepts such as 'globalization', 'difference', 'poverty', 'development', 'ethics' and 'justice' (Lucena, 2013). As such, students are presented with contemporary problems that set out some indisputable effects of neoliberal capitalism (Lucena, 2013). Students respond to this pedagogy differently; while some comment that it takes them beyond their comfort zone, others wonder why they are being asked to talk about 'non-engineering' issues at all (Lucena, 2013). In one workshop, for example, students were asked to consider the effects of corporate takeovers on factory workers by reading first-hand accounts of being fired under the guise of 'downsizing'; students were then asked to consider what other kinds of economic organization might be possible, and what they might do if they were asked to 'cut costs' and 'ensure growth' by firing the people they had read about in the case study (Lucena, 2013). Lucena reports that the perceptions of many students changed as a result, with some students stating that they have learned to recognize the complete impact that the food products we consume can have on the world, considering where they come from, how they are produced and how people are affected differently by the production of particular products. Be that as it may, many students feel that there is no alternative to capitalism and, that it is only natural to maximize profits at all costs. Questioning dominant economic paradigms is difficult for all university students, regardless of their degree subject, and it is especially challenging for engineering students who are more likely to be locked into prevailing discourses about the maximization of profits and the link between technological innovation and profitability (Lucena, 2013).

Replies that dealt with other examples of what can and should be happening pedagogically to impart transversal skills were few but powerful, in demonstrating how engineering educators sometimes have to come up with ways to do this, based on intuition rather than on practical and clear guidance from their respective departments or universities. That is, engineering lecturers sometimes experiment with teaching methods that are uncommon in traditional 'chalk and talk' engineering pedagogies. These experiments are based on the assumption that they are effective, fuelled by individual lecturers' observations or gut feeling and random student feedback rather than on formal tried and tested techniques. This is reflected well in the quote below, which captures what Professor Kleid (GER) said when asked if he thought that the innovative teaching methods he employs were resulting in the desired outcomes for his students. He answered:

> I go on that assumption, but we haven't done any research on this, but I can only work with the feedback that I get from graduates. Feedback that I have heard often is that when they are in companies and compare themselves with others, they often say we did this or we did that already, they have great project management competences and not just theoretically, so they don't only calculate the risk in the plans of a particular structure, but they have hopefully also fought with their class mates, about upholding appointments and so forth. That is something which is very important, and that one actually does it sometimes, that is also something that engineering in Germany is strongly influenced by – there is always the theory, but there must always be that element where one has understood the theory and then applies it, otherwise theory is just memorizing information. And that is an element which is common in all engineering education in Germany.

Professor Kleid (GER)'s response brings light to the fact that there is inadequate data or literature dealing with appropriate and reliable evaluative measures of the effectiveness of novel engineering pedagogies for developing transversal skills.

The examples discussed in the following paragraphs do not represent specific recommendations for reforming engineering pedagogies, but they reflect literature providing diverse and recent approaches applied by various higher education institutions in the global North and global South to amend teaching and learning in university engineering programmes. This is done in the hope to develop values, attitudes and ways of thinking that are conducive to foster public-good engineers or engineers who can function in their professional capacities as agents of sustainable human development. For example, Connor et al. (2014) challenge some common pedagogies found in Science, Technology, Engineering and Mathematics (STEM) education with a particular focus on engineering. In their paper, they argue that there is potential confusion in engineering education around the role of active learning approaches, and that the adoption of these methods may be limited because of this confusion. This is combined with a degree of 'disciplinary egocentrism', which can be defined as the lack of student or staff readiness to engage in multidisciplinary knowledge or apply alternative teaching and learning approaches to the engineering discipline. Connor et al. (2014) give examples of engineering and 'engineering-like' projects implemented at a university of technology in New Zealand that demonstrate the effectiveness of adopting pedagogies and delivery methods more usually attributed to the liberal arts, such as studio-based learning. Their paper concludes with some suggestions about how best to create a fertile environment from which enquiry-based forms of learning can emerge.

A study by Boni and Berjano (2009) reflects on the concept of ethical learning as an educational proposal. Boni and Berjano (2009) see ethical learning as a tool to aid individuals to build their own moral dimension according to which they can function effectively and responsibly in both individual and collective settings, and both as professionals in particular occupations, and as members of society. They propose the following eight dimensions for an ethical learning educational model:

1   self-knowledge: the capacity for progressive knowledge of oneself and the auto-consciousness of the self;
2   autonomy and self-regulation: the capacity to develop independence of determination and greater consistency in personal actions;
3   capacity for dialogue: the ability to escape from individualism and to talk about all value conflicts, both personal and social;
4   capacity to transform the environment: the formulation of contextualized rules and projects in which value criteria related to involvement and commitment are manifested;
5   critical understanding: the development of a group of abilities directed towards the acquisition of morally relevant information about reality, critical analysis of this reality and the attitude of commitment and understanding to improve it;
6   development of capacity for empathy and social perspective: to have greater consideration for others and interiorize values such as cooperation and solidarity;
7   social skills: interpersonal behaviour learned by the person and social performance in different spheres of relationships with others; and
8   moral reasoning: the practice of reflecting on value conflicts (Boni & Berjano, 2009).

Setting out from this model, the authors formulate a proposal for ethical learning in the university as follows: 'to educate professionals and citizens who build their knowledge individually and act in a responsible, free, and committed way' (Boni & Berjano, 2009: 206). They then argue that in order to achieve this aim, a set of conditions should be created that allows university students to acquire a set of values as ideals, reject the presence of an accumulation of opposing values and, above all, build their own set of values. This set of values ought to enable students to create personal criteria guided by the principles of justice and equality, and to act coherently as professionals and citizens (Martínez et al. as cited in Boni & Berjano, 2009: 206). In this study, the proposal for ethical learning is reflected on particularly in the context of the European Higher Education Area and is illustrated in the description of experiences gained at the Technical University of Valencia in Spain, by academic staff and students in the engineering faculty. The study examines feedback from the participants concerning the implementation of ethical learning through three courses: 'Industrial Sensors' (a technical course), and 'Introduction to Development Aid' and 'Development Aid Projects' (non-technical courses).

Results suggest that the humanities-based courses are more effective in achieving ethical learning, as students who took these classes showed increased sensitivity towards the less privileged, compared with students who did not (Boni & Berjano, 2009). This is interpreted as indicating greater interest in the subject of development, which arguably all engineers should critically reflect on in the work they do. The conclusions drawn in the study suggest that there is a value for, and need to integrate, broader soft skills alongside technical skills as outcomes of engineering education, and it seems that there is much potential in achieving this by integrating humanities subjects to help sharpen engineering students' awareness of an array of development issues (Boni & Berjano, 2009). This can be seen as an achievement of the sixth ethical dimension in the model proposed by Boni and Berjano, namely the development of capacity for empathy and social perspective, which enables students to have greater consideration for others and internalize values such as cooperation and solidarity.

A general concern raised by Boni and Berjano (2009) concerning both approaches to teaching ethical learning was the difficulty to evaluate academically the impact of the courses on students, and hence grade outcomes. A study that addresses questions of evaluating non-technical skills in engineering education is one by Fernandes et al. (2012). The study evaluated the impact of project-led education (PLE) on student learning processes and outcomes, particularly looking at students in their first semester of the first year of a five-year master's degree in engineering at the University of Minho, Portugal. As a consequence of the Bologna process,[3] new methods of teaching and assessment have been developed that focus not only on the development of technical competences but also on transversal competences (Fernandes et al., 2012), which are exemplified by aptitudes for lifelong learning, critical thinking and problem solving. The authors argue that teaching, learning, and assessment should be conceived in a way that provides students with numerous opportunities to support the development of such competences.

Findings from the study show that for some students, assessment in PLE focuses on deep-level learning and critical thinking because projects provide the opportunity to understand and link course content to real-life situations (Fernandes et al., 2012). However, many students still seem to prefer traditional teaching and assessment methods in which they play a more passive role in the learning process (Fernandes et al., 2012). The findings also suggest that formative feedback plays an important role in PLE as it helps students to recognize the utility and importance of feedback received during tutorials, group presentations and mid-term reports, allowing them to improve their performance and set out new strategies for achieving the learning outcomes more effectively (Fernandes et al., 2012).

The downfall of PLE, according to students, is the large workload and time needed to carry out the projects, which leaves the students feeling exhausted and not particularly rewarded for their hard work (Fernandes et al., 2012). In contrast to summative assessment, where students felt that they put in hard work that is then reflected in good grades, such a correlation is not necessarily observable in PLE (Fernandes et al., 2012), but PLE might bear more weight from a human development perspective, which is about more than measurable performance (e.g. good grades).

The authors thus conclude that PLE assessment practices enhance deep understanding by linking theory to practice in order to solve real-life problems, with feedback playing an important role as students are provided with opportunities to improve their work by discussing the results with their lecturers and tutors. A constraint of PLE identified in the Fernandes et al. study is the heavy workload and perceived low reward for tedious work (although results in a related study later showed above-average results for PLE students versus students taught and assessed using more traditional methods). Fernandes et al. (2012) therefore conclude that more research needs to be done to understand and combine student and teaching staff perspectives of learning and assessment and the interaction between them in practice.

A transversal skill mentioned frequently in the literature discussed above is critical thinking (see Ahern et al., 2012; Boni & Berjano, 2009; Fernandes et al., 2012). For example, critical thinking in the university curriculum is explored by Ahern et al. (2012), who focus particularly on how it is defined, understood, taught and evaluated. Critical thinking is a graduate attribute that is seen by academics as a particularly desirable outcome of student learning, and is seen by many as the defining characteristic of a university education generally, including engineering graduates (Ahern et al., 2012). The evidence used to build the authors' argument is founded on a qualitative study that was conducted with academics at an Irish university in a variety of disciplines including engineering, where the aim was to examine how academics understood critical thinking. Questions concerning the differences in the importance of critical thinking across disciplines were addressed, as well as suggestions for identifying appropriate pedagogical techniques for introducing critical thinking skills to students. The data gathered also included document analysis of module descriptions and course work.

The results show that although definitions and understandings of critical thinking are broadly similar across various disciplines, there are significant differences in the formulation and articulation of the term (Ahern et al., 2012). Ahern et al. (2012) posit that academics from non-technical disciplines such as the humanities had very well formulated conceptions of critical thinking, whereas academics in engineering disciplines had clear ideas about the importance of critical thinking in engineering education, but had difficulty verbalizing what it meant. The authors thus question how academics can explain critical thinking to students and encourage them to practise it, if they themselves are vague about what it means and how to recognize it.

Ahern et al. (2012) argue that their evidence shows that: (1) in engineering and related programmes, critical thinking is not explicitly taught, although academics have the desire to do teach it; (2) in the humanities, a more concerted effort is made to ensure that critical thinking is addressed early on and explicitly in the curriculum and across modules (Ahern et al., 2012). They conclude that if universities claim to produce critical thinkers, defined as those 'who can take the empirical and rise above this with abstraction and theory but can also use the concrete and context to ground their theory' (Ahern et al., 2012: 128), then universities need to be more explicit about what it is and how it can be realized and assessed. So, although feedback from students can be useful in helping to identify whether critical thinking is taking place or not, more systematic and reliable ways of discerning how helpful specific pedagogies are in the long run, are necessary. This might enable higher education institutions to model pedagogic shifts drawing from real examples of what works well and what does not. This is a gap in ESD literature.

Returning to lecturers' views, examples of pedagogies perceived as doing well to impart transversal skills are given by Professor Schwartz (GER), who is a proponent of project work in teams. She believes that the lessons the students take from this kind of learning range from critical thinking to effective communication and the capacity to collaborate with diverse people:

> We train them in projects where they can only succeed if they have one solution together. Where they need to arrange with other people, to learn to criticize other people, learn to take criticism, learn to think about solutions from other people. (…) Not just, 'what do I like?'/'what do I not like?' but also 'how can you improve?'. And that's something we teach them on the way in the technical aspects, it's not extra soft skills. And then also we have soft skills like presentations or moderating; we teach them, I do – teach them, how to use flip charts, meta plan, how to go through creative technology to get new ideas. We teach them about the process design, not technological but business process design, so we give them along a lot of other knowledge, but one of the basic things is that we bring them forward along the way to be a team player.

Another example is provided by Professor Bremer (GER), who tells how he encouraged students to talk about what they do. He is concerned that there are limited opportunities for students to practice articulating their thoughts, ideas, or opinions:

> (...) we suffer from the problem that, and I am speaking of Germany now, limited opportunities to articulate themselves verbally. I introduced in the example in the course technology assessment-and within the Diplom programme, I always requested that they talk about their work once, twice, three times in a seminar during their course of study. That is way under emphasized – and here we're now in the field of social sciences and humanities, so philosophers, sociologists where there is great emphasis on verbal articulation – the engineers lie far behind.

Similarly, Professor Schwarz (GER) often facilitates debates in her classroom. Through this, she tries to teach her students lessons about decision making and critical thinking processes:

> So what I can give the students is: always to be aware that they have to make decisions based on what they know and to try and be thorough about what they do, to be careful, to rethink – but then to decide. And to know that they may be wrong. And the only thing I can teach them is that they are – in the moment they decide – sure that it's the best that they can decide at that moment. We cannot do more.

Correspondingly, Professor Smith (SA) explains that encouraging students to talk more openly in class and having open-ended discussions can go a long way in helping students to practise critical reflexive thought. The example she provides below speaks both to appropriate engineering pedagogy to teach transversal skills, and appropriate course content that aims to do the same. She highlights the importance of combining case studies used in engineering courses having appropriate, relatable, context-specific content that looks at contemporary issues such as sustainability challenges, with facilitating discussions to help students realize that there are dilemmas in seeking engineering solutions, which make it difficult to judge whether one solution is better than the other:

> I guess pedagogically – where I have worked in that space and my colleagues as well has been in quite open ended classroom discussions of the sort you wouldn't necessarily expect in engineering and in project tasks which ask I mean like the one project which I was – I had two modules last year: one's a case study of a sewage plant, a waste water treatment plant and the case study has a formal settlement an informal settlement and the waste is run in particular ways [what students have to do is] look at the whole thing and ultimately come up with 'what do you think we should do?' And there's no one way to answer. You know? Should we be focusing on sanitation for informal settlement? Should we be doing this? Should we be doing that? – What's the bigger picture? I think that's quite a broad engineering

task and that's done by first years and they do a range of, I mean they do topics on bio-fuels as well so you know there's the question do you use like arable crop land for growing fuel? So, you know, they had to get into all those discussions. So I think the project work drives quite a lot of that. And then I mentioned the safety talks as well so there's quite a lot of that, let me say, sort of thinking critically about the context of engineering.

Professor Block (SA) explains the challenge in teaching such broader lessons and other values that may be conducive to public-good engineering, stating that engineering educators should be role models for the values they try to teach. Giving an example of how one might do this he states:

> Values are very hard to teach you know you've got to – you've got to model values. You've got to model values I think, I mean you can go into the – and we do in our fourth year course – go into theory behind what are ethics, and why are engineering ethics important and you know the difference between morals and ethics and what kind of constructs can we use to help you think through an ethically difficult situation; but values are some stuff you grew up with. We don't all have the same mother so we have different values and so at the same time you know people come to university in a mouldable way so when I don't rock up in the classroom that often with my cycling helmet but you know my students know I cycle to campus, I don't just teach the stuff.

With this example Professor Block (SA) refers to teaching and demonstrating sustainability practices, showing students that contributing to lowering the human carbon footprint on the environment does not necessarily happen only by using engineering knowledge to create environmentally friendly products, but can also happen when individuals choose their modes of transport more critically. Such decisions are not necessarily based on technical expertise. One can make the decision to use the least polluting mode of transport available to them, based on general (non-technical) knowledge and a disposition towards being environmentally friendly.

It is clear that the lecturers interviewed have good intentions and are genuinely interested in finding ways to help their students think in ways that are useful for their personal development. It is also clear that they are doing what they believe is appropriate or teaching in ways they perceive as conducive to critical thought and other transversal skills. However, because there is little empirical evidence on the effectiveness of the pedagogical shifts mentioned here, it is not possible to judge if these changes do/will have the desired effect. As such it appears that engineering lecturers who use out-of-the-box teaching methods do so largely based on intuition. However, this is not without value. Lecturers' willingness to attempt different teaching approaches in order to make their students aware of the complexities of engineering is an indicator of the aspirations they have for their students. It is likely that their efforts are fuelled by the hope that their students might become more than technical experts. Therefore, the value of the intuitive pedagogical shifts applied by some lecturers lies in the fact that they care about and strive towards broadening their students' professional capabilities and functionings.

What all lecturers are convinced about is the value of project work, arguing that it allows students to experience the different roles that they may have to fulfil in the world of work, and teaches students how to cooperate to achieve joint success, or how they can fail together and develop the resilience to overcome future failure. Professor Schwartz (GER) explains this well. She says:

> Something that they learn here during their studies and then something that is very important as a soft skill from my point of view; they learn to fail. They learn to fail, to stand up, get a little angry and then to speed up – and go again and succeed. And I think for the rest of their lives that is very helpful.

Summative discussion

Based on the findings from the lecturer interviews, it is clear that there are specific doings and beings that they value and seek to achieve in their capacities as engineering educators. Considering the empirical findings discussed in the previous sections of this chapter through a capabilities lens, a list of these functionings can be extrapolated. The findings also show that the lecturers have unique ideas about the purposes of engineering education, the development of appropriate engineering identities and methods to impart transversal skills such as critical thinking, open-mindedness and empathetic understanding. These findings are summarized in Table 4.1.

According to de la Harpe and Thomas (2009), in order for graduates to develop the skills in critical enquiry and systemic thinking needed to explore the complexity and implications of 'development', a deep cultural shift that promotes thinking differently about the ends of engineering education is needed. This cultural shift also requires critical reflection about what engineering students know, and how that influences how they do their work, i.e. for what purpose, by what means and for what reasons they apply engineering knowledge in their professional functionings. This speaks to Muller's (2015) argument that students, particularly in STEM fields, need to know how to make appropriate inferences and inferential relations between propositional and procedural knowledge, before going into the field of work.

Drawing on the work of Winch (2013), Muller (2015) argues that every area to be mastered educationally in the curriculum can be described in terms of: 'know that', or propositional knowledge, and 'know-how', or procedural knowledge (see Winch, 2013, 2014). More specifically, Muller (2015) refers to three different kinds of procedural knowledge. The first kind is inferential 'know-how', i.e. knowing how conceptual knowledge (the 'know that') learned in the regular courses, for example chemistry and chemical engineering, hangs

Table 4.1 Key findings from lecturers' perspectives

The purposes of engineering education are to:	Develop students' capacities to make decisions autonomously and create innovative approaches and methods to solution seeking that are founded on engineering knowledge
	Enhance students' sense of determination to be and do what they have reason to value in life as well as determine their roles in society
	Stimulate students' desire for knowledge and help them recognize opportunities where they can successfully apply what they learn, in their work and in their lives
	Provide students with opportunities for research-based learning
	Provide students with the necessary knowledge and skills that they need to become engineers and be employable
	Develop students' potential to take responsibility for running engineering organizations and be accountable for the engineering outcomes produced by them
Developing an engineering identity entails:	Recognizing that technology is ultimately the articulation of a societal purpose and that it is *not* value-free
	Developing a deep, meaningful and broad understanding of what engineers do
	Seeing engineering as a means of serving the public good to achieve positive change in society
Teaching non-technical skills requires:	Curricula that are aligned with public-good professionalism
	Unconventional engineering pedagogies
Engineering educators' valued functionings are:	Helping students to fully recognize the instrumental and intrinsic value of engineering education
	Facilitating students' development of appropriate engineering identities
	Teaching curricula that are aligned with public-good engineering
	Applying creative pedagogies that enhance students' transversal skills
	Contributing to the holistic development of students as professional engineers, and as members of society

Source: Author's own.

together, and how to negotiate the epistemic joints that link the various knowledge 'bits' to each other (Muller, 2015). Already between the subjects of chemistry and chemical engineering, the internal conceptual logic differs because of their different epistemic objectives (Muller, 2015).

The second kind is procedural know-how. It points to a 'more risky and uncertain kind of knowledge' (Muller, 2015: 414), where, for example, a novice engineer learns how to find out new things and discover various constraints, figures out what works under certain circumstances and forms new judgements that lead to effective solutions (Muller, 2015).

The third kind is personal know-how, i.e. the idiosyncratic knowledge accumulated through diverse experiences in the process of 'doing' (Muller, 2015). The humanities-based and technical parts of engineering curricula are epistemically different, i.e. they require different kinds of stipulation, they entail different recognition and realization rules, they have dissimilar evaluation criteria and pedagogic relations (see Kotta, 2011). Referring to different kinds of procedural knowledge as 'skills' does not help us describe what they are, or understand what goes wrong when students do not 'get' them, or cannot 'do' them (Muller, 2015).

Muller (2015) also emphasizes that procedural knowledge is sequential. This means that students should first have reasonable mastery of the 'know that' (the conceptual content such as thermodynamics, computer-aided design, etc.) to begin to grasp ways in which the 'know-how' (the practical application, e.g. designing sewage pipelines) works. As a result of taking a sustainable development course, engineering graduates may *know that* the results of engineering activities have led to the creation of products such as motor vehicles that contribute to environmental pollution, and they may become aware of various measures currently being taken to fuel motor vehicles with renewable energy sources to lower their carbon footprint. However, this does not mean that graduates correspondingly *know how* to design or create environmentally friendly products. Neither may they *know why* development efforts have resulted in unsustainable ways of living that potentially perpetuate inequalities or social injustice.

Recognizing these complexities and being sensitive to the interconnectivity of different forms of engineering knowledge is a capacity that all engineering educators should possess if they are to assist in developing public-good engineers. As mentioned before, engineering educators teach engineering students various natural science subjects that equip students with the 'know-how' and 'know that', or the tools necessary to be able to practise engineering. However, the data indicates that there ought to be more attention paid to the 'know why' in engineering education. 'Know why' could refer to knowledge that is concerned with the values, reasons and motives behind professional engineering functionings and technology. For example, questions that one might ask to foster 'know why' knowledge are: In what ways does engineering support sustainable development? Is engineering for human development? Is technology for social justice? Is technology for poverty eradication? Is it for profit?

'Know why' could therefore also refer to the knowledge needed to form appropriate engineering identities, as it relates to the way one sees the purpose of engineering and technology in society, and therefore how one sees the overall purpose of their work. Through the lens of the capability approach, engineering ought to be *for* all the goals noted above. But how might sustainability, human development, poverty eradication or social justice be reached if engineers have no reason to value these outcomes? Just like the lecturers interviewed in this study, engineering educators do not teach students *how* 'to engineer'. Rather, they are involved in teaching them a variety of subjects, and imparting certain values that students need in order to perform various engineering functionings.

What is needed then, is for universities to provide opportunities for both lecturers and students to develop, demonstrate and deepen their commitment to social justice and prioritize its objectives in engineering education and engineering practice respectively.

Therefore, although technical excellence is an essential attribute of engineering graduates, communication, ethical reasoning, societal and global contextual analysis skills and understanding work strategies are also necessary capacities. Neglecting development in these areas, and teaching disciplinary technical subjects to the exclusion of a selection of humanities, economics, political science, language and/or interdisciplinary technical subjects is not in the best interest of producing engineers who are able to communicate with the public, to engage in a global engineering marketplace, or to be trained to be lifelong learners (National Academy of Engineering, 2005). Moreover, education that neglects the development of transversal skills is not conducive for developing 'public-good professionals' (Walker, 2012). More specifically, as discussed in the next chapter, communication and collaboration, as well as critical thinking and open-mindedness, can be considered as transversal skills that are crucial to public-good engineers.

Notes

1 In the film, Indiana Jones has to tackle a challenge called 'Only in the footsteps of God will he proceed'. This challenge comprised a series of lettered tiles on the floor. The object was to figure out the secret keyword, and then step on the letters that correspond with the correct spelling of the word. Incorrect tiles would break through, potentially causing the seeker to plunge into a deep chasm below the floor.
2 *Produktionstechnik* is the German word for production engineering.
3 The Bologna process or Bologna Agreement refers to a process of internationalization of universities in the European Higher Education Area.

References

Acharry, Y. (2013). Developing new frameworks of art–physics–design pedagogy for future engineers. In *5th World Conference on Educational Sciences – WCES 2013* (Vol. 116, pp. 2920–2925). Procedia – Social and Behavioral Sciences.

Ahern, A., O'Connor, T., McRuairc, G., McNamara, M. & O'Donnell, D. (2012). Critical thinking in the university curriculum: The impact on engineering education. *European Journal of Engineering Education*, 37(2), 125–132.

Anteliz, E. A., Thorpe, D. & Danaher, P. A. (2015). Engineering learning connections for sustainable development futures: Towards transformative professional education for Venezuelan and Australian in-service engineers. In *13th International Conference on Education and Development. Learning for Sustainable Futures – Making the Connections*. University of Oxford, UK. Accessed 1 September 2017 from http://ukfiet2015. exordo.com/files/papers/35/final_draft/Anteliz-Thorpe-Danaher.pdf.

Bailey, D. (2009). Whole system design: An integrated approach to sustainable engineering. *Journal of Education for Sustainable Development*, 3(2), 241–243.

Bissel, C., & Bennett, S. (1997). The role of the history of technology in the engineering curriculum. *European Journal of Engineering Education*, 22(3), 267–275.

Boni, A., & Berjano, E. J. (2009). Ethical learning in higher education: The experience of the Technical University of Valencia. *European Journal of Engineering Education, 34*(2), 205–213.

Boni, A., & Walker, M. (2013). Human development, capabilities, and universities of the twenty-first century. In A. Boni & M. Walker (eds), *Human development and capabilities: Reimagining the university of the twenty-first century*. London and New York: Routledge.

Connor, A. M., Karmokar, S., Whittington, C. & Walker, C. (2014). Full STEAM ahead: A manifesto for integrating arts pedagogics into STEM education. In *IEEE*. Wellington, New Zealand. Accessed 1 September 2017 from http://dx.doi.org/10.1109/TALE.2014.7062556.

De la Harpe, B., & Thomas, I. (2009). Curriculum change in universities: Conditions that facilitate Education for Sustainable Development. *Journal of Education for Sustainable Development, 3*(1), 75–85.

Dym, C. L., Agogino, A. M., Eris, O., Frey, D. D. & Leifer, L. J. (2005). Engineering design thinking, teaching, and learning. *Journal of Engineering Education, 94*(1), 103–120.

Fernandes, S., Flores, M. A. & Lima, R. M. (2012). Students' views of assessment in project-led engineering education: Findings from a case study in Portugal. *Assessment & Evaluation in Higher Education, 37*(2), 163–178.

Fernandes, S., Mesquita, D., Flores, M. A. & Lima, R. M. (2014). Engaging students in learning: Findings from a study of project-led education. *European Journal of Engineering Education, 39*(1), 55–67. Accessed 1 September 2017 from https://doi.org/10.1080/03043797.2013.833170.

Keulartz, J., Schermer, M., Korthals, M. & Swierstra, T. (2004). Ethics in technological culture: A programmatic proposal for a pragmatist approach. *Science, Technology & Human Values, 29*(1), 3–29.

Kotta, L. T. (2011). *Structural conditioning and mediation by student agency: A case study of success in chemical engineering design*. Unpublished thesis, University of Cape Town.

Lucena, J. (ed.). (2013). *Engineering education for social justice: Critical explorations and opportunities* (Vol. 10). Dordrecht, Heidelberg, New York, London: Springer.

Male, S. A., & Bennett, D. (2015). Threshold concepts in undergraduate engineering: Exploring engineering roles and value of learning. *Australasian Journal of Engineering Education, 20*(1), 59–69.

Markauskaite, L., & Goodyear, P. (2017). *Epistemic fluency and professional education: Innovation, knowledgeable action and actionable knowledge*. Dordrecht: Springer.

Muller, J. (2015). The future of knowledge and skills in science and technology higher education. *Higher Education, 70*(3), 409–416. Accessed 1 September 2017 from https://doi.org/10.1007/s10734-014-9842-x.

National Academy of Engineering. (2005). *The engineer of 2020: Visions of engineering in the new century*. Washington, DC: National Academies Press.

Nieusma, D., & Blue, E. (2012). Engineering and war. *International Journal of Engineering, Social Justice, and Peace, 1*(1), 50–62.

Nieusma, D., & Riley, D. (2010). Designs for development: Engineering, globalization and social justice. *Engineering Studies, 2*(1), 29–59. Accessed 1 September 2017 from https://doi.org/10.1080/19378621003604748.

Petersen, R. P. (2013). The potential role of design in a sustainable engineering profile. In *EESD13*. Cambridge, UK. Accessed 31 August 2017 from www-csd.eng.cam.ac.uk/proceedings-of-the-eesd13-conference-cambridge-2013-v-2/eesd13-published-papers/premer-petersen-r.pdf/at_download/file.

Von Blottnitz, H, Case, J. M. & Fraser, D. M. (2015). Sustainable development at the core of undergraduate engineering curriculum reform: A new introductory course in chemical engineering. *Journal of Cleaner Production, 106*, 300–307. Accessed 1 September 2017 from https://doi.org/10.1016/j.jclepro.2015.01.063.

Walker, M. (2012). Universities, professional capabilities and contributions to the public good in South Africa. *Compare: A Journal of Comparative and International Education, 42*(6), 819–838. Accessed 1 September 2017 from https://doi.org/10.1080/030579 25.2012.685584.

Winch, C. (2013). Curriculum design and epistemic ascent. *Journal of Philosophy of Education, 47*(1), 128–146.

Winch, C. (2014). Know-how and knowledge in the professional curriculum. In M. Young & J. Muller (eds), *Knowledge, expertise and the professions* (pp. 47–60). London: Routledge.

5   Public-good engineering

Employers' perspectives

This chapter begins with a discussion of the makings of the ideal engineer, followed by a discussion of valuable transversal skills, then of public-good engineering. This is followed by discussing what universities can do to provide engineering graduates with the capacities to practise this type of engineering. The summative discussion at the end of the chapter looks at the implications of understanding these findings through the lens of the capability approach. For background and orientation purposes, some information is provided about the selected employers before moving on to presenting the interview findings. As in Chapters 3 and 4, for orientation purposes the responses of the participants are marked 'GER' for Germany and 'SA' for South Africa.

All but two of the interviewees were male, between the ages of 40 and 60, and had engineering qualifications or natural sciences educational backgrounds and considerable experience (on average 18 years) working in engineering firms or with engineers and engineering teams. Both female interviewees are from the South African sample of employers, with one holding a social sciences qualification. Their individual profiles are as follows:

From Germany

1   *Mr Klemp* holds a master's degree in physics and is a technical director at MT Energie, a private company that focuses on the production of electricity from renewable sources.
2   *Mr Braun* has a background in mechanical engineering, economics and mass production. He currently works as a project manager in industrial projects related to process technologies for MT Energie. In 1997, he founded an engineering firm in Graz (his home town) that deals particularly with mechanical engineering project management, offering site supervision and consulting services.
3   *Mr Lehman* is a qualified process engineer. He works as a technical director at MT Biomethan (a subsidiary of MT Energie) with engineering teams involved in the construction of biogas power plants and is in charge of the technology, production and quality management divisions.

4   *Dr Klein* has a background in mechanical and production engineering with a specialization in process engineering. He also holds a PhD in process engineering and currently works as a project manager for EWE Netz.

5   *Dr Weiss* is qualified in the field of energy and process engineering. He holds a PhD in process engineering, and he has been employed as a quality, operations and logistics manager. In 2008, he founded his own company, ProcessQ, which offers consultation services to small and medium-sized companies focusing on organizational development and quality management.

From South Africa

1   *Ms White* is a chemical engineer by training who spent her early career years working in engineering production, and moved into control engineering before getting involved with the recruitment, training and development of young graduate engineers at Sasol.

2   *Mr Kumar* is a senior project engineer at Sasol Technology, with an electrical engineering background. He has been involved in plant maintenance and leading projects at power stations at Sasol Oil and Sasol Technology for over 20 years.

3   *Mr Schrader* is a managing director of STEAG Energy Services South Africa, with a background in process engineering. Of German descent, he earned his qualification through a combination of vocational training and engineering studies at a technical university in Germany. He has 20 years' work experience (mostly in South Africa).

4   *Mr Chambers*, who holds a BSc in civil engineering and a Master of Business Leadership, is an engineering director within the engineering and construction cluster of Group Five, one of the largest construction companies in South Africa. The sectors in which the company operates include road, power, oil and gas as well as housing and transportation.

5   *Dr Shaw* (the only non-engineer amongst the interviewees) holds an MBA in organizational learning and a doctorate in organizational behaviour. She is mostly involved with management and leadership development and heads the graduate recruitment, selection and development unit of Group Five's engineering bursary division.

The qualities of an ideal engineer

The selected employers were asked a series of questions across three broad categories: their views on engineering graduate attributes, their perceptions of 'soft' or transversal skills, and their comments on engineering education in universities.

In describing the ideal engineer, beyond naming task-specific technical skills, the employers spoke of personality characteristics, attitudes, values and attributes that they found desirable for professional engineers to possess. It is notable that amongst all employers interviewed, 'the engineer' is usually referred to as male, and described as 'he'. Although gender-neutral pronouns are often used, for example 'the ideal engineer is "someone" who ...', employers never refer to the engineer as 'she'. Although this may be coincidental, it is also possible that these responses signal the awareness and acknowledgement of ongoing male dominance in engineering; Mr Chambers (SA) even refers to the industry as the 'engineering fraternity' in one of his responses. In the passages that follow, 'he' and 'his' are emphasized to highlight the frequency of referring to engineers as male. This indicates that the male engineer is still seen as the norm, and it suggests that being a woman engineer marks one out as unusual (Faulkner, 2009).

Mr Lehman (GER) describes an ideal engineer, emphasizing the necessary foundation of a comprehensive education upon which accurate decisions can be based and assessed:

> I believe the perfect engineer should first of all, have a very good education because the job consists of highly specialized tasks. And so, regardless of what one does, they should have the capacity to – based on a sound education – *he* should be able to evaluate the precision of *his* actions in terms of how close or far one gets to the desired outcome. And I think a good educational foundation sets the premise for an individual's ability to develop a sense of Ordnung.[1] And I think this is very important, in order to avoid very bad results.

Mr Klein (GER) talks about the importance of the ability to apply theoretical, analytical and technical knowledge in practice, stating that this is however a basic expectation, pointing out that this alone cannot characterize the ideal engineer:

> The ideal engineer is an engineer who can marry praxis with technique. An engineer who is a technical expert, that's great, obviously, but an engineer who knows how to apply theory to praxis – and then not just the hard skills – that means how should *he* carry *himself* in certain projects? How should *he* carry *himself* amongst different stakeholders in the project? I believe that those are the soft skills that are very important, not just that what *he* is capable of, technically, but how *he* can communicate that.

Reference to the importance of effective communication occurs frequently in the interviewees' responses, often brought up during the interviews outside the context of questions related to communication specifically, as is the case above. Mr Weiss (GER) is the only interviewee to bring up intrinsic motivation to pursue the engineering profession as a distinguishing factor of a prime engineer, referring to passion and interest in technical subject matter as 'stand-out' traits. He also talks about the difficulty of describing the ideal engineer because of the complexity and diversity of the disciplines and areas of application there are in the profession:

I think that's impossible [to describe the perfect engineer], because there isn't an ideal person (...) and I think the tasks that engineers have to do are as multifaceted as people are. So what distinguishes an engineer is, definitely fun with technology, so simply having fun with the material, the sense behind that, and the ideal engineer just like the ideal person is someone who is opportunity oriented, right? [And] not too blinded by technique and easily lost in the details.

Mr Weiss (GER) warns not to get 'blinded by technique' and 'lost in the details' – accentuating the notion that there is a certain point at which technical expertise alone has little or no added value to engineering practice if not accompanied by broader skills and knowledge.

Another desirable attribute described by Mr Klemp (GER) is persistent willingness to learn. He talks about one's learning time at the university ending, and the role industry takes over in developing the graduates:

Besides that, it's quite important that people have the ability to show the ability to learn and show the ability that they want to learn. Because being educated is just one thing and finally during the professional lifetime there is a process going on making the engineers more valuable because they learn along their working lifetime.

Mr Klemp's (GER) words allude to lifelong learning as a desirable ability for engineers and as an important outcome of university learning. The above excerpt also suggests that teaching and learning are the responsibility of the university (engineering education), the individual (engineering students) and industry (engineering employers). This reminds us of the important role that industry plays in continuing engineers' education through on-the-job training. The importance of learning that takes place once an engineering graduate enters the job market is also evident in the fact that practical experience gained through internships or vacation work is a mandatory part of engineering programmes such as those provided by the selected case sites (UCT, 2015a, 2015b; UB, 2013).

Views from South African employers mirror those of the German employers (described thus far) in most ways, with minor deviations. For example, after emphasizing the importance of a strong technical foundation and stating that she always assumes engineering graduates already possess technical skills, Ms White (SA) describes the ideal engineer as one who has a number of 'extras' in addition to technical excellence:

Beyond that, the perfect engineers or the ideal engineers are those that come with extra add-ons those are things to me like lateral thinking to be able to think out of the box, to be able to think in a slightly different direction. Those that have a bit of bigger picture, strategic thinking, and can think beyond what is currently the problem, etc. etc. and the other one that we do need a lot of is the soft skills: working with people, communication, etc.

She also comments on the type of thinking that is essential in the engineering profession, emphasizing the need for engineers to think broadly enough to recognize the interconnectivity between problems and their solutions. She underscores this fact:

> In the workplace, no problem is stand-alone. You need to understand its link to everything.

Mr Chambers (SA) points towards this in his description of the ideal engineer:

> The ideal engineer needs to be one that is interested in developing solutions for society and doing that through the theory that is learnt at the university, but also through being very open and interested in learning to apply that theory in practice.

The translation or application of theoretical knowledge into practice was mentioned often, across the interviews. Sometimes, this concern was expressed in a way that suggests that engineering graduates are often unable to develop or express their curiosity about 'how things work' in the workplace. Mr Kumar's (SA) opinion shows this:

> I think the ideal engineer is the *guy* who gets knowledge from the university but when *he* is in the environment of the work situation, *he* must be able to put that knowledge into practice. *He* must be able to ask the right questions, *he* must be able to want to know what's happening, how projects should be running, or how things should be working.

Mr Schrader's (SA) views are quite similar, but a noticeable difference lies in his reference to the rate at which technical knowledge becomes obsolete, calling for speedy learning and adaptation from engineers to try to keep up with rapid change:

> I think the most important thing for me is that *he* is always willing to learn because the science is constantly changing there is always new things coming on the (table) so you need to adapt to that. (...) [t]hen another important fact is not just heavy on theory – *he* must be able to implement that as well and must have knowledge about project management and contracts because that's the environment *he* is working in.

The environment in which engineers work is described as one that demands a myriad of soft skills that are applied in a range of contexts. Dr Shaw (SA) expresses the concern that engineering graduates often have skewed expectations of the engineering profession or the work environment in which they might find themselves upon completion of their studies. She suggests that engineering graduates often think all of their work will be carried out from an office desk.

Although this may be a likely work situation for some, Dr Shaw (SA) thinks that it is important for engineers to be willing and able to imagine their jobs outside of the office. The phrases 'out there', 'on site' and 'hands on', suggest that she values engineers who are pragmatic and eager to apply their knowledge outside the office. She also emphasizes the importance of logic. In a way, she argues that when an engineer applies common sense to different dimensions of a problem, this ought ideally to result in the development of an innovative solution:

> The way we see the perfect engineer is somebody who is hands on, who is out there, who engages with what's actually happening on site and who is able – from a very common sense point of view – to take what *he* sees and is able to come up with a better solution.

Mr Chambers (SA) shares the concern that engineering graduates often have a narrow view of the field of work in which an engineer can be engaged. This suggests that some engineering graduates are unable to recognize the potential of applying their knowledge beyond mainstream engineering projects. Again, it appears that the ability to imagine broad areas of application for engineering is limited, and it seems that Mr Chambers (SA) thinks part of the blame is on universities. He argues that engineering graduates:

> [N]eed to get a very broad viewpoint of the engineering fraternity after the university. I think they (students) aren't always shown how broadly engineering is applied in industry. You know, an engineer can be working for a bank that underwrites a big project, and because of *his* technical skills – *he* understands what the project is about and then *he'll* take a risk for the bank to provide finances for the project.

Dr Shaw (SA) also emphasizes this point, arguing that the unrealistic expectations of engineering graduates about their profession lead them to have difficulties in abandoning their comfort zones. Below she describes the challenges of working on construction sites, stating that if engineering graduates lack exposure to site work in their studies, they tend to struggle to adapt to that sphere of the work environment:

> If they haven't had that first and they get to us, it is really a huge challenge. Trying to get them to go through that personal development as well – from the shock of being on site – and that's often the reason they say they don't want to work on site because site is a very different and very difficult kind of environment. You're not with family, you can't go home to family, you're sitting in an environment out in the middle of nowhere, and the circumstances are tough.

Other challenges related to personal development as a result of being or becoming an engineer are mentioned by Mr Braun (GER), who talks about the difficulty of figuring out one's role in society as an engineer. He explains that he has reached a conclusion about what it means to be an engineer, and states that he considers his purpose as contributing, in small ways, to improvements in society:

> I would like to say something personally, which is about what actually helped me understand my place in work a bit better. I think it's all about – to make the world a little bit better. There is a need for improvement all the time.

It is interesting to note that the employers (and lecturers and students) often refer to the purpose of engineering by using phrases such as 'solving problems' or 'fixing problems' or 'finding solutions'. These phrases dichotomize 'problems' and 'solutions' as if they are always mutually exclusive. In addition, the data carries the sentiment that engineers see themselves as problems solvers who have the potential, through their technical knowledge, to help fix societal challenges. Thinking about problems and solutions as mutually exclusive is problematic because it may result in overlooking the complexities that often characterize human challenges (like those prioritized in the MDGs and SDGs). Failure to perceive the interconnectedness of challenges such as climate change, poverty and inequality may ultimately result in the development of narrow engineering 'solutions' that do little or nothing to expand the capabilities of poor and marginalized communities.

Based on employers' views, the ideal engineer is someone who: (1) has a broad view of the engineering profession; (2) recognizes the diverse contexts in which technical knowledge can be applied; (3) sees the interconnectivity between technical solutions and human well-being; and (4) has the ability to translate theory into practice, both in the office space and on construction sites. There is a consensus across both employer groups that one cannot be, at the very least, a good engineer without certain non-technical skills. These skills are discussed in the next section.

Valuable transversal skills

Critical thinking and open-mindedness

All interviewees expressed the necessity and importance of thinking critically about various aspects of engineering activities. The dangers of being an unquestioning engineer were often pointed out, and the fact that engineers have a moral responsibility towards society was highlighted. Additionally, open-mindedness emerged as a prerequisite and dimension of being able to think critically. For example, Mr Klemp (GER) likens critical thinking to taking the path less travelled, in the sense that it often requires exploring and implementing unpopular solutions. He also implies that doing so requires fearlessness:

> It is very important not to run in the path everybody is running (…) and sometimes you need to be brave (…) and to discuss topics which are

non-topics, or nobody wants to talk about (...) because every challenge you have to look for all kinds of solutions even those solutions which seem to be far off or not explored solutions. So everything has to be brought up to the table and then to find the best solution.

Mr Klemp's words draw attention to some implications of thinking critically and they serve as a reminder that the value of critical thinking is diminished by being unable to verbalize critical thought. Vocalizing unpopular ideas, exploring new terrain or bringing up issues 'nobody wants to talk about' requires confidence in the knowledge one has, the bravery to use it and most importantly the ability to communicate critical thought effectively. The dangers of not being a critical thinker include a failure to identify underlying reasons for the unsuccessful optimization of solutions, which may impede sustainable development efforts. Mr Klein (GER) expresses this notion as follows:

Without it [critical thinking] there is no functionality, without that, you can't optimize anything and you can't improve.

Based on this perspective, critical thinking is fundamental to engineering practice. Mr Chambers (SA) suggests that critical thinking also serves as a kind of moral compass for engineers, keeping them focused on their area of expertise and allowing them to make sound decisions that result in positive change, as society expects them to. He explains that without critical thinking:

They [engineers] wouldn't be in control of the work that they are doing. Because unfortunately there are a lot of people that don't stick to the facts and they [engineers] would be drawn into the hearsay assumptions which is not an engineer's area that they should be getting involved in. So critical thinking would ensure that they stick to the facts and as engineers, we're seen as being fair and transparent in our dealings, so to be able to do that you need to be quite critical.

Mr Lehman (GER) emphasizes the importance of being self-critical and his words remind us that thinking critically entails continuous questioning:

It's important. One must question oneself; question one's findings and the results that one is presented with (...)

Mr Klein (GER) expresses his opinion on critical thinking in a similar manner, also talking about the importance of questioning and the value of having a healthy degree of scepticism in order to avoid accepting information at face value:

Saying: 'yeah okay I'll do it' without questioning, that can't be. One doesn't have to be overly pessimistic but one should be open and able to ask or inquire or question certain things so not just simply to accept, but to double check.

Similarly, Mr Weiss' (GER) opinion is that critical thinking is also important in practising reasonable scepticism instead of always trusting the answers with which one is provided. He emphasizes that:

> Fundamentally, critical thinking is very important because one must really recognize the causes. So when one realizes this hasn't been successful, one has to be able to critically ask, 'Why is this the case'? And not [accept things] just because everyone says it's not working.

Some interviewees understand critical thinking as being open-minded and showing openness to ideas or ways of thinking that are different to one's own and using that information as a basis upon which to make decisions. Mr Klemp (GER) says:

> I would describe it (critical thinking) more as openness: [To] be open for all ideas coming up, [and] then to evaluate and decide.

In this sense, openness can also be seen as a guiding principle that is fundamental to tolerance, especially when one interacts or works with people from diverse professional and cultural backgrounds. Mr Klemp's (GER) words allude to the 'borderless' application of engineering solutions and the importance of the ability to recognize the often global and reciprocal impact of engineering on society:

> Open-mindedness is very important – not to be focused on your local habits because we work in a networked world where it is very likely that the projects you're working on (…) may affect other parts in the world or are affected by other parts in the world.

Notions of openness and being able to see the bigger picture of engineering and its effect on society on a global scale resonate with Nussbaum's (1997) ideas on cosmopolitan abilities. Nussbaum argues that cosmopolitanism can be cultivated through education that stimulates capacities such as a critical examination of one's own culture and traditions as well as empathizing with others and positioning oneself in another's place. Dr Shaw's (SA) response indicates that the term cosmopolitan abilities is unfamiliar to her, because she responds by saying that cosmopolitan abilities are not essential. Yet she adds:

> Given that I say that, when it comes to working across borders, there needs to be a better understanding of world culture and an understanding of where that country is politically and socially, etc.

Although awareness about the political and social conditions of a foreign country does not fully encompass cosmopolitanism, that level of awareness can be considered as a prerequisite of cosmopolitan abilities because one needs to be aware of the conditions surrounding another's life, before one can imagine themselves in that position. This kind of 'openness', as Mr Klemp (GER) calls it, is also referred to as a tool to aid collaborative solution seeking. Below, Mr Braun (GER) talks about the value of open-mindedness in the engineering profession and relates this to developing engineering solutions that people have reason to value:

> You can form, I think, a bigger group of people supporting your work if you are open minded. (...) It's also important to know the expectations of the other colleagues you are working for or who you are producing results [for] and it's not just about that you are producing the result in your own way or you are just thinking this would be correct. You need to know the expectations of the others, so that you produce results that are of good use to them.

That is to say, producing results that are of good use to people requires large degrees of openness. In capabilities language, creating valued capabilities through professional engineering functionings requires engineers to exercise cosmopolitan abilities.

The views described in this section suggest that engineers should be critically reflexive about a myriad of factors related to their occupation: the way in which engineering solutions are sought, the validity of the information presented to them, the reasons for failure to achieve optimal solutions and the value of engineering solutions to society. Openness and open-mindedness are closely related to critical thinking, and often described as prerequisites for it. The employers perceive the ability to be open-minded and practise openness to different ways of doing and being, as attributes that can foster creative thinking and enhance collaboration with culturally and professionally diverse colleagues. It is also evident that the employers see openness and open-mindedness as necessary for developing an interest in how engineering activities affect peoples' lives on a global scale. In essence, the employers are talking about the necessity for engineers to be 'broad thinkers' who can embrace and critically evaluate different perspectives, values and ideas in the process of developing engineering solutions.

The importance of openness is also reflected in the employers' views on teamwork. They all stated that engineering activities are mostly performed by project teams comprising an array of professional groups and stakeholders. Therefore the value of being open-minded or showing openness is seen as indispensable for developing the ability to interact effectively within and across engineering teams and with non-engineers. Because good communication entails being open to or receptive of the views of others i.e. people with different value sets, professional backgrounds, perspectives, etc. communication can also be understood as an aid to collaboration. The next section discusses communication and collaboration as soft skills that stood out from the data.

Communication and collaboration

Interviewees spoke about communication very broadly, emphasizing its importance in engineering in numerous ways. Mr Klemp (GER) speaks of often having witnessed project failure because of poor communication and weighs the significance of technical competence against communicative competence, saying:

> (…) sometimes, someone who is not so strong on the technical side but who is a great communicator may be more valuable than the other way around.

Mr Braun (GER) talks about the importance of communication not only in terms of engineers being able to communicate with various stakeholders on a given project but also being receptive to information pertaining to how the results of engineering activities will be employed:

> Communication is a very big thing (…) [it] enables you to know about the others' occupations (…) [and] to know what other people do with the result of your work.

With this statement, he foregrounds not only the value of being able to communicate effectively, but also the need to know what happens to engineering products once they have been successfully designed, manufactured or constructed. He puts forward that it is crucial for engineers to have a holistic view of the effects of their work on society, implying that their work as engineers does not end once a particular product is complete, but continues long after the product is in the hands of the end user. Also, we are reminded here that although concerns about engineers' poor communication abilities are mostly centred on their failing to 'send' the right message effectively, it is equally important for them to be active 'receivers' of information.

Perhaps one of the biggest disadvantages of poor communication for the engineering profession is the diminishing effect it has on their effective power. Mr Klemp (GER) expresses his concern over this, saying:

> Engineers tend to be in their cocoon of technology and [tend] not to go out. So sometimes, they have a lot of force but they cannot bring the force to the world.

The ability to 'go out' and bring 'the force to the world' triggers thoughts about agency. As discussed in Chapter 1, agency is the capacity to initiate action through formulating valued aims and beliefs, and it requires mental health, cognitive skills and opportunities to engage in social participation (Alkire, 2002). As Sen points out, there is a profound complementarity between individual agency and social conditions, and it is therefore important to acknowledge both the centrality of individual freedom and the strength of social influences on the extent and reach of that agency freedom (Sen, 1985). Looked at through the lens of the capability approach, the inability for engineers to bring their 'force' to the world, indicates that there are conversion factors that restrain engineers' agency achievement. That is, there are conditions that get in the way of engineers' capacity to use their effective power.

What are these conditions? How can they be overcome? What can engineering education do to enhance graduates' agency? These questions resulted from thematic coding of the data, coupled with thinking about the significance of the answers from a capabilities perspective. They reflect questions thought of during much of the data analysis process, especially when reading parts of the transcripts that were coded 'agency' and 'voice'. Ultimately, this led to a more nuanced understanding of communication, and recognizing how ineffective communication can signal diminished agency. For example, Ms White (SA) talks about the necessity for graduate engineers to be able to communicate assertively and eventually take on leadership roles within the workplace. She suggests that some engineering graduates struggle to acquire these abilities owing to cultural upbringings that emphasize obedience to senior members of one's community:

> For instance, somebody who is culturally brought up to 'obey your parents', 'obey your teachers' – you then want (that person) to stand up in a meeting and say 'no, no, no, this is my idea, this is what I want to do, this is what the plant needs' and persuade other people (...) but if you keep quiet, we're missing something. So the entire solution will be deficient because you haven't added what you need to be adding.

Dr Shaw (SA) expresses a similar concern giving the example that cultural principles such as respect for elders may have a negative influence on engineering graduates' assertiveness in the workplace. She says that some graduates:

> [D]on't want to push, out of respect, frequently. They don't make the kind of noise that is required to get senior management attention ... and then you end up with sometimes critical things [problems] on site.

At this point, it is interesting to note that concerns about engineering graduates' inability to communicate assertively are mentioned only by South African employers, both of them women. As described in the employers' profiles provided at the beginning of this chapter, the two women amongst the selected group of employers both work in the human resources departments in their companies. In comparison to the men's responses, at times Dr Shaw's responses offer more nuanced accounts of some complexities that characterize communication in South African engineering firms. For example, she shares her insight on the differences between male and female engineering graduate recruits and suggests that the resilience of female graduate engineers often makes them stand out from their male counterparts. She believes that women's resilience is developed throughout university learning and she argues that it is strengthened in the workplace because they have to fight to prove their worth in a male-dominated industry. She says if female engineering students:

> (…) survive all the way through and actually graduate – we find that we get them on site, and this is where sometimes – it knocks their confidence and they struggle a little. But on the other hand, you'll have the exact opposite experience with – and this is the more common experience – that if they've been through the hard knocks at the university, the women on our sites really thrive and they end up in management positions – sometimes even faster than the guys [do]. Because they've had to fight in a male-dominated environment, you see.

Dr Shaw (SA) speaks of female engineering graduates' confidence and willingness to participate in the non-compulsory training and development exercises offered by Group Five. She says that this is noticeably different from male engineering graduates and her words suggest that female graduates are more prepared to take initiative and lead:

> So that's why you see even at our summer camps that we have within the organization they're the ones [female graduates] who put their hands up first, they're the ones that are engaged with all the activities. And their management skills are usually a lot better [than the males] and so that works for us very well.

She identifies some challenges for female engineers, citing difficulties for senior white male engineers in accepting young women engineers in the profession. Difficulties are mentioned especially with regard to the challenge of learning to accept women in engineering, particularly in their capacity as managers. Her response implies that these challenges form part of the experiences that can actually enhance female engineers' agency:

> The challenge however is older white guys who have been around a long time – on site – nobody told them yet that they need to evolve and accept women as managers and so sometimes that's where a lot of the challenges are. But over a very short time, we find that those issues work themselves out because women are better attuned. They're able to – like for example with our older black supervisors – they are able to show the right level of respect to them and that kind of thing. So it's a good and bad side of things but it teaches confidence and assertiveness that they need.

Dr Shaw also shares her insight on gendered behavioural differences that she has observed amongst the female engineering graduates, attributing these dissimilarities to race and cultural factors that can inhibit black women's capability for voice. Her view suggests that the cause of this problem lies in the existence of patriarchal cultural norms that govern African traditions, which discourage black women from assuming positions of superiority over men in the workplace:

(...) if you want me to generalize there, white women tend to be a lot stronger and when I say stronger I'm talking about from a personality point of view. So this is something that we need to work on in our black ladies – that they can speak to an older black foreman and actually tell them what to do. That, from a kind of cultural perspective, is sometimes a little bit more difficult.

As mentioned earlier, some findings were unique to the views from South Africa, and this section has shown how Dr Shaw (SA) specifically mentions concerns about cultural norms that impede on assertive expression by engineering graduates in the workplace; no such concerns were shared by the German employers. In addition, resilience emerged as an important attribute from Dr Shaw's (SA) perspective, where it was highlighted as a trait that ultimately enhances female graduates' assertiveness, confidence and agency in a male-dominated industry.

Mr Schrader (SA) also attributes a significant number of project failures to the inability to speak up and communicate assertively:

[It] doesn't help you to be full of knowledge if you can't talk to anyone or you can't convey your message. And from experience in projects, all the projects I have been working in, if there was problem, it could be always related to communication problems. So that's a very important thing. And also, since you are not alone in the world you need to be able to deal with people, other human beings, ne? You often have the tendency that an engineer is a good designer but he can only relate to himself on his computer and he is not really discussing [things].

The phrase 'not alone in the world' and the idea that one needs to be able to deal with 'other human beings' articulate concern about engineers who narrowly apply their technical knowledge to a specific task in isolation, in contrast to sharing and developing their ideas with diverse stakeholders.

Examples of such stakeholders are communities on the receiving end of development aid that is planned, designed, and/or constructed with the significant contribution of engineers. For example, Mr Braun (GER) complains about the often limited communication between engineers involved in development aid projects and the individuals or groups for whom the aid is intended. He explains:

If you do projects for communities like, I don't know – bridges and houses – you have to find a strong acceptance within the community. If you realize projects without public acceptance, then it's going to be very problematic (...) it's important to get everybody within the boat to make the decision.

Top-down planning, which fails to engage communities as co-researchers and co-planners who can collaborate meaningfully with engineers, may result in the creation of artefacts that do not bring about valued opportunities. Developing engineering solutions that result in enhanced capabilities for society requires engineers who recognize the 'limitations in the 'universalistic' notion that technology can be transferred from one context to any other without regard for socio-cultural, political, economic and other systems that inform and are informed by community identity, values, and aspirations' (Schneider, Leydens & Lucena, 2008: 313). For this reason, it is important to strive towards the ideal to 'get everybody on the boat to make the decision' as Mr Braun (GER) put it.

On the other hand, Mr Chambers (SA) warns not to overemphasize the importance of communication skills. In the excerpt below, he argues that communication skills are only relevant to half of all qualified engineers:

> They're important to about probably fifty per cent of engineers. Fifty per cent that choose to go into a design/consulting kind of area where the product of their work is a calculation or drawing or specification – the lesser the softer skills [necessary]. The ones that go into project engineering – which is the execution side of engineering that deals with suppliers, contractors, clients, government bodies – need to have people skills.

This statement highlights that there is no necessary consensus amongst employers about the importance of soft skills in engineering practice. In addition, this response indicates that communication skills are applied to various degrees, depending on the type of engineering work one does. Nevertheless, the views of all employers do confirm that engineers' work, although highly technical in nature, is rarely devoid of human interaction, which usually takes the form of teamwork. For example, Mr Braun's (GER) says:

> Most of the time it's team work. It's working in a group and you need to know that you are just one part of the big picture and you are supporting something. It's not all about you and your job – it's never just what you do – it's always part of the big picture.

In the broadest sense, 'engineering teams' include individuals, community groups, and different clusters of society whose capabilities are shaped by the processes and results of professional engineering activities. The findings discussed here imply that the complexity of engineering challenges necessitates team-based solution seeking. What has perhaps been overlooked in bringing this message across is the complex nature of the 'team'. What is often described as 'teamwork', is referred to in these findings as collaboration, i.e. teamwork not only in terms of engineers working with architects, technicians, quantity surveyors and contractors on a particular project but also teamwork as community engagement. In other words, collaboration and communication between engineers (and other industry stakeholders) for the purpose of creating development solutions that help expand the capabilities of designated communities. In this sense, collaboration is both a means to and an end of communication, which can refer to, but is not limited to, activities such as:

- the exchange of ideas in the workplace amongst fellow engineers;
- receiving and critically assessing instructions from senior managers;
- consulting with stakeholders or communities to generate valuable solutions; and
- Being knowledgeable about how engineering products are used by, and affect the end user.

The terms 'communication' and 'teamwork' are therefore understood here in a broader sense as being synonymous to or necessary for collaboration involving engineers and any group of people who are affected by engineering outcomes.

What emerges clearly from the interviews is that technical excellence alone does not signify an excellent engineer. The characteristics of the ideal engineer described by the interviewees in the early part of this chapter suggest a vast number of non-technical capacities that employers would like to see in engineering graduates. Aside from a solid foundation (in mathematics, science and engineering sciences, etc.), the aptitudes desired by the employers interviewed were discussed under the three Cs namely communication and collaboration, as well as critical thinking and open-mindedness. These non-technical skills have value and relevance for the engineering profession not only in terms of potentially improving engineering graduates' capability for employment, but also with regard to developing engineers who are positive social change agents.

Having discussed employers' perspectives on the characteristics of the ideal engineer as well as the relevance and importance of transversal skills in engineering practice, the discussion turns to employers' views on questions related to the links they perceive between the work engineers do, its influence on societal development and its role with regard to sustainable development. Drawing on these views, the next section provides a theoretical, but empirically informed vision of public-good engineering education.

Public-good engineering

There is general agreement amongst the employers who were interviewed that the work engineers do contributes to positive change in, and valuable benefits to, society as well as sustainable development. However, there are mixed views on the effective power of engineers to be drivers of this change.

Mr Weiss (GER) shares his wide-ranging view on the interrelations between engineering and human development, reflecting on the fact that a joint and collaborative movement towards sustainable well-being requires the participation of stakeholders at the economic, political, societal and individual level. He argues that engineers play an important role in advancing sustainable development but acknowledges that this is not unique to the engineering profession. He also elaborates on this view by adding that the results of the work engineers do in relation to technological advancement are often the starting point to instigating sustainable development efforts:

Engineers can be part of the solution. Because there are questions of power supply, water supply, the fundamental problems that when you look at things globally, the human race has – [is] of course dependent on good technical solutions. That on its own is not enough, because it needs political conditions, it needs financing, and so forth but new technical solutions could be the initiators to ensure that solutions are found and in so far, it is a very fundamental and important role that engineers play, especially for such questions as sustainable development – and the challenges are many.

On the contrary, Mr Klemp (GER) is less keen to say engineers have effective power. His words show a more critical stance towards this assumption; for example, he talks about the role industry plays in dictating engineering activities, saying that some companies, including engineering firms, only support pro-sustainability initiatives as a front and that:

they make little projects for advertisement to show that they are 'green' but finally what they would like to do – they would like to earn money and they don't care [about sustainability].

His depiction of engineers gives the impression that they are more responsive to the demands of industry than they are initiators of positive social change. His views on the role of engineers in promoting sustainable development agendas are also not enthusiastic: he posits that the influential power of engineers is limited, stating that:

Engineers have influence of course. But I think one should not overestimate this influence. Politics has much more influence.

Additionally, he goes on to conclude that:

Engineers do not change the world, basically.

Mr Klemp's (GER) opinion is particularly sceptical, and elements of his statements are supported by the views of other employers.

On the contrary, Mr Braun's (GER) view is more balanced. He affirms that decisions made by engineers in judging the feasibility of construction projects are indicative of their strong position in society and in matters of development. He also speaks broadly about all types of employment being linked to human development:

What everybody is doing for his living I think is about the increase of life quality. And it is – if you are aware of this – I think you become aware that it's not so much about quantity or increased quantities, it's about increasing of quality. And for the engineers the relevance is that during a feasibility phase of projects (...) it very much depends on the engineers. They are, in most cases, bearing the decisions whether a project is going to be realized or not, and it's a big responsibility.

Mr Lehman (GER) sees the role and responsibility of engineers with regard to development and sustainable development in a similar way. He points out, that engineers have to evaluate the conditions and economic aspects of construction projects, and that it is ultimately engineers who ensure the implementation of development projects worth pursuing to achieve positive change in society. Mr Klein (GER)'s view corroborates this:

> We get to talking about renewable energy where the energy that is created from power plants can be reused, and we can generate clean energy. That can only happen through a vision in which we continue to question and continue to develop research and simply to keep going in the direction (…) to ensure a more secure source of power.

Ms White (SA) expresses concern that engineering graduates believe the only way in which they can meaningfully contribute to sustainable development is by being employed in companies in the renewable energy sector. She stresses that during her selection interviews she brings it to the attention of the individuals being recruited that they ought to look at other avenues to make meaningful contributions to society through their work, regardless of the engineering discipline or field:

> We have a lot of engineers who say they want to get into environmental engineering and I kind of tell them that every engineer should be thinking about environmental or sustainable development, whatever you do – every project, any way you run a plant – it's your responsibility.

Mr Chambers (SA) sees this similarly, saying that he thinks engineers are integral in the development of society's growth:

> Be it roads, schools, houses, hospitals, power stations, you know – the employment of people in society and providing society's infrastructure so that society can grow and in the end have a better lifestyle.

He goes on to provide an example of how engineers can design effective solutions to societal challenges in a manner that improves not only the infrastructure in a particular community, but also equips community members with useful skills. Through this, he alludes to community capability expansion through public-good engineering, where the results of engineering efforts e.g. designing a dam, result in creating valuable capabilities, e.g. skills that enhance capability for employment. In his example, he discusses a construction project where the engineering team that designed the dam specifically aimed to ensure that it would require community involvement. This is also a good example of what one might refer to as a participatory approach to development aid:

What the engineers are doing is that they're designing a dam so it can be built by eight hundred people. And those eight hundred people are learning skills and hopefully those skills will be used to build other dams, maybe not a dam as big as this one because it's quite a labour intensive construction project, but build maybe other farm dams and that skill then gets kept. Whereas traditionally it's been like we go somewhere, we go build something, and come back. (...) [B]ut now it's more about the sustainability of that community as well, which is quite cool.

Dr Shaw (SA) discusses some of the complexities of such efforts by engineers, where she is candid about the benefits of these approaches for the engineering firms that make use of them. She also signals the importance of processes of deliberation between representatives of the firm and community members over the engineering activities being instigated. Historically, rural communities have often been displaced from their homes for the sake of 'development' efforts, efforts pioneered with the significant contribution of engineers, but with minimal to no regard for meaningful community engagement (Lucena & Schneider, 2008; Schneider et al., 2008). Below, Dr Shaw (SA) provides an example of how modern approaches to development efforts have improved:

Some of these more remote places, we make sure that we understand who the community is before we get there and when we engage with them we appoint community liaison officers and we look at growing the actual competence of the people in that area through short skills programmes, etc. so that we can employ people. And we can't say it's just because we are marvellous people, but we do it for very pragmatic reasons, we want labour close to where we are working but we also want to make sure that we've got good relations with these people around as well. So I think you can never take the pragmatism from an engineer but there is also that willingness and the aspiration to contribute to a better society because otherwise they wouldn't be doing the jobs that they are doing. And yes, of course they do it for money, but I think the engineers we work for have a very holistic perspective.

She concludes her response by adding that engineering is about improving society, and argues that there is a keen awareness amongst engineers that all engineering accomplishments affect communities. She argues that this is part of what fuels the intrinsic desire some individuals have to become engineers and says such individuals have:

[a] very keen awareness that that's what the job is about and that's part of their kind of 'calling'.[2]

Interestingly, some interviewees expressed concern about the necessity for engineers to know their 'limits'. Mr Weiss (GER) speaks of his concerns regarding the notion that human beings and engineers in particular, generally assume a position of superiority over the environment. He argues that doing so often obstructs engineers from acknowledging the limits of imposing technical solutions on human challenges. He says:

> But when I'm dealing with technical skills, it's important for me to really understand the limits, yeah? Why does this technique no longer function in this section? Where are the limits of technical possibilities? What is the reason why we can no longer build without limits? To really understand the limits is for me a very important foundation that engineers should know as a basis. So what is important is not only to know what is being practised today, to take on the doable. Rather, when solutions are being searched for one must have understood why. When one thinks across these things you must recognize why the boundary is actually there that [has] led to the inability to build X in that dimension.

He goes on to explain that technical knowledge in itself is limited in applicability because of ever-changing problems that require engineers to come up with new ways of thinking and different approaches to solution seeking:

> I believe that in the purely technical knowledge, firstly it is very inflated, because in fact, that knowledge is permanently new. We are living in an age where at the end of your study programme what you learnt at the beginning of the programme is almost already outdated. That which has permanent value though, are other capacities that one always needs: how people work together, how people find solutions together – those are the fundamental things.

By reflecting on the limits of technical solutions to human problems, Mr Weiss (GER) brings our attention to the importance of transversal skills and the values that underpin them. He stresses that they outlast technical skills in terms of their relevance in society. He points towards the idea that the way in which solutions are brought about, although based on technical expertise, have to be merged with other forms of knowledge and principles to achieve sustainable human development. Some examples of different forms of knowledge specific to engineering are discussed in the coming section related to what universities can do better to impart such knowledge.

To summarize, the views expressed in the interviews suggest that engineers do indeed have the power to influence decisions on projects that are geared towards conceptualizing and implementing effective and efficient solutions to a variety of human development challenges. However, some responses in contrast suggest that the true authority in this matter lies at the corporate level, where *homo economicus* principles guide business activities to prioritize exclusive economic profit over inclusive human development or environmental well-being.

Seen through a capabilities lens, it can be summarized that employers' views indicate that public-good engineering could be defined as engineering that:

- is founded on principles of *homo reciprocans*[3] rather than *homo economicus*;[4]
- seeks to expand capabilities and enable valued functionings for (poor) communities;
- meaningfully engages with such communities, to ensure that engineering accomplishments benefit them in ways they have reason to value; and
- is not carried out with disregard to the environment and acknowledges the boundaries of human influence on it.

Lucena and Schneider (2008) state that since the relationship between engineering and development began to take shape, engineering work in local communities has been 'top-down', meaning that the planning, design, development and implementation of projects have been done mostly without consultation with the people that the projects are supposed to serve. This attitude towards local and indigenous communities has been reinforced by the ideology of modernization that has motivated most development work since the 1950s (Lucena & Schneider, 2008). Recognizing this problem, social scientists and development critics have been advocating participatory practices since the 1980s, and promoting meaningful participation and equal partnership with communities instead of treating them as passive recipients of development (Lucena & Schneider, 2008). As Lucena and Schneider (2008) warn, sustainable development projects that do not shine a critical, self-reflective light on their work may risk replicating traditional development projects that often disempowered the communities that they were meant to serve.

Schneider et al. (2008) contend that projects laying claim to sustainability often ignore key components of long-term intergenerational meaningfulness by ignoring significant community involvement. In engineering education, students involved in sustainable development projects are rarely offered substantial theoretical, historical or practical education in development studies or community interaction (Lucena & Schneider, 2008). So, although engineers may play an important role in development projects, their training is often limited to technical problem-solving approaches; approaches that may lead to the types of failures resulting from the fact that engineers 'plan and organize everything themselves' instead of truly engaging with the communities they aim to help (Schneider et al., 2008). Based on the four dimensions outlined above, public-good engineering would be opposed to practices that did not expand communities' valued capabilities and functions and it acknowledges the importance of community engagement. As such, adherence to these dimensions of public-good engineering could minimize the types of failures identified by Lucena and Schneider (2008) and Schneider et al. (2008).

What can universities do (better)?

Employers have often criticized universities for failing to equip graduates with broad perspectives of what professional engineering can look like in praxis. Mr Chambers (SA) shares his thoughts on this matter as follows:

I don't think they [engineering students] get given always enough insight into how broad it is so when they make a career decision to go and work in a company in South Africa they either decide to go and work for a consultant or for a contractor but they don't see anything in between and that's a pity. So what can universities do more? I don't know if it's still being done – but invite the industry to source the engineers, and while they are sourcing, get the industry to explain what they do in engineering. So while they give bursaries let them give a lecture on what they're doing in that company. So they'll get their bursaries to students but at the same time, they [students] get to see what the rest of the industry is doing.

Mr Kumar (SA) also expresses concern about the disconnect between what engineering graduates expect and what happens in practice, attributing this disconnect to the fact that engineering educators usually have little or no experience in working as engineers and therefore lack the ability to impart appropriate visions of what it means to be an engineer in industry. He concludes that the role universities can play in enhancing transversal skills is limited and he feels that practical work in industry may prove to be the better 'teacher' in this regard:

I think it's more learning on the job – because ninety per cent of the time you find that the guys that are actually in lecture rooms or the lecturers, the professors have not worked in the real world itself. They have excelled in what they were doing and they continue with their studies there to become professors, but never really work in an environment like this [Sasol]. And as a result of that what advice are they supposed to give a student who's now going to [that] environment? They would not be able to.

Mr Schrader (SA) also acknowledges the difficulty for engineering educators to impart transversal skills through their actual teaching practices, saying that it is much easier to teach content that is regurgitated in exams than to instil principles of autonomy of thought or develop students' agency. He says that engineers should be taught to synthesize and analyse information in a manner that is conducive to independent thinking. In addition, he stresses the difficulty in doing so, and argues that it is the reason behind teaching approaches that encourage rote learning. He says:

It's a bit more difficult on the teacher's side (…) it's challenging. So they [engineering lectures] just give something for the kids to chew on, and then let them repeat it in writing a test or so.

Asked if they thought the inclusion of humanities content in engineering curricula might aid the development of transversal skills, all the employers agreed that this would be helpful. Mr Schrader (SA) advocates the inclusion of 'general studies' being a good initiative. He also shares what stands out for him when making decisions about selecting graduate engineers in his company:

The engineer should remember there is a society with real human beings, not so?

What I think could help as well for these kinds of things – what we call 'Studium Generale'.[5] So that means sort of voluntary subjects you can choose as an add-on to your mandatory curriculum. And on the employers' side if I do an interview with a candidate the most important thing for me is not his standard curriculum, there are hundreds with the same curriculum and maybe even hundreds with the same results (grades). That doesn't tell a story to me at all, it just explains that a person can handle his subject matter. The most interesting part is what he is doing or what she is doing over and beyond the standard curriculum. That is what tells a story where you see okay, that's a very engaged student, he is working beyond the necessary, beyond the mandatory, he is doing things on his own.

Mr Weiss' (GER) response on the integration of humanities subject matter into the engineering curriculum is more complex. He speaks of the relevance of the humanities to all study programmes alluding to the idea that knowledge gained from the humanities is more sustainable than technical knowledge, which has the potential of losing value over time because the processes of design, construction, etc. are ever-changing. He explains this by contrasting foundational physics knowledge to knowledge of technology design and then links this to transversal skills:

> That means what one really needs, of course aside from the technical foundation, because those basic foundational technical competences will also always remain, the real technical foundation like Newton's laws will remain, or the Law of Relativity, but technology, how one constructs a circuit board was different twenty years ago with SMD technology, then ten years later and then today (…) it has a very short life span this kind of knowledge; but how people work together, how people find solutions together, those are the fundamental things.

Mr Weiss (GER) is the only interviewee to direct his attention to engineering educators in his responses, reflecting on pedagogical practices he finds inspiring. He encourages approaches to teaching that focus on highlighting the interconnectivity of various elements of engineering functions:

> I always find it admirable when the lecturers in a university (…) also engage in practical work, and that means something like: okay we're going to build a computer out of limited parts that we have to work with. How can we find an optimal solution? Exactly these types of questions should be linked or related to management tasks. I believe for example that when all semesters entail something like that: organizing seminars, taking over organizational responsibility for something during the semester – and to relate such tasks with the theoretical approaches, would really teach a lot.

When asked if he had any concluding comments at the end of his interview, Mr Weiss (GER) replies that the biggest area where universities are failing in terms of educating engineers (and other professionals) is imparting lasting or universal human values:

> We're living in exponential times. And the changes are so huge that we have to ask ourselves where are the real ground values that always remain? That is what I find crucial; which is really valuable but is not really being disseminated in universities. That's the most essential thing.

The employers' perspectives suggest that universities can aid the cultivation of engineers' transversal skills through pedagogical practices and curricula in engineering education that explicitly address outcomes in relation to 'know that' or propositional knowledge, and 'know-how' or procedural knowledge. A third form of knowledge may thus be needed: 'know why'. 'Know why' could be defined as ethical knowledge that is concerned with 'the right thing to do' or values that underpin approaches to, or motives behind engineering.

Summative discussion

With regard to what attributes characterize the ideal engineer, the responses show little or no deviation from the message conveyed in literature: that engineering knowledge and technical expertise have to be complemented by transversal skills, 'soft' skills and humane values. The general sentiment of the employers' responses is that universities sometimes fall short in providing realistic expectations or understanding of the engineering profession. Reasons for this include the idea that there are not enough opportunities for meaningful practical work during engineering courses, or that university lecturers themselves have no personal experience in the world of work and can therefore not relate this experience in their teaching. The employers' views therefore imply that more meaningful dialogue needs to take place between universities and industry concerning how students understand engineering theory and how and where they can expect to practise engineering. On the other hand, the employers seem satisfied with the technical skills engineering graduates are able to bring with them from the university. The role of industry to further graduates' development is seen as crucial because it is in this space that they gain meaningful experience of the actual day-to-day activities of engineers.

The interviewees provided some examples of the type of measures that can be taken by universities to broaden engineering education outcomes so that graduates are better equipped with the kind of transversal skills universities would like them to possess and apply. The recommendation most frequently provided related to the need for curricula in engineering education that address outcomes in relation to propositional and procedural knowledge, for example through the inclusion of humanities courses.

Only once were teaching practices mentioned in the suggestion that lecturers ought to develop engineering pedagogies that strive towards magnifying the interconnectivities between engineering functionings and human capabilities. This type of knowledge relates to non-technical skills such as critical thinking and open-mindedness, communication and collaboration, which were identified as the type of skills that could be conducive to public-good engineering. As such, what matters in the education of engineers is not only what they know, but also how that speaks to their application of that knowledge and the extent to which they apply it in the creation of products that add value to the lives of the poor, and the lives of current and future persons.

Responses that were particularly distinctive relate to gender and cultural aspects emerging from the interviews of the only two female interviewees. Despite the dis-similarities of education structures, university education and socio-historical char-acteristics, etc. between Germany and South Africa (discussed in Chapter 2), employers' views presented in this chapter proved to be similar. There were however some salient differences. For example from the female South African employers' responses, gender and culture were identified as potential constraints for assertiveness, whereas no such mention was made by either the male South African or German employers. This chapter has defined public-good engineering as engineering that, amongst other things, authentically considers the capabilities of communities, especially poor communities, and aims to secure their valued functionings through engineering endeavours. Also, qualities that characterize the ideal engineer (beyond having impeccable technical skills) are the capacity to exercise critical reflexive thought, practise open-mindedness and use communica-tion as an aid to collaboration for public-good engineering.

These findings are summarized in Table 5.1.

Having presented the perspectives of engineering students, educators and employers in Chapters 3, 4 and 5 respectively, the next chapter considers these perspectives together in an attempt to offer a cohesive description of ways in which sustainable human development can be advanced through engineering

Table 5.1 Key findings from employers' perspectives

The ideal engineer:	*Valuable skills include:*	*Public-good engineering is*
Has a broad view of the engineering profession	Critical thinking	Founded on principles of *homo reciprocans*
Recognizes the diverse contexts in which technical knowledge can be applied	Open-mindedness	Expands (poor) communities' capabilities and functionings
Sees the interconnectivity between technical solutions and human problems	Communication	Meaningfully engages with communities to ensure that they benefit from engineering outcomes
Has the ability to translate theory into practice both in the office space and on construction sites	Collaboration	Carried out with respect to the environment

Source: Author's own.

education. The relationship between the goals of engineering education (based on lecturers' views), valuable capabilities and functionings (students' perspectives), and dimensions of public-good engineering (employers' perspectives) are theorized. In so doing, a capabilities-inspired, empirically informed framework for public-good engineering is presented.

Notes

1 *Ordnung* is a German word that usually refers to order or orderliness as well as arrangement, discipline or system. It is also commonly used to describe stereotypical notions of German culture or life in Germany.
2 It is interesting to note that the German word for 'occupation' is *Beruf*, which stems from the word *Rufen*, meaning 'to call'.
3 *Homo reciprocans:* Seeing humans as cooperative actors who are motivated by improving their environment.
4 *Homo economicus*: Seeing humans as narrowly self-interested agents who are primarily concerned with meeting their subjectively defined ends optimally.
5 *Studium Generale* is the German expression for General Studies.

References

Alkire, S. (2002). Dimensions of human development. *World Development, 30*(2), 181–205.

Faulkner, W. (2009). Doing gender in engineering workplace cultures. I. Observations from the field. *Engineering Studies, 1*(1), 3–18. Accessed 1 September 2017 from https://doi.org/10.1080/19378620902721322.

Lucena, J., & Schneider, J. (2008). Engineers, development, and engineering education: From national to sustainable community development. *European Journal of Engineering Education, 33*(3), 247–257.

Nussbaum, M. (1997). *Cultivating humanity: A classical defence of reform in liberal education.* Cambridge, MA and London: Harvard University Press.

Schneider, J., Leydens, J. A. & Lucena, J. (2008). Where is 'community'? Engineering education and sustainable community development. *European Journal of Engineering Education, 33*(3), 307–319.

Sen, A. (1985). Well-being, agency and freedom. *Journal of Philosophy, 82*(4), 169–221.

UB. (2013). *Produktionstechnik – Maschinenbau & Verfahrenstechnik (Master).* Bremen: Universität Bremen.

UCT. (2015a). *Faculty of engineering and the built environment* (Postgraduate Handbook). Cape Town: University of Cape Town.

UCT. (2015b). *Faculty of engineering and the built environment* (Undergraduate Handbook). Cape Town: University of Cape Town.

Part III

6 Advancing sustainable human development through engineering education

The SDGs offer a new vision of education (Boni, Fogues & Walker, 2016). For example, Goal 4 of the SDGs is to: 'ensure inclusive and equitable quality education and promote lifelong learning opportunities for all' (UN, 2014: 10). There is one target proposed for monitoring SDG 4 that is related directly to ESD:

> By 2030, ensure that all learners acquire the knowledge and skills needed to promote sustainable development, including, among others, through *education for sustainable development* and sustainable lifestyles, human rights, gender equality, promotion of a culture of peace and non-violence, global citizenship and appreciation of cultural diversity and of culture's contribution to sustainable development.
>
> (UN, 2014: 11)

Keeping this in mind, this chapter brings to light questions about the reach of engineering curricula and pedagogies in teaching students values associated with sustainable development. Data is drawn from the student focus group discussions and the lecturer interviews. What is different about this chapter is that it contains a combination of students' and lecturers' voices, as opposed to the previous chapters, which looked at the findings for each group of participants separately. To begin, the chapter describes the role of engineering curricula in teaching sustainable development and then explores the challenges of teaching sustainable development as a fixed concept. Thereafter, the chapter discusses students' understandings of this concept and its implementation in engineering praxis. Students' views on their ability to advance sustainable development in their capacities as engineers in the future are also discussed, before revisiting the capability approach and drawing conclusions.

Learning about sustainable development through the engineering curriculum

One of the criteria used to select the university case sites studied in this project was the institutions' commitment to, and explicit engagement, with the topic of sustainable development or sustainability in their engineering curricula.

A good example of a course that is dedicated to creating awareness and broad understandings of issues related to sustainable development includes 'Sustainability and Organizational Leadership' from UB. This elective course addresses fundamental questions of sustainability from an interdisciplinary perspective, where the aim is to offer students a language and/or order system with which they can evaluate companies' statements about, and commitment to, sustainable development. It also allows for detailed discussion of the concept of sustainability and new tools of sustainable resource management are presented to students (UB, 2015). Another example is the elective course 'Sustainability in Chemical Engineering' offered by UCT. This course provides graduate students with an awareness of issues surrounding sustainable processes in the chemical engineering industry and an appreciation of its importance. It examines the central role of chemical engineering in achieving balance amongst economic, environmental and social benefits and the impacts arising from projects conducted by companies operating in the oil, chemicals, minerals and energy sectors. The course also addresses the related challenges of intensive agriculture and the provision of water, and seeks to provide a framework and a set of tools that will assist the process engineer in providing rational input in terms of sustainability to the decision-making process (UCT, 2015).

The courses mentioned above are illustrative of the manner in which themes related to sustainable development are being addressed through engineering curricula at the selected universities. It is apparent from the empirical chapters that courses dealing with sustainable development questions help students gain awareness of, and interest in, factors that influence the natural environment. Such courses also show potential to stimulate students' critical thinking. However, the fact that they are usually offered as electives limits the possibility of *all* students learning from them. For instance, Phillip (GER) gives the example of the 'Industrial Ecology' course that he studied, stating that one learns about the complexity of factors that need to be considered when aiming for sustainable development in car manufacturing. He provides the example that switching to electric cars cannot in itself be a solution to the problem of pollution caused by motor vehicles, because one would first have to consider the source of electricity used to fuel electric cars. He attributes such knowledge to the Industrial Ecology course. He says:

> I find it good that one has courses like Industrial Ecology where you learn how complicated it [sustainable development practice] is (…) One cannot say 'okay we're switching to electric cars, and we'll get that electricity from coal fired power plants'.
>
> That wouldn't make any sense, and that is something one does learn from such courses.

Phillip (GER) states that such considerations have to be borne in mind by engineers when carrying out their work. However, his response also indicates that sustainable development problems are not considered by some engineers, implying that ideals of sustainability do not necessarily characterize the value systems of all engineers:

> I mean, one does have to consider this question [of sustainable development] throughout the whole process (...) [but] there are those who say: we're doing it that way, those who say it is important and those who say it isn't.

If the ideals and values of sustainable development do not influence engineers' values, and if those ideas and values are confined to elective courses, good as these might be, this is not conducive to widespread public-good engineering. Therefore, an important question is: To what extent do universities instil values associated with sustainable development in their engineering students (beyond electives)? Such values would include those aligned with public-good engineering, e.g. that engineering should enhance valuable capabilities and functionings for communities and promote *homo reciprocans* instead of *homo economicus* approaches to solutions. While some students do feel that their values have shifted as a result of engineering education, others are less convinced that this is a result of their studies. While students such as Phillip (GER) quoted above, suggest that there are courses that enlighten and perhaps inspire students to be agents of sustainable development through their professional work, other students suggest that this remains a personal choice. As Anna (GER) states:

> I think it is in some way a personality thing, but I do think that, I mean it's often said that this is ecologically better this way, or these are the consequences for the environment – that is said in our studies. And maybe it gets embedded in your mind that way, but it also depends on the person, I'm sure there are other people who don't live their lives according to sustainability.

Similarly, Lisa (GER) says that learning from subjects that are related to sustainable development prompts students to think about the role of engineers in development more carefully, but her response also suggests this may be the limit of the effect of such courses:

> I think it does result in us reflecting a bit more on the topic, but there are people who think well, maybe – not that it's complete nonsense – but rather see it differently, so it's not every engineer who is then brought up to be sustainable.

Likewise, Markus (GER) attributes much of his knowledge on sustainable development to courses offered in his engineering programme in the university:

> Yeah, like in this general studies I mentioned before, I think there were two subjects which were about sustainability and renewable energy and everything like that, so we learn a lot.

While some students were keen to say their engineering studies had influenced some of their values, other students ask if such changes are due to their education or due to other factors. The passage below, which is an excerpt from a German focus group, illustrates this debate well:

KURT: When I started studying, I thought when I finish my studies I will buy the biggest car, but now it [has] changed, so now I think a small useful car is better.

RUPERT: But I don't know if it has anything to do with your studies, maybe it's just a change of your life that you think differently about it, maybe. Maybe it's not because of the engineering part.

MARKUS: Yeah, I must say I think during our studies we learn a lot of how things work and as soon as you think about how things work you think about 'what does it mean to me?', and I think that starts the progress to think about sustainability, yeah so I would agree, yeah.

Rupert's (GER) comment challenges the notion that engineering curricula shape students' values surrounding issues related to sustainable development. Similar doubt is apparent in responses from students who feel that sustainability principles are underpinned by values that cannot necessarily be taught explicitly through higher education. Through the eyes of some students, the media and the state or politics were often referred to as the main drivers of a sustainability agenda. Arnolds' (GER) words imply this, where he says that concern for sustainability is:

> (…) maybe personal and influenced by the media and politics – what's good and what's not good.

Arnold's (GER) statement implies that the media and politics are co-teachers of sustainable development and that this ultimately shapes an individual's affinity for, or indifference towards, sustainability. It is clear that students supplement what they learn about sustainable development through their studies, with messages portrayed in the media. What is interesting to note about students' views on these conduits of knowledge about sustainable development is that information from both the university and the media is often perceived as ambiguous. It is not clear whether the ambiguity stems from the fact that the term itself is contested and can be used in different ways, or whether it is because there are mixed messages about what sustainable development is.

What is perhaps most important to note is that students are engaging in the process of questioning the way things work and what that means for them. This signals that some students are engaging with issues of sustainability in personal ways. This is important because it shows that students are exposed to knowledge about sustainable development in a way that does not result in only one way of understanding sustainability. It also signals the potential for engineering education to provide students with opportunities to deepen their commitment to sustainability in ways that they have reason to value. Nevertheless, most students argue that they do not learn the 'how' of sustainable development or sustainable engineering. Anna's (GER) words indicate this, and suggest that the onus is on the individual to take initiative and inform themselves on what sustainable development looks like and how to implement it:

> I also think (…) it's not being communicated properly [through media] because we're also not told: 'you should save on heating' they say: 'coal should be used less'. So, actually, I think in our studies it's also not well communicated, just the theory what sustainability is [is taught]. But how sustainability can be implemented, I find is not really taught in the studies. That is more of a personal interest thing I would say.

Likewise, Tendayi's (ZIM) response suggests that the bulk of what he knows about sustainable development comes more from his general personal interest and observation, rather than as a result of a taking a course with sustainability content. He says that he learns about sustainable development:

> through general awareness, reading and also some journals and people speaking at maybe conferences (…) so my knowledge is based on general awareness, getting to hear around, and also reading.

Similarly, when talking about the value of elective courses, some students think that they do not learn much 'know-how' from courses geared at developing soft skills. Instead, they feel they learn a combination of soft skills from project work. Communication skills are often highlighted as an outcome of project work:

MAYITA: We go through a lot of group work, we communicate all the time with each other, with the class like I can meet like ten different people in one day because I have a project.
VALERIE: And everything you do you need a presentation really.
THANDI: Yeah, everything is group work, everything is a presentation – these communication courses actually don't help that much.

In the same focus group from the UCT, students debate the value of elective humanities courses. While Mayita (ZIM) sees the value in courses such as sociology and anthropology for the research she is conducting for her master's, other students argue that the range of elective courses is too broad, or that they cannot find a course that they feel has added value to their engineering knowledge:

MAYITA: I did Anthropology, Sociology and Mandarin as my electives and I've seen that I've used a lot of knowledge from Anthropology and Sociology, for the study I'm doing at the moment, and just looking at that connect between being an engineer and using the social aspects to design technology

– and I don't see that a lot in engineering, particularly in chemical engineering education, so maybe they need to advise better in terms of the soft skills you should be attaining, to solve problems holistically.

VALERIE: Or maybe they should like in the programme incorporate those, because if they give you two electives, that could literally be anything. People end up taking statistics, or whatever is easiest. Things that are easy or don't develop your soft skills to begin with.

THANDI: Or what's available between 12:00 and 14:00 – the easiest one that fits into that period.

MANDY: Because you don't have time to do other subjects that aren't gonna bring you anything – it's like a whole bunch of excess knowledge that's never meant anything in my life.

To summarize, findings suggest that 'sustainable development' courses are conducive to building appropriate propositional engineering knowledge ('know that') but, appear to do little for students' procedural knowledge ('know-how').

It is clear that students appreciate the knowledge they gain from courses offered by the university that address sustainable development problems. However, some students questioned the extent to which their values were being shaped by this knowledge. The fact that students engage in the process of questioning 'the way things work' and how best to make sense of sustainable development indicates personal ways of engaging with issues of sustainability. This suggests that engineering education generally, or sustainable development courses specifically, may implicitly shape students' values towards sustainability. It is also clear that the engineering curriculum is not the only source of knowledge that students draw from to formulate understandings of sustainable development. Sustainability courses seem to provide a foundation upon which other sources of information (particularly from the media) are interpreted, and made sense of in order to complement students' comprehension on the topic of sustainable development.

It appears that engineering curricula are effective in contributing to students' intellectual or cognitive understanding of sustainable development, but courses on sustainable development on their own have limited reach in shaping students' values. However, the purpose of ESD is to allow students the opportunity to be better informed about various aspects of development, and encourage them to re-evaluate their role and responsibilities in the development process (UNESCO, 2014). Particularly in engineering education, ESD also challenges students to re-evaluate their understanding of broader social issues and their capacity to construct appropriate solutions for human needs (Cruickshank & Fenner, 2007). Therefore, if engineering students' understanding of sustainable development is limited to intellectual comprehension and their values are not meaningfully influenced by their studies, engineering education falls short of enhancing students' opportunities to function as agents of sustainable development.

It thus also appears that, following advocates of ESD, university leaders, faculties and students should introduce sustainable development into all elements of engineering education to safeguard sustainable development as its golden thread. This requires universities to explore how academic courses interact with other knowledge sources and individuals' personal experiences in the formation of sustainable development values. This implies that measures taken by engineering education institutions to teach sustainable development should focus on both the content of courses that are designed for this purpose, and who is teaching this knowledge. Engineering educators clearly have a responsibility to help instil values associated with sustainable development in their students, regardless of the course they teach.

The next section explores this aspect further and considers the values that underpin engineering lecturers' understandings of sustainable development and how they perceive its teaching.

Teaching 'sustainable development' as a disputed concept

The discussion in this section shows how some lecturers perceive complex interactions between societal forces that fuel their uncertainty of the meaning of 'sustainability' and therefore 'sustainable development', which creates difficulty in teaching the concept as a fixed ideal.

In one of her responses Professor Schwartz (GER) suggests there is a lack of consensus about the meaning of sustainability, implying it is almost impossible to define it because our moral judgements of what is sustainable changes depending on a number of complex variables. The questions Professor Schwarz poses are good examples of the kind of questions that engineering students should be grappling with in order to exercise critical thinking towards notions of sustainable development. She asks:

> What is sustainability? What does that mean? Does that mean that we do not use any energy anymore to keep the planet stable? Do we all want that? Does that mean that we do not produce any garbage anymore? (...). The question 'what is sustainability?' is not really answered right now.

She goes on to give some examples of what could be considered as sustainable practices in agriculture, manufacturing and design; in each case highlighting the difficulty in labelling something as a sustainable process. She uses the example that arable land is being used for growing crops that are used in bio fuel, instead of growing crops for human consumption, citing this as a good debate for thinking about the meaning of sustainability. She argues:

> We are using bio energy, and killing places where food could grow – the question is very difficult to answer, 'what is sustainability?'

Professor Schwarz's responses show that she believes sustainable development is a multifaceted and fluid concept. This implies that she would rather teach her students to think critically about approaches to sustainable solutions than promote the idea that one particular solution is necessarily more sustainable or beneficial to society than another.

On the other hand, in defining sustainability or teaching what sustainable development means, Professor Smith (SA) explains how chemical engineering might lend itself well to exploring ways in which the environmental dimension of sustainability can be addressed by teaching aspects of cleaner production or waste management systems. She does however note that it is very difficult to engage students deeply with the broader dimension of sustainable development that is concerned with societal issues:

> (...) at the post graduate level they use life cycle analysis and so on, so very much a chemical/process engineering kind of take on the notion of cleaner production. So we're not debating so much the issue of like social inequity which is a part of the broader definition. Given [that] the kind of discipline here (chemical engineering) is less an area for serious engagement in that sort of thing, you know as compared to your course in sociology.

Concern for neglect of the social dimension of sustainable development in engineering education is shared by Professor Jones (SA), who speaks against the shallow use of the term 'sustainability' implying this is done inappropriately and takes away from the impact of the word:

> I think the term sustainability is used too loosely and applied too often to think that just basically means commercial sustainability. And in the university specifically in a setting in South Africa tends very strongly towards the commercial sustainability aspect of it. In engineering, in chemical engineering, I don't want to speak for the whole university – and that is by virtue of the fact that the interested industry, the chemical process industry influences very strongly what is going on in chemical engineering, by research contracts that they give, by stipends that they give to the students and also by being on the advisory boards of the committees that are set up.

Professor Jones' (SA) concerns allude to the idea that there are structural constraints imposed on university departments because of the financial ties certain institutions may have with companies that contribute to funding the university. He argues that such situations allow industry to dictate universities' commitment to sustainable development, or at least influence universities' stance on the issue of sustainability. It is interesting to note that concerns about academic freedom and autonomy are not related only to the issue of funding from industry, but also to the impact that state funding has on the governance of universities.

Like the answers on how to teach transversal skills (discussed in Chapter 5), many responses from lecturers pointed to the curriculum for answers on how to teach 'sustainable development'. For example, Professor Bremer (GER) refers to courses that can prompt students to think about the social, environmental and economic aspects of engineering outcomes, saying that they go a long way to getting students thinking about issues surrounding the concept of sustainability. He also suggests that there is a level of what Connor et al. (2014) refer to as 'disciplinary egocentrism' amongst engineering educators, which can be defined as a lack of student or staff readiness to engage in multidisciplinary knowledge or apply alternative teaching and learning approaches to engineering. Professor Bremer (GER) explains:

> The course 'Technical Assessment' stems from a critical stance towards the consequences of technology. As such, this is a course which lends itself to that excellently. (...) We need lecturers, and as such, also professors who say we want to deal with questions and problems of technology, and consequences on society, consequences on the environment and so forth – unfortunately there are too many hard liners amongst us engineering professors who say we don't need that, I think that's a catastrophic mistake.

Professor Kleid (GER), however, argues that teaching sustainability through elective courses is inadequate, explaining that issues to do with sustainable development have to be integrated throughout engineering curricula, and in the curriculum of other education programmes, to explore what the principle of sustainability might look like when applied in different disciplines:

> One then has to ask what is the purpose of an exclusive course? because it can't be about telling people that they can decide to be either pro or anti sustainability – that's total rubbish (...) these issues belong in the regular curriculum, in the course content, not as here an extra course, there an extra course, because then you have a lot of extra courses, and in the end you don't know what it's about anymore (...) we have to communicate what influences what, for example the topic sustainability in this field, in that field, [and so on] ... that belongs in the message.

On the other hand, Professor Hunter (SA) posits that there is enough awareness of sustainable development challenges created through the media, which reduces the pressure on engineering programmes to do this for students. Instead, he argues that the bigger challenge lies in creating more awareness of these complex issues amongst older engineering educators. His response also indicates his reflection on the fact that sustainability issues in the curriculum interact with sustainability debates in the public domain. As mentioned previously, there should be more attention focused on the nature of this interaction if we are to understand how values associated with sustainable development are best formulated:

> I think all over the world today in engineering education – you don't need to tell young people that they have got to look after the environment. They see it in the movies, they read it in the newspaper; the world is full of the story of environmental impacts and the green economy and so on. And in fact my

view is that the older generation such as myself need to play catch up because when we started engineering we didn't worry about that.

Similarly, Professor Jones (SA) is of the opinion that engineering students come to the university already having the necessary awareness and values in place, arguing that although specific ethical values may be difficult to instil through teaching technical courses, it is something towards which universities should strive. He explains that in his experience students come to the university and enrol in engineering programmes with bold intentions of helping to 'save the world' through sustainable engineering outcomes, saying that such ambitions are:

(…) kind of simplistic [naïve] – but the value is there, you now just have to build that value and bring more sophisticated understanding that we're not 'saving the planet', that will take care of itself, we're saving humanity, that's more of the challenge here. So you can take that good intent all the way through your technical work all the way into detail all the way out of detail back to the big picture.

By contrast, Professor Marco (GER) argues that this type of knowledge can be learned later in life, and that universities should maintain their focus on imparting technical skills, because it is the only space in which students can perfect foundational engineering knowledge:

However still the vast majority of what the university provides is fundamental science and technical knowledge because otherwise – where do you get that? It is in my opinion easier to acquire the skills required to work in sustainable, or human development engineering later in your career rather than acquire the technical knowledge in your later career, this is exceedingly difficult.

On the other hand, Professor Kleid (GER) speaks of the importance of interdisciplinary knowledge, explaining that he is a proponent of such approaches to engineering education:

I myself, have, here in Bremen, before I got my professorship, I was a planner of the study programme Industrial Engineering; and as a result I am a strong believer of interdisciplinary knowledge, which engineers need. So I do not represent one who looks exclusively at engineering sciences, I look very much at the intersections, and I regard it important that we educate people who are capable of on the one side, to develop technology and at the same time to understand the consequences of technology, and who are also capable of communicating technology.

Correspondingly, Professor Schwartz (GER) emphasizes the need for engineering students to be cognisant of the fact that on the one hand technological advancements in themselves are not necessarily pro human well-being or sustainable development. On the other hand, she also teaches her students that one cannot look at technology as a bad thing per se. She also argues that the state and society are stakeholders who should be making decisions on some fundamental questions about the pursuit of development through technology. She says:

> When people say 'technology is bad' I say okay. How is your life today? What is your medical supply? What is your dentist doing? It's engineering. Yeah? Why do we grow so old? How come so many children survive the first three months even those with heart diseases. What do you think are the machines that keep them alive during the operation?

Professor Schwartz (GER) poses these questions to illustrate the good that can and does come from technological advancements that result from engineering and to indicate the tensions that arise from this. At the same time, these words counter popular arguments against technologies that do little to improve human lives in just ways. Her words also serve as a reminder that technological advancement is not necessarily synonymous with development.

In the quote[1] below, she explains her understanding of the role of engineers in society using an analogy on different levels of participation for a particular cause, arguing that the engineer's role is to be an active agent of positive change in society:

> And when I tried to explain this I say we have different roles in society, there are people who climb on the trees to say save the trees, and that's one role. And the engineer can say what can I invent that I do not need them [trees] anymore for my product? So I wanted to be the one who thinks about the better solution, the best solution instead of just saying I'm against it. Of course it's important that people say I'm against [something] but that's not enough. That's just the beginning. It doesn't help us to be against everything. We've got to be for something. So the question is what is it for? And that's from my point of view the engineering subject. To be 'for' something.

To summarize, while some lecturers seem confident that the media or engineering curriculum adequately addresses sustainable development concerns, other lecturers call for more interdisciplinary engagement with the subject and challenge themselves to prompt students to think critically about the meaning of sustainability. This difference in the views of lecturers is important, because it shows that engineering educators have different value sets that underlie their conception of teaching and of sustainable development. It is apparent that teaching sustainable development comes with the challenge that the concept itself is multifaceted and fluid, making it a difficult subject to teach across engineering disciplines.

A study that offers empirical evidence on the effects of teaching sustainability as an elective course shows that most engineering students, after taking a course on sustainable development, focus on the technological aspects of environmental sustainability and neglect the social/institutional aspects (Segalás, Ferrer-Balas & Mulder, 2010). This hypothesis suggests that addressing sustainable development through the curriculum alone may result in students developing narrow understandings of the concept. This conclusion supports findings by de la Harpe and Thomas (2009) that indicate that there is no single approach or formula for implementing ESD curriculum change that has been found to be effective, and bringing about such change is challenging. However, if students' engineering knowledge is combined with non-technical skills such as open-mindedness, critical thinking, effective communication and collaboration skills, they are arguably in a better position to make appropriate judgements about sustainable development.

Therefore, rather than gearing efforts towards teaching fixed ideas about sustainable development, more attention should be focused on making sure that students are able to engage with ideas about sustainability critically and personally.

The findings therefore also suggest that more attention should be focused on exploring engineering pedagogies in relation to sustainable development. In particular, the values that frame lecturers' understandings of sustainable development may have an important influence in shaping students' perceptions of the concept. For these reasons, it is important for universities to provide opportunities for engineering educators to develop values that are aligned with social justice goals. An example of such a value is public-good engineering.

Students' understandings of sustainable development

In the focus group discussions with students, the intention of questions surrounding sustainable development was to establish the various ways in which students understand the concept and how they articulate their understanding. Also explored in these parts of the discussions was how much of their knowledge on sustainable development students thought could be attributed to their studies, as well as their views on their perceived capacity to function as agents of sustainable human development once they were practising engineers.

When asked what came to mind when they heard the term 'sustainable development' or 'sustainability', responses such as 'the environment', 'I think about the future' and 'managing the resources' were very common across both groups of students. Even more common were utterances that were almost identical to the WCED's definition of sustainable development, i.e. 'development that meets the needs of the present, without compromising the ability of future generations to meet their own needs' (WCED, 1987:43). For example, Anna (GER) states that:

> Sustainability means I only use resources in a way that there are enough for other generations to come (...) that resources are used in a way that future generations can also use them in the same way that we do.

Likewise, Rupert (GER) explains his understanding of the notion of sustainable development with the words:

> It's like you give the next generation the chance to live a life like we do – same chances, same resources.

At times, the answers of the students on the question of defining sustainability were nuanced. Some students were even reluctant to say that sustainability meant anything in particular.

Vimbai's (ZIM) words also indicate that discussions about sustainability have been integrated into the curriculum to some extent. She says:

> It's been an ongoing discussion since first year – it keeps changing. The definition keeps changing.

This also indicates that sustainable development is a topic that is being well covered in the curriculum. On the other hand, Mayita (ZIM) explains that sustainability:

> Is a holistic approach to understanding what the need is, and when you bring in a solution that solution should be self-reliant in some form, from a social end, from an environmental end, [and] from a technology end. That's what I view as sustainability.

Students' responses also show that they are aware of the difference between how sustainable development is defined and how it is implemented. This indicates a distinction between students' perception of the concept on an intellectual level, and what the implications of this ideal are in engineering practice. For example, when Valerie (ZIM) responds to the above quote she comments that Mayita's (ZIM) understanding is based on a 'text book' definition, to which Mayita responds:

> Pretty much – but the dictionary definition compared to what actually happens in reality is completely different. So I'm still trying to figure it out.

Furthermore, the students share the rather bleak outlook that engineering efforts and innovations will always prioritize economic profit above the other two pillars of sustainable development. Similar to some lecturers' views on the glib use of the term, students from UCT in particular talk about how sustainable development is used as a marketing gimmick in industry:

THANDI: It's just thrown around: green! sustainable!
VALERIE: And then you can just mark the price up because you have something that is 'green' or 'organic' (...) they'll capitalize on anything.
MAYITA: It always goes back to money.

Based on these views, it is clear that engineering students are being made aware of, and taught about various aspects of sustainability and sustainable development through their study programmes. The students showed that they grasp the concept of sustainable development with references to commonly used definitions in sustainability discourses. The most important observation across the data is that the discussions on this particular topic were almost constantly in the form of a debate, as opposed to a discussion characterized by consensus. These debates showed that the students regard sustainable development as an ever-changing concept, although they could articulate popular definitions of the term very well. The debates also suggest that the concept is valued by the students – at least enough to be the basis for debate and discussion. Also, students have a keen awareness of the ways in which the three pillars of sustainable development (the economy, the environment and society) 'compete' against each other, although this should not be the case. Ideally, the longevity of all pillars ought to be safeguarded. The students' views clearly indicate their belief that the economic dimension of sustainability is over prioritized at the expense of the other dimensions.

In the following section, students' suggestions on what engineers can do to address this problem are outlined and their perceptions on the role of engineers as agents of sustainable development are provided. Again, discussions on this topic mostly took the form of debates across both groups of students, indicating its complexity.

Students' perceptions of engineers as agents of sustainable development

Students' views on their roles in society as future engineers suggest that they are sceptical about their effective power to function as agents of sustainable development. There is often concern expressed about the limitations imposed on engineers by industrial and economic constraints, which students fear will hinder their ability to reach the ideals of sustainable development. For example, Markus (GER) states:

> We haven't been in industry and I think there – it's different there, because it's much more about money than about your idealistic thinking.

On the other hand, Kurt (GER) believes that engineers' knowledge and skills gives them effective power to influence decision makers in industry in ways that can gear more efforts towards sustainable development. He also argues that this is more likely to be the case if more engineers end up in managerial positions within the corporate sphere:

> Because you have a technical background and you can explain and see the possibilities, and if you talk to the decision maker then you can still influence whatever is planned. And I think in the industry, even like the powerful people sometimes are engineers.

But Lisa (GER) has apprehensions about limitations imposed on engineers to exercise their agency in large corporations. She argues that it is easier for engineers to advance sustainable development values in small to medium-sized enterprises or companies that explicitly focus on environmental sustainability:

> I would rather work in a small to medium-sized company where you can still actually influence something, and where it's about making people's lives easier through sustainable development and so on but also to unburden the environment so like, maybe renewable energies, maybe electric cars or that kind of thing.

Kurt (GER) also sees this issue in the same fashion but emphasizes that the problem lies in too many decisions related to sustainable development having a political dimension. His words describe engineers as pioneers of change, where the mandate of that change is predetermined by the state:

> I think a lot of it is more from the politics but the engineers are the people who – like if politics says there is a power plant and we have to reduce the CO_2 – then the engineer has to think about how to do it. So the engineers are the people who are trying to reach what politics decided before.

Kurt's response reflects an 'engineer-as-employee model', which is based on the assumption that organizational and market incentives will adequately guide engineering towards outcomes that serve the public good (Nieusma & Blue, 2012). This view assumes that the economy and the state will do a good job of filtering out projects that ought not to be undertaken and that anything that makes it through the filter is most likely good for society (Nieusma & Blue, 2012). According to this model, the key role of the engineer is to make available (as instructed) one's technical knowledge, deferring decision making on their part, as it is seen as the responsibility of the organization to ultimately make decisions that are aptly guided by rational economic and political logics (Nieusma & Blue, 2012).

In this approach, engineers use existing organizational logics rather than providing a distinct logic of their own, and adhere to chain-of-command decision-making structures that direct and constrain the input provided by individual engineers (Nieusma & Blue, 2012). Nieusma and Blue ask (2012: 57): 'Does engineering best serve the public interest when engineers work merely as employees in organizations (directed as they are primarily by financial and/or political logics) or when engineers exercise professional autonomy?'

That engineers fit in so well into this model, suggests a reciprocal relationship between the training of engineers and command-and-control problem solving (Nieusma & Blue, 2012). This arrangement increases the effective power of engineers by structuring and constraining their roles, but, at the same time diminishes their political will (Nieusma & Blue, 2012).

Arnold's (GER) opinion supports this notion, and his views allude to the fact that *homo economicus* principles are over emphasized in industry. He argues that this is the reason engineers do not have the voice they should. On the other hand, it also reflects minimal political will. He says:

> I mean you would have to convince the people who earn a lot of money with their company, and if that income is decreased it's really hard to convince someone to do research into renewable energies and stuff like that, and I think often, for example, I think they [politicians] don't even know what is the potential of engineers' techniques, what is possible, what is not; and so I think there is an influence, but as I said before as long as society and politics don't want to, like, change the way we live, it won't really be possible.

Again, the intricacy of various aspects involved in determining who gets to decide on the pursuit of sustainable development agendas is highlighted.

Below, Rupert (GER) explains the cyclic result of engineers being 'fixers' of what industry identifies as problems, asserting that the very efforts engineers in the past have geared towards development have inadvertently contributed to current challenges:

> I mean many problems we are facing today are at least influenced by engineers, I mean maybe they didn't know better, maybe they were not as open-minded as we are now, but I mean carbon emissions [are] often done by industries and industries are done by engineers. So sometimes I think we have to solve problems other engineers initiated before.

This statement from Rupert sparked a debate amongst the students concerning accountability for creating technologies, processes and products that have in the long run not benefited humanity in a just way:

MARKUS: Yeah, I would say it's more the company itself not the engineer, I don't know ...
RUPERT: Yeah maybe it wasn't the intention but ...
MARKUS: Yeah, well, I don't know ...
ARNOLD: But normally engineers are not the people who make the decisions ...

The perception that 'engineers are not the people who make the decisions' is echoed by most students. Vimbai (ZIM) explains:

> I think the power is really not in our hands because it all boils down to the economic aspects of like, if the company says 'we have a budget of this much' you have to work within that budget or else – I guess you lose your job.

Vimbai's statement reflects some fears about the perceived potential consequences of not conforming to company demands. However, engineers are not simply employees whose only social responsibility is to obey hierarchy. In extreme cases, blowing the whistle and taking the risk of bypassing their obligation of loyalty towards their employers may be necessary (Didier, 2010), while in other situations, exercising agency for positive change will require engineers to contribute to improving the structures in which they act in order to turn them into fairer and more responsible institutions (Didier, 2010). This point of view fits well with a definition of ethics as 'an aim of the good life with and for others in just institutions' (Didier, 2010: 186).

Unlike Vimbai (ZIM) Mufaro's (ZIM) opinion alludes to the notion that engineers remain a powerful professional group in contributing to human well-being, sustainable development and social justice. She argues that engineers have the responsibility to help strike a balance between all three pillars of sustainable development (economy, environment, society):

> I think we have the power in our hands to determine the outcome of every process – so whenever we're going to design something we can still design something that has like a lot of economic benefit but also has advantages to the society because in the end it's [not good] for us to have all this benefit for the elite and then ignore the rest of the people (…)

On the other hand, Mayita (ZIM) questions the ability of engineers to help 'strike a balance' between the three pillars of sustainable development, again expressing concern about the voices of engineers not being heard:

> But the question is: how effective are you as an individual in that company if you want to have a say in something – do you have a voice?

Valerie (SA) responds to this question by asking another question, which suggests that it is a fundamental task for engineers to come up with solutions within conditions that are characterized by constraints:

> Isn't that the challenge for an engineer? To come up with creative solutions in a space where you are limited?

Most focus group participants respond by suggesting that the spaces that exist for graduate engineers in industry are not wide enough to allow meaningful engagement with corporate heads or application of their agency. Valerie (ZIM) argues that:

> If you're a graduate process engineer at Sasol you will do what they are doing at Sasol (…) like you would have a good idea to say reduce emissions by this amount but they'd rather get a management consultancy firm to transfer the accountability and get them to do the ground work, so the question is: how much say do you have as an engineer within that company to try and change [things] you know? I don't think we have that much of leverage.

Some students argue that engineers can make incremental changes in the way that they carry out their day-to-day work activities, but the overriding sentiment of students' views is summarized well in the words of Kopano (SA), who says:

> In most cases financial wise you can try and improve the process in terms of emissions and all that but in most cases if it's financially better off and within the regulations of the government, that's [all that matters].

The profitability of sustainable engineering ideas formulated to take on challenges related to reducing carbon dioxide emissions is often cited as an example of the financial constraints within which engineers have to work. For example, Tendayi (ZIM) says:

> Engineers face resistance especially when it comes to finances when like (…) there's a project and you see that this project is going the wrong way, and you know that it should be going [another] way, there's always that friction or resistance to actually implement the decisions that engineers would have made.

Tendayi's words suggest that it is the responsibility of engineers to position themselves in the corporate spaces that allow them to make decisions that are more influential. He argues that engineers need:

> [to] grow in terms of learning how to get ourselves into leadership positions where we can actually be the people making the big decisions for ourselves. Because mostly you'll find the people who are making the decisions will be like from other fields like accountancy, they're the ones who are managing directors of the companies so they understand the financial flows and statements and then the engineer now would face resistance from such a counterpart in industry. So the best way would be for engineers to also learn to position themselves into very influential leadership positions so that whatever decision needs to be made, whenever a project is to be implemented it can easily be done, because we will be talking of someone who understands better what is supposed to happen.

Literature suggests that engineers are generally regarded highly in public opinion surveys for their honesty, integrity, and diligence (Kulacki, 1999). Also, according to Boni, McDonald and Peris (2012), engineers have come to regard themselves as appropriate leaders of society who can solve social problems using science and logic as agents of industrial development, while also showing qualities of being impartial, rational and responsible for ensuring positive technological change. Moreover engineers perceive themselves as having better aptitude to make decisions than lay people, and having a professional identity and status that qualifies them to exercise power in organizations through their capacity as technical problem solvers (Trevelyan, 2014). However, engineers are sometimes avoided in legislative processes and public affairs because of a tendency to approach subjective matters from a technical angle, where rigorous methods of objective analysis are used to make recommendations and decisions (Kulacki, 1999). This means that engineers usually have to rely on other people to deliver the results of their work (Trevelyan, 2014).

This is problematic because simply finding a solution to a technical problem may not provide any value in itself; the value is only created once the technical solution is applied to result in improving human capabilities (Trevelyan, 2014). Therefore, when engineers take leadership positions in industry, they should have the capacity to balance their engineering knowledge with a keen awareness of human and social dynamics.

A capabilities-inspired, empirically informed framework for public-good engineering education

As indicated in Chapter 1, literature that illustrates the contribution of the capability approach in provoking critical reflection on conceptions of sustainable development is growing (see for example: Crabtree, 2013; Lessmann & Rauschmayer, 2013; Pelenc, Lompo, Ballet & Dubois, 2013). However, as Crabtree (2013) warns, we should not blindly apply the capability approach as a lens through which sustainable development should be seen. There should also be a focus on examining the limits of our freedoms because our beings and doings have consequences that need to be accounted for, and hence need to be part of the conceptual evaluative space of our judgements on sustainable development (Crabtree, 2013).

Crabtree (2013) defines and defends a concept of sustainable development as 'a process of expanding the real freedoms that people value that are in accordance with principles that cannot be reasonably rejected by others' (Crabtree, 2013: 41). By so doing, he draws in issues of morality and ethics to interrogate how individuals evaluate their actions as right or wrong, in relation to how they may affect other people. Crabtree (2013) argues that it is important to take this into account because the moral choices that we can make, and we can be blamed for, are limited by the knowledge we have. For example, carrying out an act of pollution, when there is an option to do otherwise, while being aware of the negative consequences that will be suffered by others, is morally wrong. Thus conceived, one could similarly judge engineering decisions as morally wrong if they are carried out with disregard for poor and marginalized communities.

Although different students gave diverse accounts of their understanding of sustainable development, there is a clear sense across most responses that they value the concept. There are also clear indications that the students are critically reflective, and that they have developed 'dialogic habits of mind' (Wood & Deprez, 2013). However, their responses do not immediately indicate that poverty reduction is valued. This does not necessarily mean that the students are indifferent to the existence of poverty, nor does it necessarily suggest that they have no reason to value reducing it. It does however show that their understanding of sustainable development does not automatically trigger thoughts of concern for communities living in poverty. Yet it should.

To reiterate a capabilities-inspired description of the goals of engineering education: engineering education should enhance the professional capabilities and functionings of engineering graduates, provide them with meaningful opportunities to develop, demonstrate and deepen their commitment to the cause of poverty eradication, and enhance their ability to exercise agency to promote sustainable human development in society. Thus conceived, students' understandings of sustainable development indicate that the reach of engineering education in teaching for sustainable human development is limited.

This leads to a number of important questions regarding engineering education in universities. First, with regard to the lives people can actually live, what opportunity does each student have to explore connections between engineering curricular topics and contemporary inequities involving power, privilege and material resources? Second, with regard to 'development' what effective opportunity does each student have:

- To unearth and interrogate assumptions about development?
- To engage in critical reflection and dialogue on competing notions of human progress?
- To explore power relations and their impact on development?

Third, with regard to reasoned values, do students have effective opportunities:

- To interrogate embedded economic and political values in the engineering curriculum?
- To reflect critically on the relationship between learning, values and engineering functionings?

If these opportunities are not effectively available to each engineering student, then the potential for universities to develop students' capacities for public-good engineering is restricted. Figure 6.1 illustrates the opposite situation: what engineering education can look like, and what it can achieve for engineering graduates and what it can do for society when it is well aligned with and seeks to promote sustainable human development.

More specifically, the goals of engineering education (based on findings from lecturer interviews), valued engineering functionings (based on findings from student focus groups), and dimensions of public-good engineering (based on employer interviews) are juxtaposed. The potential links between the various dimensions are suggested by the arrows drawn between and across the three columns. Based on these links, it can be seen that one goal of engineering education (i.e. enhancing students' sense of determination to pursue valued functionings and determine their roles in society) might have more significance for public-good engineering than others do, because it is essential to, and directly linked with, all four public-good engineering functionings (and hence capabilities).

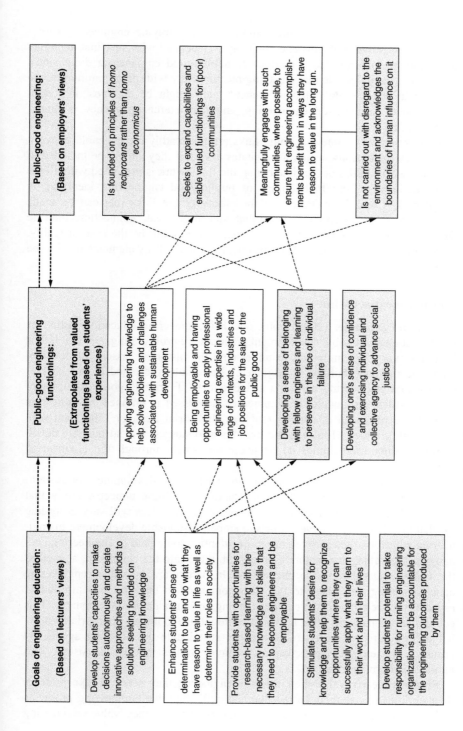

Figure 6.1 A capabilities-inspired, empirically informed framework for public-good engineering education.

It can also be seen that a functioning, such as applying engineering knowledge to help solve problems and challenges associated with sustainable human development, is central to a number of public-good engineering dimensions. Similarly, it is noticeable that engaging meaningfully with poor communities to ensure that engineering outcomes benefit them might be the most important dimension of public-good engineering, and that exercising agency is fundamental to this.

It is important to note that some links are not readily recognizable between the various dimensions, which necessitates asking if they should be included in the framework at all. For the time being, the framework is presented with all the goals, dimensions and functionings of public-good engineering identified in Chapters 3, 4 and 5, regardless of the clarity of the links that can be made between them. Although it may seem that unclear or 'weak' connections indicate the irrelevance of a goal, functioning, etc., this may not be the case in reality. Therefore, until the framework is empirically tested, all its elements need to be considered.

Summative discussion

Lucena and Schneider (2008) point out that engineering education initiatives incorporating sustainable development practices are proliferating, and that it thus becomes ever more important to understand the historical lessons of development and the contributions of engineers. The results presented in this chapter suggest that engineering curricula at UB and UCT provide good examples of ways in which sustainable development is addressed in engineering education through the provision of courses (such as 'Industrial Ecology') that deal with sustainability issues. However, the findings also suggest that sustainable development cannot (nor should it) be addressed solely through the engineering curriculum.

The lecturers' perspectives on teaching sustainable development or sustainability principles, and students' understandings of these concepts imply that engineers' judgements of sustainable engineering practices will vary according to what they know or believe. Efforts to embed sustainable development in engineering education therefore require more attention to be paid to engineering pedagogies, the values that lecturers bring with them into the classroom, as well as the values underpinning the curriculum. In particular, the values engineering educators bring with them to the classroom need to be explored empirically; especially in relation to their understandings of sustainable development. This could uncover pathways that universities might use to impart appropriate knowledge for future engineers to function as sustainable development agents, by ensuring that engineering pedagogies convey values that are consistent with public-good professionalism.

Students clearly value their roles as engineers; they seem to take pride in their abilities to use their knowledge and skills to solve engineering problems and have the desire to effect positive change. That is, they value engineering functionings, or *being* engineers and *doing* engineering work.[2] In addition, students see engineers as important role players in helping to shape or even initiate positive change towards sustainable development. The general logic behind this view is that engineering knowledge is fundamental to any development process. Students also expressed doubts about the extent and reach of engineers' effective power as a professional group. This doubt is generally fuelled by the idea that engineers are not the ultimate decision makers in the corporate world, implying that engineers have limited voice and agency within industry, despite their pivotal knowledge that is used to advance 'development'. Students take the view that engineers' voices can best be heard within companies that explicitly address sustainable development challenges, or when engineers are in managerial positions in large companies. This shows that the students are able to recognize, discern and articulate some of the economic and material constraints to engineers' professional freedom and agency; particularly in relation to advancing sustainable development through professional functionings.

According to Didier (2010), the highly compartmentalized work situation of engineers and the labour division that characterizes the large corporations in which they work create a dilution of responsibilities and loss of orientation. This can result in an accepted 'blindness' for the actors involved (Didier, 2010). However, the work engineers do carries a moral obligation not to be ignorant, or worse indifferent, to the goals they are working to achieve (Didier, 2010). This is important because one cannot be held accountable for something about which one is ignorant (Didier, 2010). As discussed in the first chapter, engineers have an ex-ante responsibility to contribute to solving sustainability challenges in a manner that is just. Thus conceived, engineers should neither lose sight of their objectives, nor be indifferent to social justice concerns. Therefore, both students and lecturers must learn to analyse different elements of the ideologies underpinning engineering, contextualize these historically, and then identify them in their sites of engineering education and practice (Lucena, 2013). Only once these ideologies are recognizable will engineers begin to realize how taking them for granted diminishes their contribution to sustainable human development, and only then can they begin to wonder where and how else we can integrate it in engineering curricula, pedagogies and practice.

Notes

1 This quote is used previously in Chapter 4 under the discussion on developing an engineering identity. It is repeated here because of it is also a good example of the kind of questions one might ask when thinking about the instrumental value of engineering, particularly in relation to sustainable human development.
2 This finding corresponds with conclusions made by Case and Marshall (2016).

References

Boni, A., Fogues, A. & Walker, M. (2016). Higher education and the post 2015 agenda. A contribution from the human development approach. *Journal of Global Ethics*, *12*(1), 17–28.

Boni, A., McDonald, P. & Peris, J. (2012). Cultivating engineers' humanity: Fostering cosmopolitanism in a technical university. *International Journal of Educational Development, 32*(1), 179–186.

Case, J. M., & Marshall, D. (2016). Bringing together knowledge and capabilities: A case study of engineering graduates. *Higher Education, 71*(6): 819–833.

Connor, A. M., Karmokar, S., Whittington, C. & Walker, C. (2014). Full STEAM ahead: A manifesto for integrating arts pedagogics into STEM education. In *IEEE*. Wellington, New Zealand. Accessed 1 September 2017 from http://dx.doi.org/10.1109/TALE.2014.7062556.

Crabtree, A. (2013). Sustainable development: Does the capability approach have anything to offer? Outlining a legitimate freedom approach. *Journal of Human Development and Capabilities, 4*(1), 40–57.

Cruickshank, H. J., & Fenner, R. A. (2007). The evolving role of engineers: Towards sustainable development of the built environment. *Journal of International Development, 19*(1): 111–121. Accessed 1 September 2017 from https://doi.org/10.1002/jid.1352.

De la Harpe, B., & Thomas, I. (2009). Curriculum change in universities: Conditions that facilitate Education for Sustainable Development. *Journal of Education for Sustainable Development, 3*(1), 75–85.

Didier, C. (2010). Engineering ethics and anti-corruption. In *Engineering: Issues challenges and opportunities for development*. Paris: UNESCO.

Kulacki, F. A. (1999). Engineering, engineers and the public good. *William Mitchell Law Review, 25*(1), 157–179.

Lessmann, O., & Rauschmayer, F. (2013). Re-conceptualizing sustainable development on the basis of the capability approach: A model and its difficulties. *Journal of Human Development and Capabilities, 14*(1), 95–114.

Lucena, J. (ed.). (2013). *Engineering education for social justice: Critical explorations and opportunities* (Vol. 10). Dordrecht, Heidelberg, New York, London: Springer.

Lucena, J., & Schneider, J. (2008). Engineers, development, and engineering education: From national to sustainable community development. *European Journal of Engineering Education, 33*(3): 247–257.

Nieusma, D., & Blue, E. (2012). Engineering and war. *International Journal of Engineering, Social Justice, and Peace, 1*(1), 50–62.

Pelenc, J., Lompo, M., K., Ballet, J. & Dubois, J.-L. (2013). Sustainable human development and the capability approach: Integrating environment, responsibility and collective agency. *Journal of Human Development and Capabilities, 14*(1), 77–94.

Segalás, J., Ferrer-Balas, D. & Mulder, K. F. (2010). What do engineering students learn in sustainability courses? The effect of the pedagogical approach. *Journal of Cleaner Production, 18*, 275–284. Accessed 1 September 2017 from https://doi.org/10.1016/j.jclepro.2009.09.012.

Trevelyan, J. (2014). *The making of an expert engineer*. Netherlands: CRC Press.

UB. (2015). Modulhandbuch und Bescreibung der MSc. Produktionstechnik. Bremen: Master-Prüfungsausschuß Produktionstechnik/Studienzentrum Produktionstechnik. Accessed 30 September 2017 from www.fb4.uni-bremen.de/pdf/Produktionstechnik/Modulhandbuch_MA_PT_Teil_A.pdf and www.fb4.uni-bremen.de/pdf/Produktionstechnik/Modulhandbuch_MA_PT_Teil_B.pdf.

UCT. (2015). *Faculty of Engineering and the Built Environment* (Undergraduate Handbook). Cape Town: University of Cape Town.

UN. (2014). *Open Working Group proposal for sustainable development goals* (No. Sustainable Development Knowledge Platform). New York: United Nations. Accessed 1 September 2017 from https://sustainabledevelopment.un.org/focussdgs.html.

UNESCO. (2014). *Roadmap for implementing the Global Action Programme on Education for Sustainable Development*. Paris: United Nations Educational, Scientific and Cultural Organization.

WCED. (1987). *Our common future* (World Commission on Environment and Development). New York: Oxford University Press. Accessed 1 September 2017 from www.un-documents.net/ocf-02.htm.

Wood, D. R., & Deprez, L. S. (2013). Re-imagining possibilities for democratic education: Generative pedagogies in service to the capability approach. In *Professional education, capabilities and the public good: The role of universities in promoting human development*. New York: Routledge.

7 Being a public-good engineer and doing socially just engineering

This chapter describes what has happened to 15 of the 18 engineering students with whom focus group discussions were held in 2014, and whose perspectives inform Chapters 3 and 6. In particular, the chapter describes the professional progress made the young engineers since graduation. This provides empirical data that can tell us how well or to what extent they are able to function as public-good engineers or do socially just engineering. As such, the framework of public-good engineering provided in Chapter 2, is tested here by addressing the questions:

1 How robust is the list of public-good engineering capabilities developed theoretically and empirically in this book?
2 How robust is the framework for public-good engineering education developed proposed in this book?

The chapter begins with a brief description of the work, company and location of each participant, based on data gathered in 2017. Thereafter, the chapter focuses on five individuals whose cases lend themselves particularly well to demonstrating how becoming and being a public-good engineer are influenced by gender, race and socio-economic class.

- Anashe is a graduate engineer at an oil and gas extraction company in Johannesburg South Africa.
- Anesu works as a product development engineer at Axis House, Johannesburg, South Africa.
- Anna is an operations manager at nextbike GmbH, Bremen, Germany.
- Arnold is a PhD candidate and research assistant at UB, Germany.
- Kopano is a PhD candidate in chemical engineering at University of Queensland, Australia.
- Mandy is pursuing a PhD between the UCT, South Africa and Southampton University, UK. She also works as a research assistant at HySA Catalysis, Cape Town, South Africa.
- Mayita is a PhD candidate and research assistant at the Leibniz Institute for Functionalized Polymers, Dresden, Germany.

- Mufaro is employed as a water sector analyst at GreenCape, Cape Town, South Africa.
- Phillip is a PhD candidate and research assistant at UB, Germany.
- Rupert is also PhD candidate and research assistant at UB, Germany.
- Tendayi is a freelance engineer currently seeking employment in Harare, Zimbabwe.
- Thandi is employed as a proposal engineer at WEC Projects, Johannesburg, South Africa.
- Tinashe is a researcher in Stellenbosch, South Africa.
- Valerie is a production engineer at Unilever, Johannesburg, South Africa.
- Vimbai works as a management consultant and business analyst at EIU Canback, Johannesburg, South Africa.

The descriptions that follow focus particularly on Mandy, Mayita, Phillip, Mufaro and Tendayi. Each section can be read as a short story that gives us a sense of who they are, and the role engineering education has played in shaping their aspirations and career choices. More specifically, the section that follows describes where they are, what work they are doing, how they find the work, whether or not the work they do contributes to sustainable development and how they now understand the concept of development. Also described here are reflections on their educational journeys to becoming engineers, what being an engineer means to them and what they like best about their work.

Each short story is unique, varies in length and follows a different chronology. This is done for two reasons. First to present the data, as far as possible, the way each individual described their post-graduation circumstances. Second, each story emphasizes different aspects of the factors that influence being a public-good engineer and practising socially just engineering. Each story is concluded with a discussion of the lessons we might pull from it, drawing from literature to unpack the key messages that one might take, based on the analysis of the data. The stories are followed by a discussion on what, read together, they can tell us about the robustness of the framework for public-good engineering proposed in the previous chapter and the list of valued capabilities and functionings identified in Chapter 3.

'I get to do what I love and I don't have to sacrifice my earnings' *– Mandy*

Mandy is white, female and South African. She graduated from UCT with a master's degree in chemical engineering in 2016. She is currently pursuing a PhD between UCT, South Africa and Southampton University, United Kingdom. Her research is based on hydrogen fuel cells, which is a green technology for electricity production. This project is partially funded by the South African Department of Science and Technology, through the Hydrogen South Africa (HySA) project, which looks into fuel cells as a sustainable energy solution. She finds the research very interesting and enjoys it thoroughly, although she is surprised by the toll that doing the doctoral degree is taking on her:

> I didn't predict the mental and emotional struggles that come with doing [a] PhD.

Asked if her expectations had been met in terms of the work she is doing, she explains that she thought she would be doing much more practical work and that she never anticipated that she would end up doing research:

> I wasn't expecting to go into research after I finished my chemical engineering degree and post grad has been very different from what I was expecting it to be. There is a heavier emphasis on core sciences like chemistry and physics than I was expecting, it's a far cry from thinking you would end up with a hardhat on an oil rig one day.

Mandy describes the chemical engineering undergraduate degree at the UCT as 'very good' and she is happy with how it has prepared her for both postgraduate studies and research, and she sees her undergraduate degree as a fall back if she decides to transition into industry.

> My post grad degrees have exceeded my expectations, I've been very privileged to learn from leaders in my field of research and my work has progressed successfully because of it. Sustainable development is incredibly important to me, and I think with South Africa still developing its economy and infrastructure (for instance, the electricity grid) we have an incredible opportunity to mould that development to a more suitable future.

For Mandy, the best thing about her work is that she is actually able to do what she is passionate about and earn a good living from it:

> I get to do what I love and I don't have to sacrifice my earnings. I've always been thankful that my calling was not to become a painter or actress.

She is very happy with her choice of degrees, including postgraduate studies, and says she wouldn't change anything about her academic trajectory. She thinks that she should have voiced her need for help more than she did at the time:

> I suppose I would tell myself to ask lecturers and tutors for help more often than I did in my undergraduate degree.

Mandy volunteers at Habitat for Humanity at the UCT and she has also spent some time on the committee. Her understanding of development is:

Improving or creating a situation or physical structure which serves society for the better.

She has the following to say about her role as an engineer:

> I think my age and gender play a significant role in breaking the stereotype of what an engineer or scientist typically looks like. I suppose it's not just looks, it's also actions, I am a very feminine person and I think it's important to show younger women that they don't need to give up their femininity to be respected in science or as an engineer. As a white South African, the best I can do is try to uplift communities and advocate for affordable education and better living conditions for people living in poverty.

Mandy's story reminds us that it is important that research on engineering education finds ways to foreground and celebrate heterogeneous understandings of engineering and heterogeneous engineering identities (Faulkner, 2009). Faulkner (2009) provides two strong reasons for this. First, every aspect of engineering is heterogeneous; even the most apparently technical roles have social elements embedded inextricably within them. Second, foregrounding and celebrating more heterogeneous images of engineering can only serve to make the profession more inclusive (Faulkner, 2009, 2010).

According to Fuchs (1997), the history of engineering occupations shows that they have evolved exclusively on the basis of men's experiences. The dualism of rational/irrational and its relationship with masculinity and femininity has long functioned as a process of including men in and excluding women from the fields of technology and engineering (Holth, 2014). Holth (2014) argues that individuals, life stories and everyday practices that deviate from this stereotypical division pave the way for more diversified perceptions of the gender practices performed in engineering when both women and men choose it as a career (Holth, 2014). The empirical data for Holth's (2014) study comprise the life stories of 46 computer and mechanical engineers; 26 of whom are women and 20 men. The findings show that there are significant differences between the gender stereotypes of engineers and engineers in reality, and that the ideology of 'rational men' and 'irrational women' in engineering is mistaken (Holth, 2014). The findings also imply that neither gender nor technology is a constant or a given, but that they should both be continuously reinterpreted (Holth, 2014).

Masculinities and femininities are set up as opposites and mutually exclusive and they can be exemplified in the technological/social dichotomy and in the idea that women are socially inclined and hence non-technical, while men are technically inclined and therefore seen as non-social (see Faulkner, 2007, 2009). This is a part of the cultural distinction between women's presumed emotionality and men's presumed instrumentality (Holth, 2014). Thus conceived, technical competence is constructed as a part of what it means to be a man, and of masculinity, and in the process women and femininity have been constructed as non-technical (Faulkner, 2007, 2009, 2010).

Holth argues that technological artefacts have also been associated mainly with men and seen as part of masculine identities. Artefacts traditionally associated with women, e.g. the sewing machine, have not achieved, unlike their male-encoded counterparts, the status of 'real technology' as they belonged mainly to the private sphere and hence were valued less than the technology used in public-sphere production by men (Holth, 2014). Likewise, technical artefacts have been categorized as 'hard' and 'soft', and associated with different stereotypical modes of thinking (Holth, 2014). The hard masculine mode of thinking is symbolically associated with emotional distance, objective rationality and abstract reductionist problem solving, while the gendered stereotypical view of women as emotional and irrational has been deemed incompatible with technological development and has contributed to women's exclusion from the technological sphere (Holth, 2014). Rational intellectual thinking and abstract reasoning have therefore symbolically formed the ideal of the engineer as a knowledge-seeking individual, described in terms of a collected, calculating and rational *man* (Holth, 2014).

A study by Faulkner (2007) draws on ethnographic fieldwork in two United Kingdom offices of a building design engineering consulting company, where data collection methods involved job-shadowing six engineers over the course of five weeks (Faulkner, 2007). Findings discussed include that 'technicist' engineering identities are as strong as they are partly because they converge with available masculinities in at least two important ways: they evoke a sense of hands-on 'nuts and bolts' work (even though engineers rarely do this themselves); and they make engineers feel powerful (i.e. they make things such as buildings, machines and cars that 'work'). As such, many men engineers assume a technicist engineering identity, Faulkner argues, because it feels consistent with versions of masculinity with which they are comfortable.

While women engineers also take pleasure in and identify with the material power of the technologies they build or use, the majority nonetheless identify more readily with the science base of engineering than with hands-on engineering (Faulkner, 2007). So, the traditional association of men with engineering tools still marks professional engineering as masculine and makes the 'nuts and bolts' identity feel 'manly' (Faulkner, 2007).

The tendency to see 'the technical' and 'the social' as mutually exclusive reinforces some men's resistance to embracing a heterogeneous engineering identity (Faulkner, 2007). Although a growing proportion of the men now entering engineering do not come from a technicist background, and although some women opt for hands-on work, still considerably more men than women engineers have been socialized into a hands-on relationship with technology. As women engineers testify, this can seriously undermine their confidence and their sense of belonging, especially when they first enter engineering degrees (Faulkner, 2007).

A study by Beddoes (2012) examines the current state of feminism in the emerging field of engineering education and identifies barriers, challenges and tensions experienced by scholars and educators who have been involved with feminist engineering education initiatives. Using data from 15 in-depth interviews, she identifies a number of changes that would facilitate deeper engagement with feminism in engineering education research. These changes include that engineering education researchers should stop: asking how to change women; using men as the unacknowledged reference point; and conflating gender and sex (Beddoes, 2012). Another problem that gets in the way of good engineering education research is the classic stereotype of the engineer as a man who is brilliant at, and passionate about, technology but not so good at interacting with people (Faulkner, 2010). This image not only says 'technology is for men', it also says being 'into technology' means not being 'into people' (Faulkner, 2010). As women are stereotypically 'into people', the image carries the implicit message that women engineers are not 'real women', or perhaps not 'real engineers' (Faulkner, 2010).

I agree with Fuchs (1997) that being a woman and being an engineer clearly represent two forms of being that can be difficult to integrate. But as we can see from Mandy's story, they do not have to be.

'I always wanted to help people' – Mayita

Mayita is black, female and Zimbabwean. She spent most of her life in South Africa, where she lived and studied, graduating with a master's degree in chemical engineering in 2015. She is now a research assistant and PhD candidate at the Leibniz Institute for Functionalized Polymers (IFP) in Germany, where she does research on smart, bio-responsive coatings for use in maintaining water quality in the water purification process. The overall aim of her work, she says, is:

> Making use of human-centred design to introduce affordable nanotechnology in the developing world – if it is needed.

Her work is very different to what she is used to. She has never been one for lab work or regular working hours. Her past engineering work was mostly freelanced and tackled in her own time. She struggles to work with a routine nine-hour working day that does not give her the: 'luxury of 80% thinking and 20% actual work', because she likes to 'let things simmer'.

Mayita got into chemical engineering by default:

> Medicine, I believed was my calling. I always wanted to help people.

She describes her alternative choice, chemical engineering, as very difficult and not well suited to the way she learns best, but still feels that her studies were worthwhile:

> It was a super tough degree that didn't or couldn't accommodate my learning style (which I have only learnt recently is slow, practical, visual and

immersive). However, the knowledge, opportunities and problem solving capabilities acquired, far outweigh the challenge.

She expected the job hunt to be difficult but it turned out to be worse than she anticipated. Being a non-permit holder worked to her disadvantage as it does for many fellow foreign nationals. She had to figure out ways to find work experience on her own, through networking and freelancing: 'It is really a game of who you know' she says.

Her current work at the IFP came from work she did with previous colleagues for water systems in Nepal. She says that she is sceptical of the work she is doing for the following reasons:

> It is a technology that is being developed in the 1st world for the 3rd world – I feel it may be far removed from the needs of the people we intend to serve. Nanotechnology is very complex and I am not sure it is necessary or applicable to any context. The greater question I am looking to answer (I suspect it would be negative), [is] what place does nanotechnology have in [the] developing world? – It would be great to write a PhD on 'negative' findings. But alas, science does not leave space to document failures.

She once wrote this for a past interview:

> The world's failure to solve simple global sustainability issues is due to detachment from nature and our inability to evolve, survive and thrive within our respective environments; while we strive for global modernization. Clean water is a vital and scarce resource in rural communities. These households already sustainably manage water by effectively reusing grey and black water. Practices such as composting, using natural materials like dung and thatch, are examples of traditional rural African solutions, which are basic and sustainable. Sustainable solutions lie within communities themselves and the real challenge in Africa is aligning these solutions in terms of health, safety and functionality; making them not only more efficient but more effective.

Mayita is involved in community development work. She works on the ongoing roots on top project,[1] works part-time as a senior consultant for 180 DC – a global consultancy firm that offers free management consultancy services to non-profit organizations and social enterprises – and volunteers some of her time to help manage a multidisciplinary, creative co-working hub[2] in the heart of Cape Town's east city district.

She is excited and inspired by innovation that arises when 'designers speak to scientists, through nature's lens'. She says that she aspires to be an 'engineering translator' who 'works on the interface between the complex systems that are engineering and society; even more deeply between nano, and micro-scale science'. Her ultimate goal is to 'use biophillic design to create functional and simple, socio-technological interventions that improve how people and communities function'.

There are many things that Mayita appreciates about her undergraduate studies. She says the degree as a whole is a great problem-solving tool, and she is glad that she had the opportunity to take courses in the Humanities Faculty:

> Two years of that dreaded professional communications course has really put me, and I am sure many other UCT engineering graduates, a cut above the rest!

On the other hand, she does wish that she had had a little more practical work, and says:

> I still cannot tell you the difference between a distillation column and reactor on a plant, but I can design one theoretically! I also have problems with estimating size and space, but maybe that's just me.

Mayita says the undergraduate degree on its own was not enough to get a job, or at least not the job she wanted. She says doing her master's degree and postgraduate research prepared her well for research work. But she emphasizes that this is dependent on the supervisor one has. Her postgraduate studies gave her time to think, network and take courses for her future career path. She would have loved to have done more inter- and transdisciplinary work with other engineering departments and in various faculties, especially in the social sciences. She also says that there should have been more 'empathy work'. Mayita is also aware of discourses that have dominated the media, and academic debate in recent years in the field of higher education, particularly in South Africa:

> There is of course the talk of decolonization of education – I strongly believe in this. Students and lecturers need to speak more openly about race and privilege in the classroom. The racial divide when I was studying was strong.

With regard to changes that can be made to improve the engineering curriculum at postgraduate level, Mayita says:

> Policy, policy, policy is all I hear – something tells me a course along these lines needs to be integrated into engineering degrees.

According to Mayita, too few students are offered, or even allowed, to take vacation work outside a typical engineering plant and/or field:

> The two students who were allowed to complete their vacation work at 75 Harrington is a step in a new (and right) direction. Engineers need to know

how their knowledge can be used in 'alternative' fields, which are not always technical.

She also thinks more social skills and entrepreneurial training are necessary inclusions in engineering curricula, adding that she has failed in two start-up ventures to date. In reflecting on her journey to becoming an engineer she says:

> I was never an A or even a B student (only in 4th year when work became more application based!), so I spent a lot of my free time networking and pursuing voluntary positions here and there. Through this I was exposed to Biomimicry and have worked with them in a freelance capacity ever since. All [my] jobs were through this network – including my work at 75 Harrington. To further emphasize the power of networking: once I joined the 75 Harrington team (which has an open door policy), I was offered a job with Green Cape, Greenhouse and McKinsey – not a single application. All networks. A lot of credit can go to my master's supervisor, who is very open-minded and pushed me to explore new avenues in and outside of engineering. Supervisors are very important! He pushed me to apply for the Green Talents award which has opened every door for me in the past two years. – I was headhunted by my current institute via the Green Talents network.

Mayita describes eloquently her aspirations for the future and her understanding of the role she can play as an engineer in society:

> The human-made world has lost touch with nature and fails to design sustainable eco-systems that work with, not against nature. I want my work to highlight the dynamic variables that lie on the interfaces between the complex systems. Between science and society; nano- and micro-scale science; engineering, natural sciences and social science. The links between these realms are not made nor are they understood. They do not talk to each other, but have a lot to say about each other. It is understanding the complexity of these interconnected systems that are essential to achieving truly sustainable/regenerative/resilient (insert any buzz word here) development. This can only be done from a trans- and multidisciplinary angle. I am an advocate for transdisciplinary work in science. Science used to be curiosity about the world and how it worked. Now it is about excess, efficiency, optimization, control and status. I do not want to be a part of that. Science *is* about curiosity. Accept that you do not always have to understand it, enjoy the complexity, see it, observe and do not try to manage or control it. Work with it and around it.

Mayita clearly thinks critically about the role of technology in enhancing human capabilities and this indicates that she has the desire to use her knowledge for the public good, but particularly in developing regions. Her story reminds us that the whole point of development is to determine what constitutes progress. As her reflections indicate, it is unhelpful to think that human problems can be resolved by educating more engineers and creating more sophisticated technology in order to increase wealth, improve education and research, to minimize pollution, conserve wildlife, discover new sources of energy, and arrive at more functional agreements on peaceful coexistence (Schumacher, 1973). Of course, all these things are necessary for progress, but what is most needed is a reconsideration of the ends that these means are intended to serve (Schumacher, 1973).

Engineering education may impart all the knowledge required to help promote sustainable development, but systematic, imaginative effort to bring technology into active existence and make it generally visible, available and most importantly accessible to those who need it most is still needed. Goal 1 of the SDGs (eradicating poverty in all its forms, everywhere) compels us to recognize the limited opportunities of people living in poverty, and thus from a capabilities perspective, engineering that is for sustainable development should explicitly seek to expand valued opportunities for the poor by helping to design and produce technologies that enable them to live the lives they have reason to value, or what Schumacher calls 'democratic technology' – technology to which all people can gain access and that is not reserved to the already rich and powerful (Schumacher, 1973).

Public-good engineering is a framework that can be used to identify guidelines to facilitate engineering education for sustainable development and help us turn this potentiality into a reality to benefit all people. To do this, the task of engineering education would be, first and foremost, the transmission of ideas, of values and of the technologies worth pursuing to advance social justice. Indeed, know-how must be transferred, but this should be secondary, because it is unwise to put effective power into the hands of engineers without ensuring that they have reasonable ideas about what to do with their hands or that power. At present, not all engineering promotes sustainable development. This is not because we are short of scientific and technological know-how, but because not all engineering is geared towards it. Yet it should be. Thus conceived, the essence of engineering education ought to lie in the transmission of values associated with sustainable development. However, these values:

> do not help us to pick our way through life unless they have become our own, a part, so to say, of our mental make-up. This means that they are more than mere formulae or dogmatic assertions: that we think and feel with them, that they are the very instruments through which we look at, interpret and experience the world.
>
> (Schumacher, 1973: 52)

This is what Mayita achieves.

'I am doing something that no one else has worked on' – Phillip

Phillip is white, male and German. He graduated with a master's degree in production engineering from UB in 2016. He currently works at the same university as a research assistant in the area of structural mechanics/engineering, in which he is pursuing a doctoral degree. His research, he says, has the potential to achieve new and improved formulae for calculating bearing structures used in construction analyses.

He finds his work very pleasant. The department in which he works has flexible working hours, and he is happy that he may come and go as he pleases, as long as he puts in the total number of hours stipulated in his contract. The learning aspect is his favourite part of the work and he is considering a profession in engineering education once he has completed his PhD. He is ambivalent about the topic of his PhD research: on one hand he finds it very interesting and enjoys working on it; on the other hand he has doubts about its usefulness. This is part of the reason why he thinks he might go into teaching engineering instead. The expectations he had for his current job have been met completely. And he feels that the education he received at university has prepared him well for his current work, because he still works within the university. His undergraduate studies alone would not have been enough, he says, but his master's studies provided him with the foundation he needed for his doctoral research.

Phillip finds it unfortunate that his PhD studies do not have much to do with sustainable development. Because his research is purely theoretical, there is no opportunity to integrate it with practical problems to 'save the world', he argues. However, he is currently also working on a small project, where he is engaged in testing and improving the mechanical load-carrying capacity of medical products after their original use. Phillip says that this project is not aimed directly at sustainable development, but that it will, if it works, at least help some people. His thoughts on being an engineer, development and sustainability:

> The best thing about being an engineer is that one can solve problems technically, and that these technical solutions can be mathematically explained. I believe that neither my age, gender nor skin colour have any kind of influence or bearing on my being an engineer. The best thing about my work is the learning, which I find a lot of fun. The best thing about my PhD research is that I am doing something that no one else has worked on, and that I can discover something that no one else in the world has known of before. That is a nice feeling.
>
> As an engineer, I understand development as, first and foremost, the invention of new products and their technical application. So, the creation of products. Aside from this understanding, I see development as a process in which something or someone in a certain situation or circumstance, transforms into a higher form.
>
> Sustainability is something that is important to me, as it should be to everyone. I read a lot about the planet's sustainable development and I know that engineers can help to improve certain things, but they cannot solve the world's big problems. All people have to help with that. The small project I do [on the side] is a community project. I work there with some of my colleagues and people from other institutes. The best thing about the community project is that I can really help a medical firm to develop its

products, and improve them, and with that also, help many people in the future.

Reflecting on his journey towards becoming an engineer, Phillip says:

In hindsight I wouldn't change much about my studies because they prepared me well for the work an engineer does. The best thing about my undergraduate studies is that I learnt 'engineering thinking', – logical, and problem oriented thinking. I would however recommend that all study programmes have a compulsory 'International Studies' semester for every student. I think there are too many 'smart heads' nowadays who really do not know what is going on in the world. Economics should be included in this course, where we ask the question: where does our money come from? What happens when we borrow money from the bank?, etc. Politics also belongs in this course: How did the injustice we see today in the world come about? What wars are going on and why? And of course, sustainability should also be included: For how long can we continue to live in this world under the current circumstances? How long is oil going to last? What will the natural environment look in the future? I think that every university graduate should be able to tackle these questions, otherwise it will not be at all possible to be for sustainable development, or one will not be able to make a positive contribution to the world's development.

At this point, I would like to add another question, which I think is the reason why many students want to become engineers today: What role does money play for engineer? For me, money is not very important. As a research assistant with a full-time contract at the university, one gets 2000€ net per month. With this money, one can live very well alone, or also well as a couple, or even as a small family if one's girlfriend also has a job. In any case, I think earning over like 10,000€ is not justifiable for anyone or any job, and that no one really becomes happier with that amount.

Like most of the young engineers interviewed for this book, Phillip is interested in sustainable development and wishes that his research was more explicitly geared towards it. His educational journey has made him appreciate learning processes so much that he is considering becoming an engineering educator instead of a practising engineer.

It is easy to assume that the best way for engineers to apply engineering knowledge is through working in industry, applying technical knowledge to help design, construct and implement technologies that advance development. However, using it to teach future engineers is public-good professionalism too. Like Mandy's story, Phillip's reminds us to foreground and celebrate heterogeneous understandings of engineering identities. It tells us that there are different areas within which qualified engineers can work and still use their knowledge to enhance valued capabilities and functionings for future engineers. Given Phillip's passion for sustainable development, engineers like him may be better positioned to transfer values associated with sustainable development than an engineering educator who does not have this passion. As discussed in Chapter 4, lecturers who themselves care about issues of social justice and sustainable development make concerted efforts to integrate these topics into their classes by facilitating discussions and debates where students are challenged to think about and reflect critically on the role that engineering plays in improving or worsening both human and non-human life. What we can therefore take from Phillip's story is that qualified engineers can make valuable contributions to society, be it in laboratories, on site or in the classroom. Reminding engineers of the diverse landscape in which they can be employed is important.

Another useful reminder that can be drawn from Phillip's story is that there are opportunities for qualified engineers to get involved in community projects where they can practice public-good professionalism without the typical constraints found in large companies in the public or private sector. That is, if, like Phillip, an engineering graduate is passionate about sustainable development but currently employed in a company, or doing work that does not explicitly promote it, they can look for opportunities outside of their formal employment to find projects that do. Since the early 1990s, engineering activities dealing with humanitarian and community development activities have proliferated. Stimulated by the involvement of other professions in humanitarian relief, such as Doctors without Borders (founded in 1971), Reporters without Borders (1985), and Lawyers without Borders (2000), engineers took up the challenge and independently organized a number of groups under some form of the name 'Engineers without Borders'. These groups include France's Ingénieurs Sans Frontières (late 1980s), Spain's Ingeniería Sin Fronteras (1991), Canada's Engineers without Borders (2000), Belgium's Ingénieurs Assistance Internationale (2002), and others (Lucena & Schneider, 2008). In 2003 these groups organized 'Engineers without Borders International' as a network to promote humanitarian engineering for a better world (Lucena & Schneider, 2008). Engineers against Poverty is another organization that has humanitarian ambitions for engineering.

According to Lucena and Schneider (2008), engineering organizations in the early twenty-first century heeded the call to sustainable development and began taking action, from attending hosting regional and world conferences to declaring their position with respect to sustainable development. Some organizations revisited their codes of ethics, and requested members to address these principles in their work, and others created international professional partnerships such as the World Engineering Partnership for Sustainable Development or the Federation of African Organisations of Engineers (1994). These are just some examples of initiatives across the world that allow engineers to get involved in work that aligns with sustainable development.

'I expected that I would earn more' – Mufaro

Mufaro is female, black and Zimbabwean. She graduated with a master's in chemical engineering from UCT in 2016. She currently works at GreenCape, which is a sector development agency that aims to advance the green economy.

She works as a research analyst. She enjoys her work at the moment, although 'just like any other job, it has its highs and lows'.

Her expectations have not been met in terms of what she thought she would get out of her degree and what kind of work she would do after her studies:

> I expected that I would earn more than I am now and I expected the work to be more technically challenging. The work is relevant but not as tough as I initially expected it to be.

University prepared her very well for the work she is doing, she says:

> I think undergrad helped me to be able to tackle technical problems head on and postgrad helped me to develop my soft skills (self-management, writing and verbal communication).

Mufaro has previously been involved in community development work, mostly in mentorship programmes. She has also done volunteer work for Innovate SA (under Engineers without Borders) and also for Women in Engineering. Answering the question on whether or not she thought her age, gender, nationality or race affected her potential to make a positive impact in communities or in society as an engineer, Mufaro says that now that she is working, she realizes that 'it is indeed true that the engineering field is white male dominated'. This has affected her confidence and she felt a little intimidated from time to time:

> If I nurture this attitude it will ultimately affect my job performance so now and again I try and reaffirm myself to prevent that. To sum it up, I think the only way race and gender will affect my potential for impact is that it presents an opportunity to feel insecure and to lack confidence. I don't think age will have any impact at all, even though I am at a disadvantage due to limited experience.

Her view on development:

> Development is when the quality of lives (food, education and health) and surroundings/environment of a community/country/continent get better.

Asked about the best thing about her work and being an engineer Mufaro says:

> I love technology and innovation and it is exciting to see how everything keeps getting better and how people keep finding ways of tackling everyday problems. To be consistently exposed to that, I think, is the best part of my job.

Mufaro says her job is very much linked to sustainable development as 'the aim of the company is to advance investment in the green economy'. Her engineering studies and current work have increased her interest in this issue significantly:

Sustainability has not always been important to me but with my master's research project and my new job, I am starting to care more and more about it.

The general sentiment of advocates of ESD is that university leaders, faculty and students should be empowered to catalyse and implement new paradigms by introducing sustainable development into all courses and curricula and throughout all other elements of higher education activities. Doing so, Lozano (2013: 8) argues, would safeguard sustainable development as the 'golden thread' or 'leitmotiv' throughout university systems. According to (Tilbury, 2011), education and learning for sustainable development refers to gaining knowledge, values and theories associated with sustainable development, including learning to:

- ask critical questions;
- clarify one's own values;
- learn to envision more positive and sustainable futures;
- think systematically;
- respond through applied learning; and
- explore the dialectic between tradition and innovation.

As mentioned in Chapter 1, there are many examples of ways in which universities are responding to calls for ESD, and literature on this topic is proliferating. Across this literature, there are interesting lessons that can be drawn. For example, Carew and Mitchell (2008) argue that sustainable development should be taught as a contested concept. In their paper, they demonstrate that there is substantial variation in the way that individual engineering academics conceive of environmental, social and economic sustainability (Carew & Mitchell, 2008). In their study, a variety of sustainability themes and actions that were described by the Australian engineering academics who participated in a professional development workshop were documented. The findings suggests that a significant part of the challenge for individual academics attempting to infuse concepts of sustainability into undergraduate coursework is to acknowledge that sustainability is a concept with both factual and value-based components, and therefore should and does/will manifest in diverse ways (Carew & Mitchell, 2008). Carew and Mitchell (2008) consequently suggest that rather than advocating specific tools, sets of actions or particular outcomes as 'sustainable', academics might develop approaches to teaching and learning that consider the role of values and assumptions in sustainability discourses.

A survey carried out by Azapagic, Perdan and Shallcross (2005) suggests that, overall, the level of knowledge and understanding of sustainable development is not satisfactory and that much more work is needed to educate engineering students in this field. A total of 3,134 students from 21 universities across Europe, North and South America, the Far East and Australia participated in the survey (Azapagic et al., 2005). While on average students appear to be relatively knowledgeable about environmental issues, it is apparent that significant knowledge gaps exist with respect to the other two (social and economic) dimensions of sustainable development (Azapagic et al., 2005). Also, students' awareness of sustainable development policy and standards was reported to be low (Azapagic et al., 2005). Azapagic et al. (2005) assert that engineering students see sustainable development as important for them personally and even more important for them as engineers. Building on this finding, the authors argue that it should not be difficult to capture students' imagination by teaching sustainable development so as to make it as relevant to engineering as possible. This, Azapagic et al. (2005) argue, can be done through a series of lectures and tutorials on sustainable development, supplemented by practical examples and case studies integrated into the core modules of the engineering curriculum.

In another study, Von Blottnitz, Case, and Fraser (2015) demonstrate the feasibility of reforming core undergraduate engineering curricula to incorporate a focus on sustainable development, from the first year of study onwards. Their paper reports on a curriculum reform process in chemical engineering at a South African university. Departing from traditional curricula, the new first-year course incorporates a 'natural foundations' strand that introduces nature not just as a resource, or as imposing parameters on engineering dexterity, but also as 'mentor and model' (Von Blottnitz et al., 2015). Sustainability problems are interpreted as systematic violations of nature's grand cycles and contrasted with development needs, particularly in relation to provision of water and energy (Von Blottnitz et al., 2015). It is reported that by the end of the course most students rated their knowledge of environmental and sustainability issues as good or excellent. The authors cite the significant achievement of this new programme as the interweaving of sustainable development into a mainstream undergraduate engineering curriculum, and predict that such an approach may become a trend in chemical engineering programmes.

De la Harpe and Thomas (2009: 83) state, 'We would be more than halfway there if we can ensure that time in such efforts is spent on getting a critical mass of people on board to form a group to lead, champion and implement change'. They also state that it is necessary to develop a vision and a clear plan, and to ensure that there are sufficient resources and staff development opportunities available to achieve that vision.

Mufaro was fortunate to study at a university where the engineering programme integrated and encouraged students to learn about sustainable development. This gave her the opportunity to learn to 'care more and more about it'. Not all engineering students have this opportunity. Yet they should; regardless of where their education takes place, because caring, defined as an 'active compassion, empathy, and concern for the well-being of other living things', is a key and necessary element for engineering education to embrace social and ecological justice (Campbell, Yasuhara & Wilson, 2012).

'I have to be selfish and focus on developing myself first before giving back to the community' – Tendayi

Tendayi is male, black and Zimbabwean. He graduated from the UCT with a master's degree in chemical engineering in 2015. He worked for Citrine Informatics as a Freelance Data Analyst. The work involved data extraction in the field of material science and metallurgy. He is currently unemployed, and living in Zimbabwe.

He did not like the work he did at Citrine Informatics. He found it monotonous and he felt like it was not making full use of his engineering know-how. Tendayi has been having difficulty finding work. The difficulties are linked to his residential and work permit status:

> I am not sure my point of view would be valid regarding available opportunities in South Africa. Unfortunately due to the permit application process complications when applying from Zimbabwe, I have found it hard to secure a job as the companies [in South Africa] are not willing to aid in the permit application process as it is said to take too long. In general, I would say opportunities in the engineering field are hard to get into as graduate programmes are more inclined to be given to undergraduate graduates [BSc graduates] as we [MSc graduates] are deemed too qualified. And in the roles that an MSc is an advantage, some three to five years of experience are required. Hence management consulting firms end up being the option left and they pay well.
>
> I initially had to go into Master's so that I could apply for the special skills work permit so as to be employed. The immigration laws were amended, and unfortunately I have been unable to get the new critical skills work permit from last year [2016] September. My initial application was denied and I had to lodge a second application and I am still waiting for the outcome. The unfortunate part is the application requirements that are stated in the immigration act and accepted in applications submitted in South Africa are apparently not the same as the home affairs in Zimbabwe. As a result, I have lost a number of employment opportunities due to the work permit situation.

Tendayi's education prepared him well for work, he says:

> I would say undergraduate deadlines helped in preparing me for that. With reference to my postgraduate, it helped me get used to managing my time on my own and giving myself personal targets and deadlines which helped a lot with my personal time management. The report writing skills gained over the years have come in handy as well.

There was no relation to sustainable development in the work Tendayi did at Citrine Informatics, and he seemed indifferent about this. He has also never done any work for, or volunteered to work in, community development projects:

I tell myself that I would have the time and resources to give back to the community later in life when I am financially and socially stable. In terms of achieving in life (...) most of my age mates have been working for a number of years and accumulated assets in the time. As a result, I feel like I have to be selfish and focus on developing myself first before giving back to the community.

He says the following about development:

I believe it's the presents of a society that provides opportunities for its members to be safe, get employment opportunities, or create businesses that will allow the people to be self-sufficient, and grow to whatever heights they dream. In terms of personal development it is achieving the goals which you set or continue to set and be able to sustain yourself and your family.

For Tendayi, the best thing about being an engineer is:

The ability to solve a number of problems that most people cannot, and feeling valuable at the work place.

He adds:

And the salaries are also reasonably well as compared to most of my peers [who are not engineers].

If he could have changed anything about engineering studies he would add financial/business courses in the curriculum. He says:

This is very evident with my other classmates who end up being required to provide technical solutions with a bit of the financial aspect in the presentations. So the basic undergraduate knowledge will not cut it. I would also add a project management course in the curriculum, as most of us end in some management role to some extent with minimal know-how on that besides solving calculations on our desks.

Asked what it was like to be back in his home country, Zimbabwe, he says:

With the economic situation that is still far from functional, most production companies are not functional, hence potential employment opportunities are next to none if you don't 'know someone who knows someone'. And as I mentioned [before], the problems with the embassy, it's the same story with most of the graduates who were not able to secure a work permit in South Africa before their study permits expired. As a result, it just feels like you are stuck in one place and you can only keep trying out all the options until something gives.

In the future, Tendayi hopes to secure a job in either the mining field or a management consulting industry ideally in South Africa for a couple of years. He also wants 'to live in a first world country for a few years' before returning to Zimbabwe. And then:

> After I have achieved my targets in growing my network and going up the ladder, if you can put it that way, I would want to open an engineering consulting company in Zimbabwe.

Tendayi's story provides a good example of how being a public-good engineer can be shaped by nationality. Tendayi would have liked to get a job in South Africa after completing his undergraduate degree, but he had difficulties finding a job. He then decided to again apply for a study visa and pursue a master's degree so that he could continue staying in South Africa. His study visa expired soon after he completed his master's degree, and without a job offer at the time, he had to return to Zimbabwe.

Tendayi's education has clearly enhanced his sense of empowerment, confidence and personal development, but it did not necessarily enhance his individual agency to forge pathways into employment. This highlights issues of structure and agency. It shows that it would be helpful if engineering education in universities also developed and strengthened graduates' potential to exercise agency so that they are able to initiate and create employment opportunities. At the same time, public-good engineers as entrepreneurs would also need to take on projects that are consistent with social justice values while they navigate personal, environmental, and social conversion factors or constraints, and cope with the contradictions that they are likely to encounter in this work. Tendayi's being unemployed gets in the way of him living a life he has reason to value, but also limits his potential as a public-good engineer. He is stressed by the prospect of having to go without work for longer, and being stuck in a country where there are no signs of impending improvement in the economy and the job market. While fellow Zimbabwean, Mayita, was able to get numerous job offers through networking (which was based on advice she received from her then supervisor), Tendayi did not experience this.

The views of employers on the ideal engineer reflect a range of technical and non-technical skills they would like graduate engineers to possess. These skills reflect attributes that the employers consider valuable in industry. Assuming that Tendayi has the required technical skills, the data reported on in Chapter 5 suggests that his capability for employment might improve if:

- he has a broad view of the engineering profession;
- he recognizes the diverse contexts in which technical knowledge can be applied;
- he understands the interconnectivity between technical solutions and human problems;

- he is able to translate theory into practice both in the office space and on project sites;
- he is a critical thinker with an open mind; and is able to communicate and collaborate effectively.

Read separately, Mandy, Mayita, Phillip, Mufaro and Tendayi's stories provide us with examples of the kind of work engineers may end up in, and the kind of attitudes they might have towards the concept of sustainable development, if their education resembles the curricula and pedagogies that these young engineers were exposed to at the UCT and the UB. Their stories show that engineering education in universities can enlarge a wide range of valued capabilities and functionings that have different degrees of relevance to public-good engineering and hence, to sustainable human development. However, it does not always do so. A new normative underpinning developed in this book is therefore advanced.

Read together their stories tell us that the capabilities, functionings and framework for public-good engineering identified in this book hold well. To recap, the educational capabilities and corresponding functionings identified as those that are arguably most important for public-good engineering are:

- solving problems; not just any problems, but those particularly that get in the way of achieving sustainable human development;
- being confident and feeling empowered; not only for the sake of personal development, but also in order to enable the application of individual and collective agency to advance social justice;
- being resilient and having a sense of affiliation, both to encourage the development of appropriate engineering identities and to learn how to persevere in the face of individual failure; and
- working in diverse fields, in which professional engineering expertise is applied in a wide range of contexts, industries, companies and job positions, for the sake of the public good.

Identifying these capabilities and functionings was an iterative process that required going back and forth between data and theory, i.e. describing what emerged from the analysis of the findings, reflecting on how the findings relate to the ideal-theoretical, capabilities-inspired normative account of engineering education (in Chapters 1 and 2) and then referring again to the data. In brief, students' valued functionings were extrapolated from the data, and then the list was shortened to eliminate any beings and doings that were theoretically irrelevant to public-good professionalism (see Chapter 3). The remaining functionings were then considered for their relation to the goals of engineering education (see Chapter 4) and the dimensions of public-good engineering (see Chapter 5) before refining the list again. Finally, corresponding capabilities that are necessary for the achievement of the identified functionings were extrapolated.

To recap, the goals of engineering education were described as seeking to:

- develop students' capacities to exercise agency, make decisions autonomously and create innovative approaches and methods to solution seeking founded on engineering knowledge;
- enhance students' sense of determination to be and do what they have reason to value in life as well as determine their roles in society;
- stimulate students' desire for knowledge and help them recognize opportunities where they can successfully apply what they learn to their work and in their lives;
- provide students with opportunities for research-based learning;
- provide students with the necessary knowledge and skills that they need to become engineers and be employable; and
- develop students' potential to take responsibility for running engineering companies and be accountable for the engineering outcomes produced by them.

Public-good engineering was defined as engineering that:

- is founded on principals of homo *reciprocans* rather than homo *economicus*;
- seeks to expand capabilities and enable valued functionings for (poor) communities;
- meaningfully engages with such communities where possible, to ensure that engineering accomplishments will benefit them in ways that they have reason to value in the long run; and
- is not carried out with disregard to the environment and acknowledges the boundaries of human influence on it.

And non-technical skills conducive to this type of engineering are:

Critical thinking and open-mindedness, along with communication and collaboration.

Mapping out the functionings, dimensions of public-good engineering, non-technical skills associated with it, and the goals of engineering education, a capabilities-inspired, empirically informed framework for public-good engineering education was generated (see Chapter 6). It outlines what engineering education might look like, if it is to enhance future engineers' opportunities to use their agency to practice public-good engineering.

In this way, the capability approach offered a foundation for normative descriptions of processes that aim to result in development. Examples of such processes include engineering education, because it produces a workforce of professional engineers who often work at the forefront of development. At the same time, descriptions of what engineering education ought to do are also helpful in identifying what it ought *not* to do, thereby providing grounds for criticism. Following this line of thinking, engineering education for sustainable human development was described as:

> Education that enlarges the professional capabilities of engineering graduates, whilst providing them with opportunities to develop, demonstrate and deepen their commitment to causes such as poverty eradication, and at the same time enhances their ability to exercise their agency to promote sustainable human development through their work.

Drawing from this definition, the following can be said about engineering education:

> Engineering education that does not provide students with opportunities to engage meaningfully with knowledge about poverty, and sustainability, falls short of its contribution to sustainable human development.

In this way, the capability approach aptly provided a framework for normative critiques of engineering education. More specifically, the capability approach can be used as a theoretical basis to help broadly describe what the outcomes of engineering education should be, if future engineers are to advance sustainable human development through their work.

Original contribution

This book makes an original conceptual and empirical contribution to how we can think differently about engineering education in both global South and global North contexts; the combined conceptual and empirical application is important. On its own, rich qualitative empirical data on engineering education in universities tell us much about the aspirations, experiences and opinions of engineering students, lecturers and employers. This is important because it provides the evidence needed from which we can then build our understanding of engineering education and practice. However, using the capability approach as both a normative lens for theorizing, and a site for analysing this data, enriches the value of the data because it provides valuable conceptual grounds for critically assessing, and problematizing engineering curricula and pedagogies in universities.

This has book shown how the capability approach could be informed by the concept of sustainable development to result in a view of human flourishing as 'sustainable human development'. It has also shown that much work has been done to promote infusing the concept of sustainable development into engineering education. However, there are no studies that explicitly describe the normative objectives of engineering education according to a capabilities-inspired conceptualization of sustainable human development. That is, although there are global action plans and institutional responses to ESD, similar efforts have not been made to advance a capabilities approach to engineering education or 'Engineering Education for Sustainable Human Development'. This is an original theoretical contribution to engineering education literature.

Combined perspectives (in this case from the global North and South) are more than the sum of individual views; they provide a new window through which to perceive the value of engineering education. In the same way that the colour green results from mixing blue and yellow, combining German and South African perspectives creates a new outlook, which allows us to see some 'blind spots' that may otherwise not have been achieved had the perspectives merely been *compared* to one another. Thus conceived, this book also advances a critique of comparative engineering education research, opting instead to showcase the value and synergy created from combining global North and global South perspectives on engineering education.

Limitations of the book

Notwithstanding that the book enables a fresh and innovative look at engineering education, the qualitative nature of the research undertaken means that the findings are not generalizable. This book also contains data that were collected from two universities that were specifically selected because of their explicit commitment to addressing sustainable development in their engineering curricula. Therefore, the findings arguably reflect examples of exceptional engineering education in global South and global North countries respectively. They do not reflect what students and lecturers at 'average' universities might perceive or what they might get out of engineering education there. Nonetheless, the book's findings point to possibilities, but also to challenges that can resonate in other contexts and universities or higher education institutions. These identified limitations are, however, also avenues for future research.

Future directions in research

Gaps in engineering education research that could help us to get a sense of how well we are doing in developing public-good engineers are summarized below.

Most engineering education reform efforts appear to be ad hoc, fragmented institutional attempts to broaden outcomes, often based on measures that lack empirical evidence of their long-term effectiveness. That is, there is lack of longitudinal empirical evidence showing which courses are most effective in imparting the kind of knowledge required for sustainable development. There are studies that discuss engineering students' understanding and evaluations of 'sustainable development' courses (for example, see Boni et al., 2012; Case & Marshall, 2015; Connor et al., 2014; Fernandes et al., 2012; Segalás et al., 2010; Von Blottnitz, Case, Heydenrych & Fraser, 2013; Von Blottnitz et al., 2015). However, most studies do not go as far as evaluating the long-term effect of these courses on students' professional functioning, nor do they assess the long-term results of the reform measures or new courses they propose for their education institutions.

When it comes to teaching sustainable development, most attention appears to be focused on engineering curriculum change, and fewer studies consider how integrated engineering pedagogies could make a positive contribution to reform efforts. Those that do have reported a failure to address sustainable development through engineering pedagogy owing to lecturers' ambiguity on the concept and confusion about how they can infuse related issues in their actual teaching (Carew & Mitchell, 2008; Jones, Trier & Richards, 2008). That is, there appears to be a gap in engineering education literature concerning how sustainable development principles can be infused in the actual teaching practices of engineering educators (regardless of the course they teach). No clear and comprehensive conceptual framework or practical guidelines are being employed as a normative and evaluative basis for engineering education reform efforts in general (Karatzoglou, 2013).

Finally, we do not know much about how becoming and being a public-good engineer is shaped by gender, race or socio-economic class. Especially in countries like South Africa, this is much needed to inform both educational and social justice policy, practices and outcomes.

Public engagement

This book is also concerned to engage in discussions about public-good engineering beyond the academy, given the influences of employers, colleagues and the work context not only on the engineering curriculum, but also on practices post-university. To this end, this process was initiated by presenting a paper in July 2015 entitled 'We think we're helping, but are we really? Critical reflections on engineering for sustainable development', at an annual meeting of a group of members of the German Association of Engineers (VDI) in Pretoria, South Africa.

In our discussions, the VDI members generally had similar ideas about the concept of sustainable development that were presented in Chapter 6. They also see sustainability as a vague concept and worry that it is used too loosely and frequently. They also placed an emphasis on the structural constraints that get in the way of engineering that seeks to reduce inequalities. The South African political climate was described as one that does not allow this adequately. They spoke about the opportunities and possibilities for more sustainable engineering projects that could be implemented in South Africa (especially in response to the ongoing energy crisis) but cited corruption and cumbersome red tape as the biggest constraints for this to happen. They also echoed the sentiment that, too often, non-engineers make the final decisions about the engineering projects that are implemented. Some points were then made about the importance of incremental changes in this regard; that sometimes the only way to change something is by doing 'a little bit at a time'. The VDI members appreciated having a non-engineer present at their meeting and said our discussion allowed them to step back from the typical technical engineering content that is usually talked about at their monthly meetings. Doing so, they said, gave them an opportunity to think about their work more broadly than they allow themselves to do on a daily basis. This is an important because it shows that this book has the potential to prompt critical reflection about the purpose and value of professional engineering functionings amongst practising engineers.

Sharing findings in this way is important in order to receive feedback on the research, but also for participatory dialogue, which is emphasized strongly in the capability approach (see Sen, 2009) as integral to the process of agreeing which capabilities ought to be prioritized and developed. Making this book public and engaging with diverse audiences is thus part of the process of defending the framework for public-good engineering education and inviting other voices to review it critically. This process can contribute to the refinement of the framework and the list of educational capabilities for public-good engineering. Public engagement also creates avenues for thinking about teaching and learning in engineering education, and for 'speaking' to policy and policy makers.

Concluding remarks: changing the way we think about the ends of engineering education

In the same way that this book speaks to some of the central questions about development and engineering outcomes from a capabilities perspective, it also approaches the question of the relationship between universities and the public good from a human development viewpoint. As the discussion of public-good professionalism has shown, a capabilities lens on engineering professionalism points to multidimensional freedoms and functionings – particularly those of the poor – as proxies of development that is just.

If every engineer were to be educated and to practise in environments that questioned the implications to the capabilities and functionings of people living in poverty, the idea of socially just or public-good engineering could play a different sort of role: to prompt a re-examination of engineers' central assumptions about development, the role engineering plays in it and its sustainability. In this way, a capabilities framework has the potential to upset old habits in engineering, not removing them, but making them noticeable and inviting scrutiny. And rather than encouraging the idea that there is one right way to advance sustainable development through engineering, a capabilities approach points to robust public democratic deliberation, a process that includes engineers, but also members of different groups and communities impacted by engineering decisions and actions. Ultimately, then, a capabilities-inspired framework for public-good engineering opens a discussion of what engineering is and ought to be – not only conceptually and methodologically but in terms of professional practice.

The process of carrying out this research resulted in my hoping to see engineering defined and practised differently so that engineers can work in a variety of contexts from and on behalf of social justice values, rather than against them. It is clear that the engineering students want their work to matter outside of corporate or profit driven contexts, yet some of them struggle with their commitments to traditional engineering values associated with objective 'problem solving'. Work on engineering education for sustainable human development should continue to explore these tensions, and discover how they might be overcome so that future engineering endeavours might contribute more ardently towards eradicating poverty.

Notes

1 For further information see www.facebook.com/rootsontop75HS/?fref=ts.
2 For further information see www.facebook.com/75harrington/?fref=tse.

References

Azapagic, A., Perdan, S. & Shallcross, D. (2005). How much do engineering students know about sustainable development? The findings of an international survey and possible implications for the engineering curriculum. *European Journal of Engineering Education, 30*(1), 1–19. Accessed 1 September 2017 from https://doi.org/10.1080/0304 3790512331313804.

Beddoes, K. D. (2012). Feminist scholarship in engineering education: Challenges and tensions. *Engineering Studies, 4*(3), 205–232. Accessed 1 September 2017 from https://doi.org/10.1080/19378629.2012.693932.

Boni, A., McDonald, P. & Peris, J. (2012). Cultivating engineers' humanity: Fostering cosmopolitanism in a technical university. *International Journal of Educational Development, 32*(1), 179–186.

Campbell, R. C., Yasuhara, K. & Wilson, D. (2012). Care ethics in engineering education: Undergraduate student perceptions of responsibility. In *Frontiers in Education* (pp. 1–6). Seattle: Institute of Electrical and Electronic Engineering (IEEE).

Carew, A. L., & Mitchell, C. A. (2008). Teaching sustainability as a contested concept: Capitalizing on variation in engineering educators' conceptions of environmental, social and economic sustainability. *Journal of Cleaner Production, 16*, 105–115. Accessed 1 September 2017 from https://doi.org/10.1016/j.jclepro.2006.11.004.

Case, J. M., & Marshall, D. (2015). Bringing together knowledge and capabilities: A case study of engineering graduates. *Higher Education, 71*(6), 819–833. Accessed 1 September 2017 https://link.springer.com/article/10.1007/s10734-015-9932-4?no-access=true.

Connor, A. M., Karmokar, S., Whittington, C. & Walker, C. (2014). Full STEAM ahead: A manifesto for integrating arts pedagogics into STEM education. In *IEEE*. Wellington, New Zealand. Accessed 1 September 2017 from http://dx.doi.org/10.1109/TALE.2014.7062556.

De la Harpe, B., & Thomas, I. (2009). Curriculum change in universities conditions that facilitate education for sustainable development. *Journal of Education for Sustainable Development, 3*(1): 75–85.

Faulkner, W. (2007). 'Nuts and bolts and people' : Gender-troubled engineering identities. *Social Studies of Science, 37*(3), 331–356. Accessed 1 September 2017 from https://doi.org/10.1177/0306312706072175.

Faulkner, W. (2009). Doing gender in engineering workplace cultures. I. Observations from the field. *Engineering Studies, 1*(1), 3–18. Accessed 1 September 2017 from https://doi.org/10.1080/19378620902721322.

Faulkner, W. (2010). Women and gender issues in engineering. In *Engineering: Issues, challenges and opportunities for development*. Paris: UNESCO.

Fernandes, S., Flores, M. A. & Lima, R. M. (2012). Students' views of assessment in project-led engineering education: Findings from a case study in Portugal. *Assessment & Evaluation in Higher Education, 37*(2), 163–178.

Fuchs, M. (1997). Like fathers-like daughters: Professionalization strategies of women students and engineers in Germany 1890s to 1940s. *History and Technology, 14*(1–2), 49–64. Accessed 1 September 2017 from https://doi.org/10.1080/07341519708581921.

Holth, L. (2014). Passionate men and rational women: Gender contradictions in engineering. *NORMA: International Journal for Masculinity Studies, 9*(2), 97–110. Accessed 1 September 2017 from https://doi.org/10.1080/18902138.2014.908629.

Jones, P., Trier, C. J. & Richards, J. P. (2008). Embedding Education for Sustainable Development in higher education: A case study examining common challenges and opportunities for undergraduate programmes. *International Journal of Educational Research, 47*(6), 341–350.

Karatzoglou, B. (2013). An in-depth literature review of the evolving roles and contributions of universities to education for sustainable development. *Journal of Cleaner Production, 49*, 44–53. Accessed 1 September 2017 from http://dx.doi.org/10.1016/j.jclepro.2012.07.043.

Lozano, R. (ed.). (2013). Advancing higher education for sustainable development: International insights and critical reflections. *Journal of Cleaner Production, 48*, 3–9. Accessed 1 September 2017 from http://dx.doi.org/10.1016/j.jclepro.2013.03.034.

Lucena, J., & Schneider, J. (2008). Engineers, development, and engineering education: From national to sustainable community development. *European Journal of Engineering Education, 33*(3), 247–257.

Schumacher, E. F. (1973). *Small is beautiful: A study of Economics as if people mattered.* London: Blond & Briggs.

Segalás, J., Ferrer-Balas, D. & Mulder, K. F. (2010). What do engineering students learn in sustainability courses? The effect of the pedagogical approach. *Journal of Cleaner Production, 18*, 275–284. Accessed 1 September 2017 from https://doi.org/10.1016/j.jclepro.2009.09.012.

Sen, A. (2009). *The idea of justice.* Cambridge, MA: The Belknap Press of Harvard University Press.

Tilbury, D. (2011). *Education for sustainable development: An expert review of processes and learning.* Paris: UNESCO.

Von Blottnitz, H., Case, J. M., Heydenrych, H. & Fraser, D. M. (2013). More complex from the outset: Theory, practice, laptops and natural foundations in a new 1st year chemical engineering course. In *6th Conference of Engineering Education for Sustainable Development.* Cambridge, UK. Accessed 1 September 2017 from www-csd.eng.cam.ac.uk/proceedings-of-the-eesd13-conference-cambridge-2013-v-2/eesd13-published-papers/von-blottnitz-h.pdf.

Von Blottnitz, H, Case, J. M. & Fraser, D. M. (2015). Sustainable development at the core of undergraduate engineering curriculum reform: a new introductory course in chemical engineering. *Journal of Cleaner Production, 106*, 300–307. Accessed 1 September 2017 from https://doi.org/10.1016/j.jclepro.2015.01.063.

Index

Page numbers in *italics* denote tables, those in **bold** denote figures.

For Product Safety Concerns and Information please contact our EU
representative GPSR@taylorandfrancis.com
Taylor & Francis Verlag GmbH, Kaufingerstraße 24, 80331 München, Germany